Letters Home

Letters Home

World War II Though the Eyes of a Soldier

By W. Scott Westerman, Jr.
(Edited by W. Scott Westerman, III)

Published in 2015 by
W. Scott Westerman, Jr.
Ann Arbor, Michigan

ISBN: 978-1522830535

PREFACE

A "Preface" is typically the place to acknowledge the contributions which others have made to the content which follows. Therefore, I use this occasion to express gratitude to my parents who thoughtfully preserved all of the letters I had written to them from the time of my induction in the United States Army at Fort Hayes in Columbus, Ohio, until I left Germany to return to the United States following the end of the war in the European Theater.

As will become evident in reading the letters, no one could have had more loving and supportive parents. I had not realized that their caring had extended to the preservation of my correspondence until a year ago when I came upon a large brown envelope, which contained the letters. I was sorting through a variety of miscellaneous items in a file drawer when I discovered the envelope.

Typing the letters (more than 175) gave me a great sense of communication with my parents, almost as if they were still living. The need to travel "army light" made it impossible for me to save their correspondence. Nevertheless, my frequent references to what they had written helped to recreate the feeling of a genuine and loving exchange.

Why preserve these letters in this form? There has been little occasion to talk about WW II with family. Now, as we are about to celebrate the 50th anniversary of the war's conclusion, it seems reasonable to anticipate greater interest in that historic event. Moreover, those years were formative not only for the world and for me, but also for the family. Among the many themes within the letters is the central event in our family's history, the evolution of the love, which resulted in the lifetime partnership between Marcy and me.

So, thank you, Mom and Dad. No son could have had

better parents. I've enjoyed visiting with you again.

WSW JR.

When dad moved from the family home at 1926 Hampton Court in Ann Arbor, Michigan to the Glacier Hills Retirement Community, simplification and downsizing became an important task. Dad was somewhat of a hoarder and among his treasures was the Apple MacIntosh SE on which he had typed "Letters Home". He had printed a few copies on a dot-matrix printer to share with family members and thought that, with ever evolving technology and the demise of the floppy disc the opportunity to upgrade this document for digital distribution had passed.

One day, not too long ago, he produced his bound edition of "Letters Home" and asked if I might take it to the copy store to make a few additional copies for friends. I remembered that I still had both his Mac and disc collection in my own basement (hoarding like father, like son). Having the good fortune to work at Michigan State University, I reached out to Ryan Edge at our library. Ryan wrote some code to translate the original data into a document format I could edit.

This is the result.

Our generation grew came of age during Viet Nam and have been sobered by the now ever present threat of terrorism. Our enemies don't wear uniforms and the attack from among us. And yet, there are still heroes who put themselves in harms way. Today we each fight for freedom and the American Dream in our own ways. As I re-read Dad's "Letters Home", I only wish I were again young enough to follow in his footsteps.

WSW 3

INTRODUCTION

On Sunday, December 7, 1941, at 7:55 a.m. Hawaiian time, the Japanese began the devastating bombing of the Pearl Harbor Naval Base. The next day President Roosevelt addressed Congress saying December 7 was "a date that would live in infamy." The United States declared war against Japan. Four days later, on December 11, Germany and Italy declared war on the United States. The U. S. then declared war on those countries.

I was sixteen at the time and a high school junior in Gallipolis, Ohio. Everyone recognized the dramatic implications of being at war. However, I did not begin to think of the personal implications until the beginning of my senior year.

As best I can recall, early in the fall of 1942, an announcement was circulated in the high school inviting boys who wanted to qualify to attend college while in the army or navy to take a test. Apparently policy makers in Washington had decided that a pool of college men would be needed from which to draw for service-related positions, which required some college education. Only a few of us took the test. Out of the 88 seniors, fewer than a dozen were following the college-prep curriculum.

The test proved to be a defining moment for me. There was a place on the form to indicate a preference for either the army or the navy. I checked "army" even though I had not previously given the matter any serious thought. I soon learned that I had passed the test and was officially enrolled in the Enlisted Reserve Corp (ERC), with the understanding that I would not be called to active duty until after my 18th birthday. As a result of this initiative, I was assigned an identification number of 15121772. indicating that I had "volunteered" for the army. Volunteer ID's began with a "1." Draftees carried an ID number beginning with a

"3."

Also in the fall of 1942, three colleges in Ohio announced a special program for senior boys who wanted to experience college before going into the service. These were Oberlin, Miami University and Ohio Wesleyan. The plan was to begin college at the end of the fall semester of the senior year with the understanding that once the college semester was completed successfully the high school would award a diploma. That plan was attractive to my parents and was of interest to me, although it meant leaving in the middle of the basketball season and discontinuing my responsibilities as student council president and editor of the school newspaper.

It is appropriate at this point to describe another defining moment which is a part of our family's lore. I was accepted at Oberlin and had expected to attend. My parents, however, had stopped there while traveling in that part of Ohio and had observed co-educational dining. They saw that as a distraction for both sexes - and very likely for their son. A coincidental visit in Gallipolis from a recruiter for Ohio Wesleyan, and the promise of a scholarship ($250) for a minister's son, redirected me to OWU - and within a few weeks to Marcy Percy.

Ohio Wesleyan had instituted a continuous schedule to accommodate navy men (V-5 and V-12) who were on campus preparing to become naval officers. Consequently, I was able as a civilian to complete two full semesters between January and October, 1943.

Ohio Wesleyan was an excellent transitional experience between high school and the army. During the first semester, I roomed with Bard Battelle in Mrs. Leady's rooming house. Bard and I had been good friends in Dayton, Ohio during our elementary school years. We both pledged Delta Tau Delta fraternity, having been recruited by Bob Rahn, the pledge master. We were both very serious students regularly "burning the mid-night oil." (In my two semesters at OWU I earned seven A's and seven B's. Two of the B's were in physical education. Bard did even better.) We would occasionally take breaks from our studies by playing duets on his clarinet and my flute.

The second semester we moved to a boarding house operated by Edith Swartz and her mother. Bob Rahn and Walt Routson were among the other roomers.

I sang in the a cappella choir, was active in the campus "Y," played on the fraternity's basketball team, the university's 150 pound football team (instituted chiefly for the navy men), and edited the fraternity newspaper during the summer. Best of all, I met Marcy.

I entered the army full of confidence, in good physical condition, and absolutely certain that the war was for a just cause.

Now, in this post-Viet Nam War era, it is difficult to understand the total commitment of the nation to World War II. Two of my high school friends did not pass their physical examinations and were classified 4-F. They were devastated. All of my buddies were eager to become involved. Two friends at OWU who were pre-ministerial became conscientious objectors. They, however, participated in alternative non-service activities. My father, nearing fifty, considered becoming an army chaplain. He reluctantly conceded that the curvature of his spine would disqualify him. Everyone wanted to do his or her part.

Severe measures were undertaken to assure that the nation's resources were directed to the war effort. Gasoline was rationed. As a minister, my father was awarded a "C" card providing for him more gas than others were allowed. Sugar was scarce. Major campaigns were instituted to collect scrap metal. New cars were no longer manufactured. Manufacturing was dedicated to the production of the materials and weapons required for war.

The letters include a variety of topics many of which were treated repetitively:

1. My enthusiasm for army life: While I may have protected my parents a bit by not reporting some disagreeable aspects of the army, I really did enjoy the life.   Part of the pleasure resulted from being with some very compatible men. Also, I welcomed the physical challenges. In addition, I was genuinely excited by the many new experiences. I should acknowledge. also, that in comparison to the service assignments of some of my age-mates, I was very lucky. \

2. Training experiences: I attempted to describe what I was learning and doing.   This was done especially during the seventeen weeks of basic training.

3. Attendance at church: From the time my father baptized me in Grass Lake, Michigan in 1926, until I left home, I was wrapped in the arms of the church. Going to church was like breathing for me, an unexamined and natural act. It was a habit, which kept me in touch with God and my roots.

4. Marcy Percy: I first saw Marcy at OWU when she appeared before my speech class as a student guest speaker, chosen by her instructor to demonstrate for us what a good speaker could be. Her topic was "Why Women Should Stay in College." After dating her roommate once,   I was able to meet her personally. While it might be an exaggeration to say that it was love at first sight, I was impressed! We became good enough friends to recommend staying in touch. And stay in touch we did!

5. Family: Sisters Joanne and Ellen were constant in their support through their letters and personal

services.   References to "Joey," Joanne's first-born, are frequent.   I was, of course, vitally interested in my parents' activities.

6.   Packages: A considerable amount of space is devoted to expressions of gratitude for all the packages I received from many different sources. My mother provided a constant flow of delicious edibles.   I received much more than any of my buddies, and was shameless in asking for even more.

7.   Friends: I often report on or ask about friends. Since most of these are unknown to the readers, I have described who they are in small print in parentheses.

8.   Furloughs: Rumors about and planning for furloughs was a subject for much discussion.

9.   Combat situations: Censorship rules prohibited reporting anything about our actions or whereabouts in Europe.   Therefore, I have supplemented the letters written while in combat with some descriptions of what actually occurred. It is important to remember, however, that the 86th Division was in actual combat for only 42 days, a very small number in comparison to other veteran infantry divisions.

No letters were saved relating to my time in the Philippines. Consequently, I have written a brief addendum to complete the story of my thirty months in the service.

I hope this will be of some interest to members of the family, specifically Scott, Colleen, Shelby, Brandon, Judy, Ed and Tommy. Ellen may enjoy parts of this, too. Marcy is already familiar with most of the story, but may be surprised by some of the references to her. All readers will want to skim most of what is recorded.

In typing the letters, I was honest to the original

content, grammar and general style, as painful as that was. I copied each letter word for word, including all the "swells," "greats," and other repetitive superlatives and expressions.

CHAPTER ONE

INDUCTION

Fort Hayes, Columbus, Ohio
November 10-24, 1943

November 11, 1943

What a wonderful life! So far everything has really been great. The train was an hour late but I called Marcy anyhow, and we had a nice visit. After that I went to the "Y" where I slept like a log in a fine room. I ate breakfast in the "Y" (in Columbus) with Carter Ashleman (from Gallipolis) whom I met in the restaurant. Since I didn't get up until 9, when I finished eating I hopped a bus and came out here to Ft. Hayes. I arrived here at 11, slow time, and they gave me blankets and assigned me to this barracks. I started to fix my bed when I met "Packy" McFarlane, a buddy of mine from Wesleyan, he was making his bed only two bunks away.

Our physical was given to us this afternoon. Of course, I'm in top shape. In the evening Bob Rahn (pledge master for Delta Tau Delta at Ohio Wesleyan) popped in and we went to a free movie here in the camp movie house. We visited for awhile and he left. We went to bed at 9 and slept well. We get up at 5:30 a.m. Today we haven't done much. We got reimbursed for our trip expenses and just sat around. The meals are really super. You'd almost think it was Thanksgiving every meal. Our bunch in this barracks is tops. All the new fellows were in E. R. C. (Enlisted Reserve Corps) and most of them college boys. Of course other men are with us. It's swell having "Packy" to bum around with.

We might get our intelligence tests, etc. this afternoon, but I doubt it. We'll probably get our uniforms and equipment tomorrow. I don't think we'll leave here until Monday or Tuesday and maybe later. I plan to spend Sunday afternoon in Delaware, if we get it off.

It's O. K. to write here to the induction center. As you see on the envelope, I have an address. I brought everything I needed, thanks to you. They issue everything, combs, etc., but the extras will come in handy. Mother, we do sleep between sheets, have plenty of blankets, good place to wash, and everything is really nice. You'd think this place was a classy summer resort instead of an army camp. I can see I'm really going to like this life. I do hope we get our uniforms soon.

I'll keep you posted on things.

P. S. That A-12 card seems to have more influence than I expected.

November 14, 1943

Yesterday we got all our equipment. Several of us fellows went into Columbus and saw a show, "The Iron Major." It was fine. After the show we went to the U. S. O. We got out of camp at 6 p.m. and had to be in at 12.

Yesterday I took out $10,000 insurance. It costs me about $6.50 a month. Also I'm having a bond sent home every month. This army really gives you everything.

I don't imagine that I'll be leaving here until next Thursday or Friday. We haven't had our classification tests yet. Those come tomorrow. This come tomorrow. We've seen about four hours of movies on hygiene, army organization etc. They were good shows.

Lights are out every night at 9 o'clock. I'm getting about 8 hours of sleep every night. The food is still great, and I can just feel the pounds adding. I am still meeting people I know, a couple of more Wesleyan men, and two fellows from Oberlin who know Wes. A nice boy from Cleveland is going to Delaware with me. We're leaving in about 15 minutes and hope to get there in time for church. The camp has church, of course, but I'd rather go to "Bill Street."

Marcy sent me the other picture and it is swell. She still writes very nice letters. Rushing is still going on, but I hope to see her for a while today anyhow. I tried to call her last night to make a date, but she was at a rushing dinner. (Marcy was in charge of Gamma Phi Beta rushing.) I spoke to her friend so I think it's O.K.

How are things in Gallipolis? How'd the game against Jackson come out? Wesleyan beat Bowling Green yesterday. I guess they're starting too late. Ohio State was a lucky one. Michigan is still tough.

Well I guess I better start for Delaware. You should see me in my uniform!   Oh well, we all can't be snappy marines. If I'm still here

next weekend I might try to get a weekend pass so you can see the "suit." I doubt very much that I'll still be here, though.

November 16, 1943

Finally I'm all done with everything. All the tests are finished. Yesterday morning we took four hours of classification tests. This morning I had an interview to be placed. I got 136 on the general intelligence test, 125 on mechanical aptitude test, and 118 on radio test. These are good scores, much better that I expected. The man was swell and put me down for "personnel." Also, I'm eligible for A. S. T. P. (Army Specialized Training Program). The army is very, very efficient. They certainly try to place you where you are best qualified.

Last night we had typhoid shots. My arm was only a little sore. Today I am on "special detail." I sit at a desk and ask men questions: "What church do you prefer?" "Are you a citizen?" "Mail this stuff home to your wife." It's really an interesting job. It's similar to several corporal's positions. I was lucky to get it instead of sweeping or something else.

I had a swell time at Delaware Sunday. Another boy went with me and we thumbed. I saw lots of my friends and, of course, Marcy. We had lunch and dinner together, and the evening., Marcy was great, as usual. It was fun showing my uniform off. An army suit is really rare in Delaware. I spent time with Kenny (Kenny Morgan, a Gallipolis friend attending Ohio Wesleyan) and all my buddies. I got back an hour late due to the snowstorm, but luckily no one said anything.

Now we get up at 5 o'clock. I am still getting to bed at 9, so that gives me a good 8 hours. I'm crazy about this army! So far it's great. Honestly, I'm enjoying every minute. I've made so many good friends. I can hardly wait to get started on basic training. It will get tough then, and that's what I want. I might go any day now. I hope to leave by Thursday or Friday.

Please excuse this sloppy note. I'm scribbling it between "customers." Whenever there's a pause, I write. I've been so busy the last two days that I haven't even had a chance to get my mail. I'm anxious to hear how Gallipolis came out against Jackson.

Bob Rahn was in Delaware Sunday. He hasn't yet received his orders. Believe it or not he was getting ready to give his pin out.

Everyone is kind to the soldier. Everybody speaks to me as if I were a brother or son. What a life. I'm afraid I'll get spoiled with all the attention. If you just walk down the street, cars stop with nice people in them and ask if you want a ride.

5:30 a.m. Wednesday.

Mail goes out at 6 so I'll have to rush this off fast. I got a haircut last night. My hair was really getting long. This afternoon at 1 o'clock a bunch of us are to see the flight surgeon because of our good scores on the tests. My ear (I had had a ruptured ear drum four or five times which left scar tissue.) will eliminate me anyway.

I hope you are both well and happy. The service flag sounds swell. Maybe I'll get to see it soon.

November 22, 1943

It was certainly grand talking with you on the phone. You both sounded well and happy.

I am writing this on duty, so to speak. I told you about our working on special details. Today I am working in the Captain's office downtown here in the depot. I was told to rest, so I guess it's O. K. to write a letter. These special details are very interesting. Every day, except today, it's something different. None of the jobs are really hard work.

Yesterday I went to Delaware as planned. I got there in time to go to church at Bill Street. Rev. Bayliff preached on Youths' Thoughts and it was a fine sermon. Especially interesting to us youths. Marcy and I had lunch and dinner togther. Don't worry about me getting too involved. There are far too many handsome navy men around Delaware to allow a girl to give her heart to the army. (Ohio Wesleyan had special wartime training programs for navy men who had been classified as V-5 or V-12.) Anyhow, I was born a slow "operator" when it comes to women. We are swell friends and she'll write me once a week or so. That's about as far as it goes.

Did I tell you Bob Rahn gave his pin out. He gave it to a very, very lovely girl, a Tri-Delt. He went with her whenever he went with a girl last year. Bob is lucky and so is she. Her name is Janet Stancil, a really fine girl.

This morning we had another shipping call. Fifty more men went out. I'm hoping our numbers will turn up in the call tonight or at least tomorrow. "Packy" is really a fine fellow and I do hope we'll be shipped out together. His father drove us back from Delaware last night.

Saturday night I stayed in camp and washed out underclothes, socks, and handkerchiefs. I straightened my barracks bag and shined my shoes and was in bed before 9 o'clock. We could have stayed out until 5 a.m., but what I would want to do beyond 11 o'clock is beyond me. I got about 9 hours of sleep and that really felt good.

Many of the fellows drink and run around with women. When a fellow has already established his mores, as I have, this offers no problem at all. You can always find men with interests similar to yours too. We have already formed a little group of college fellows who don't smoke or drink, etc. Of course we don't exclude association with others, but when we go into Columbus, we naturally stick together.

Saturday night I weighed myself in just my regular uniform and the scales read 159. Taking seven pounds off for clothes, I still have gained two pounds. If I gain a pound every week, I'll be more than satisfied.

The food is still swell. Here's an example of one of our noon meals. (Our biggest meal is at noon.) Mashed potatoes and gravy, roast beef, beets, pear plus juice, celery, cake and ice cream, cocoa, bread and butter. This is just a common example. Really, food is extraordinary.

I don't believe I have ever told you exactly what equipment was issued to us. Here it is: 2 winter shirts, 2 winter pants, one blouse (similar to suit coat), 2 pairs of shoes, 6 pairs of socks (3 wool, 3 rayon), 2 pair of long undies (pants and shirt separate), 3 pair of underpants, 3 undershirts, 1 winter overseas cap, 2 summer shirts, 2 summer pants, fatigue outfit (pants, shirt and cap), 2 ties, six hankies, woolen cap, crash helmet, two towels, shaving brush, razor, blades, toothbrush, comb, mess kit, canteen, fatigue coat, overcoat, belt, 2 barracks bags, and other minor things which I can't remember. We're given two books, one on health, one on army rules, etc. We are truly the best equipped army in the world.

The letter you forwarded to me was interesting. Thanks. I would certainly like to see that flag in the window. I have so much to talk about already after only almost two weeks. When I do see you I probably won't be still a minute.

I guess I better quit. There still isn't any work to do, but I've written enough anyhow. If you get a chance to see the "Iron Major" you might enjoy it. The man had ten children, my idol. The show has bad parts but on the whole it's fine.

I hope my next letter is from some nice sunny southern camp. Stay well and I'll be seeing you soon via mail again.

P.S. I really apreciated those good jokes. (Wow) Packy and I really laughed over them, especially your little sly notes, Mother.

November 23, 1943 (Postcard)

At last I leave.   I'll probably be traveling over Thanksgiving. I'll let you know for sure as soon as I arrive. It is rumored we'll be very near "snook" country. (This is a reference to Florida where I had caught a snook in Tampa Bay when I was twelve years old.) Next time I see you I plan to have a tan. Have a Happy Thanksgiving. We've lots and lots to be thankful for.

CHAPTER TWO

BASIC TRAINING

Second Company
   Fourth Training Regiment A. S. T. P.
   Harmony Church Area
   Fort Benning, Columbus, Georgia
   November 25,1943- March 20, 1944

November 25, 1943

What an interesting, interesting Thanksgiving this has been. So much has happened since I left Columbus that I don't know where to begin to tell you about it.

We left Columbus at 1 o'clock November 24th. Thirty of us were in the group with a corporal in charge. We all expected to be going to Florida, but as you see from the letterhead, we were quite wrong. We got a nice car on the train with plenty of room. At Cincinnati we had an hour stop. While waiting I attempted to call Ted (Uncle Ted Wuerfel) and Eileen (a girl I had dated while in high school). We ate cookies at the U. S. O. in the station to pass the time. When I speak of "we" I mean "Packy" (Wayne MacFarland) , my buddy from Wesleyan, a nice Phi Gam from Dennison, and a swell fellow from Cleveland. The four of us traveled all the way together, and we weren't separated until we reached camp where we were put in different barracks. From Cincinnati we traveled steadily until we reached Birmingham, Alabama. There we ate breakfast in a hotel while waiting for connections to Columbus, Georgia. We ate our dinner the night before in the diner. The trip from Cincy to Birmingham was beautiful. Scenery was tops ! We had a fine meal on the train, consisting of 4 pieces of chicken and other things which made up a good Thanksgiving meal. Of course, I thought of Thanksgiving at home and how nice it would be, but the army certainly did us fair.

When we arrived at camp we realized that we were really segregated as A. S. T. P. trainees. Our basic is the ordinary infantry basic and it's really going to be plenty tough. All of us A. S. T. P. fellows are in the same company. The meal tonight was really shocking. Shocking because our mess hall has curtains, we eat off of plates, and everything was tops! After "mess" I wandered down to the gorgeous Service Club where they give away this stationery, and there, lo and behold, I met Merrill Niday (a Gallipolis friend). Boy, is he looking great. Wow, I hardly recognized him. He weighed 153 when he entered the army and now he hits the scales at 169. If only basic training will do the same for me. We talked together for a while, then I left him to write this letter.

This is really a great experience. I know I won't be home for four more months because no home passes are allowed before the end of basic. This is the stuff that will make a man out of me. Next time you see me I want to be hard as iron physically. Mentally, this is a fine place to keep morale up. A fine theater and excellent recreation facilities are offered. And, being with men who use little profanity, etc., is also a great asset. My, but I have a lot to be thankful for. The background you have given me has been my life.

I'm certainly grateful for parents such as I have!!! I'll never waiver from their standards.

The barracks I'm in are nice. Our corporals seem to be exceptional. One thing you could send me would be about a dozen hangers. Also, six hankies would be swell, plus a finger nail clipper. Our clothes are kept in barracks bags, but we have a big shelf and a place to hang coats, pants, shirts, etc., so the hangers are most important.

More shots are coming soon. I guess we take more A. S. T. P. tests tomorrow, too. Best of all, we don't wake up until seven o'clock for three or four days. Basic doesn't really start until next week. The we'll have to buckle down, but definitely.

I hope you're both fine, and I hope Thanksgiving was great for you too. Give my regards to everybody. I may not be able to write a whole lot for we're going to be busy pretty soon.

November 27, 1943

UNITED STATES ARMY
Fort Benning, Georgia
"A great organization"

Now, being almost fully adjusted to my new surroundings, I find I'm in one of the most extraordinary camps in the U. S. There are almost 100,000 men here. Men are trained for paratroops, infantry, armored division, and almost everything, including cooks. One whole training regiment is made up of A. S. T. P. candidates.

Last night Merrill called his mother. She probably called you to tell you where I was. It certainly was a surprise meeting Merrill. Also last night Brian Aherne, the movie actor, was here in the service men's club. I got his autograph and sent it to Marcy. We really get exciting things around here. Right now there is a fellow playing the

Rhapsody in Blue on the piano, and he is good! The army is, absolutely, a wonderful experience.

The psychology program of A. S. T. P. has been discontinued. If I make it it will be as an engineering student. We have more interviews about it next week. Our basic doesn't start for a week or so. It is the real infantry basic, the toughest there is. All the men around here who have just finished their basics looks so great, I can hardly wait to get started. We're already being molded into soldiers. I really love it. None of us are anything special here. We're all equal. That's the way I like it

I've had to work hard. I fired furnaces for a while, then today we scrubbed the whole barracks with brushes. I eat like a horse! the food here is even better than Fort Hayes.

You will notice my addrress is changed a little from the last letter. If you will please write "4th Platoon" down in the right hand corner of the envelope it will facilitate faster separation of the mail, and I will get your letters faster.

Tomorrow we are going to church. Our Sundays will always be free. In fact, we can sleep through breakfast if we want to. I never want to miss any meals though, since adding weight is one of my big army aims. The weather here is perfect, cool at night and warm in the day. I am told that after Christmas rain begins and it is very sloppy. There is lots of clay and sand around. Have you ever been in this county? Were we around here when we went to Florida?

Don't forget the hangers. Hope you're both well.

November 28, 1943

Today is Sunday and truly a day of rest in the army. This morning I slept in until 8 o'clock, ate a leisurely breakfast, went to church, ate a steak dinner and then had the afternoon and this evening free to do what I wish.

Always Sunday is a day of rest in the army, and I think that is great. Of course, sometimes a very special duty may change that, but not often.

Church this morning was very interesting. A swell men's glee club sang "Beautiful Savior." It was good enough to make you weep. It was the same arrangement we sang in choir, Daddy. The sermon was only fair. It was a swell service. A certain spirit of worship seems to prevail among the men. The church services are very well attended.

If time allows, I think I shall try to get in the glee club. This afternoon I washed all my socks and hankies. Washing service starts Thursday at a very small cost. I like doing washings, but I will take advantage of the washing service.

I am really meeting some swell fellows. I Think almost every man in our barracks has had some college. The other day the captain asked our whole company how many men drank beer. So few held up their hands that a planned beer party was postponed. How's that?! A University of Michigan man sleeps near me. Also, a Harvard man and a Yale man are nearby. Most have had only a year like myself.

The initials or abbreviations on my address stand for the following: Private, etc., Army Serial Number 15121772, 2nd Company, 1st Battalion, 4th Training Regiment, 4th Platoon, Army Specialized Training Program, Basic Training Center. I Thought perhaps you wondered about it. It's a long address, isn't it. Don't forget to write 4th Platoon down in the right corner.

It's raining outside, and I better go back to the barracks before it gets too muddy. I'm getting in the habit of writing letters. This is my tenth one since I've been here, believe it or not. To seven different people too.

How was church this morning? I plan to make one of my Christmas events a long distance call. Merrill has phoned a couple of times, and connections aren't difficult.

See you again soon via mail.

P. S. I still have $30, so don't worry about money. I got the travelers checks cashed. We get paid in a few days.

November 30, 1943

Strange as it may seem, I am enjoying this life more and more. Today we had a big day. This morning I took tests for basic engineering. Not having any interest in the test, and not being able to develop even an artificial interest, I am afraid I flunked it. Nevertheless, I will probably be shoved into A. S. T. P. basic engineering anyhow on the basis of my other intelligence scores and my college record. We find out tomorrow for sure. The army continues to treat you fairly. So far I have been interviewed by not less that five interviewers. All of them complimented me on my college grades.

I guess I told you psychology was closed as is chemical engineering. The only thing I can possibly qualify for is basic engineering.

This afternoon we drilled for about four hours. We are developing a wonderful platoon spirit, and each one of us is doing his best to make our platoon tops in this company. It's really just like football or something. I've already told you what swell fellows are in our platoon. There are about fifty of us. Almost all are college men and our three corporals are all college men. Also our sergeant is a college graduate. We are treated as individuals not merely robots. We all have our names printed across our crash helmets which we wear most of the time. Our captain is tops\

What a great guy. Really, I'm so enthusiastic about it all I could pop.

Of course there are thorns with the roses. I came into my barracks yesterday to find my bed completely torn apart because of a wrinkle. Then tonight we all had to stay here and hand scrub the whole barracks because an officer found a little dust somewhere. Also, we are getting up a half hour earlier tomorrow to scrub some more.

Our spare time is used partly by shining shoes (shoes have to be polished always) and making sure mess kit, packs, gas mask, etc., are in proper shape. We get our guns soon and they will mean more work. In the evenings after checking on these things we always have at least four hours or so to ourselves. In the future I hope to work in some serious reading in this spare time, for in the army a person is very apt to lose his intellectual interests. Obeying orders and acting passively is too easy.

Our real "basics" starts next Monday. Our training will be finished March 5 at which time we will be assigned to our college (if I do get in). Perhaps then we might get a furlough long enough to go home.

I got a letter from you today which had been written the 23rd. It was nice to hear since it had been a week since I have had any mail. Letters will probably take 3 days at least to come from Gallipolis.

As for Christmas, I don't need anything. A box I could share would be swell. Also an army colored pull-over short sleeved sweater would be nice. I bought some nice shower slippers, so forget those. Some white hankies would be appreciated. This is early to ask "Santa," but there you are.

Tomorrow eve six of us fellows have challenged six others in football. It will be fun. Saturday our whole company is going to have its picture taken. A week from Saturday we get our first day off. That will be nice!

I guess I'll turn in early tonight. I want a shower first. We have to shave every day regardless of how tough our beards. I use a blade every other day (ha, ha). I'm correcting my posture and putting on weight already.

How are things at home? I'll probably get a letter tomorrow from you, but I wanted to write this evening. I'll drop you a note to let you know how I come out finally for A. S. T. P

December 2, 1943

It was so nice to get your letters. Also your box was really welcome. It came this afternoon and is just about cleaned out already.

Today we had our final interviews for A. S. T. P. I am accepted for basic engineering. After basic I will be assigned to one of a possible 225 colleges to take this engineering course. As you said, it surely should prove some value to me later in life. I guess the entire course runs for a 21 month period with seven days furlough every three months. It starts out with the fundamental course for engineering, so I shouldn't have too much trouble.

Yesterday we had three shots all at once. Tetanus, vaccination, typhoid were the weapons. "Believe it or not," they hardly phased me. The fact that we have been kept busy may have something to do with it.

Did I tell you I got called in to see the Company Commander? He is a captain, and I wondered what I had done. He merely wanted my opinion on how the company was being run. He was picking men at random to find out if there were suggestions for betterment. He's a swell fellow and we had a great talk. He asked me all about Gallipolis, you, etc. I told him I thought the army was swell, and he was pleased. It's nice to know we have such an excellent commander. (Actually, after some general conversation, the Company Commander gave me a secret mission: I was asked to keep an eye on two or three men in the platoon who had family connections in Germany. My assignment was to write a letter to the CC every so often reporting any suspicious or seditious behavior or comments. I remember writing some letters, but only to report that everything was OK.)

We got our rifles today. We drilled all afternoon on "present arms," "parade rest," etc. The movements are tricky and I have to stay on my toes or I get mixed up. We are getting more and more drilling. It's pretty hard work.

Does Mark (Mark Tanner, one of my best friends in Gallipolis, who had gone into the air corps) like his work? I was glad to hear Dr. Martin's opinion on ears. Even though I had decided to accept A. S. T. P., I had had a little yearning for the flashy air corp. Now I am satisfied it would be an unwise move

There are chances to get in bands and glee clubs, but I'm afraid I don't have the time. Perhaps later I might. I want to use my free time working on that all-important vocational choice which I must make. I expect to help this along by some reading. We have a fine library from which I may draw books.

I got a nice letter from Ellen today. I haven't heard from Marcy yet, but will probably hear tomorrow. Thanks again for the box, hankies, etc. Already I have clipped my nails with the clippers.

Laundry service starts tomorrow, so I won't have to be doing so much washing. It's such a good feeling to be directly responsible for every article you have. It gives one a sense of responsibility and independence. Also starting tomorrow we take doses of Sulfathiazole tablets to make sure we get rid of all germs. This army makes sure we stay healthy. They're very strict about windows at night, and all that mothers used to tend to so well.

December 5, 1943

Well shut mah mouth and call me Corporal Westerman (for one week only). Yes, the Sergeant just called me in his room to tell me I was to have the honor of being acting corporal over a squad of fourteen men for the first week of basic training. Every week it will change to another fellow. Being one of the first men chosen really enlarges my head. Especially since we were chosen because of outstanding work in drilling. I say "we" for four of us were chosen out of our platoon of 60 men. Only a minute ago I was given this honor so I missed bragging about it to Joanne and Ellen both of whom I wrote this afternoon. I even get to wear two stripes on my sleeve for this week Whoopee!! This as as near as I'll get to being a corporal since I'm going into A. S. T. P.

Today has been beautiful. I slept until 8 o'clock. We went to church at 9:30 and it was again a pretty good service. We were told in church that Christmas Eve a program with 300 male voices was going to be given. I guess I'll again get to hear Christmas music.

The Messiah sounds wonderful. I'd love to hear it. Is Daddy still singing some solos in it? I hope so. If I weren't so busy I would attempt one of the glee clubs.

Your cartoon on rifle drilling was really appropriate. We were given our rifles and we've been drilling constantly with them. I put the cartoon on the bulletin board and all the fellow got a big kick out of it. We've been working hard. Tonight (even Sunday) we scrub barracks. Thursday night we scrubbed the whole building only to be told to scrub it over again. As a result we won the inspection contest.

This afternoon I lounged around and wrote letters. Sundays certainly are welcome. Tomorrow "basic" officially starts. I hope it's tough 'cause that's what I want. This is a hurried note so forgive the brevity and sloppiness.

December 12, 1943

Here it is another glorious Sunday. Time is just whizzing by. It goes so fast that it is easy for me to get way behind in my correspondence. We are really kept busy in this basic. Almost each minute is planned for us. Here's a schedule of what our time was spent for:

- Orientation films and lectures 1 hour
- Military courtesy and discipline 3 Hours
- Equipment and clothing, and tent pitching 4 hours
- Chemical warfare 4 hours
- Dismounted drill 4 hours
- Physical training 4 hours
- Rifle M-1, 30 caliber 4 hours
- Military sanitation and first aid 6 hours
- Organization of the army 1 hour
- Interior guard duty 4 hours
- Extended Order (tactics, etc.) 4 hours
- Marches and bivouacs 4 hours
- Inspection 1 hour
- Co. Commander lectures 4 hours

This totals up to 48 hours for six days. That sounds like a nice 8 hour day; but when you realize you have to clean rifle, shoes, and equipment, plus eat three meals a day and keep the barracks sparkling, you can see that the only time left is for needed sleep. Of course, when we get the swing of things we'll be able to squeeze more time out for ourselves. Also, the first weeks are probably more intense to get us acclimated to working.

All our work is very, very interesting. Even though we are kept hopping, I still like it immensely. In fact, if someone gave me the chance to leave the army, I would not take it. Being a squad leader this week was a factor in my enjoying the work so much. I led my squad in all of our extended order work. (This is field formations for attacking the enemy.) I signal my men with various hand signals and they follow me thusly. We get a lot of realistic practice.

Next week I get to continue to wear an armband with stripes. I've been boosted to assistant non-com (assistant to our non-commissioned officers). I take charge of barracks scrubbing. It's fun to be on the other end of the order giving. Also it gives me an opportunity to express individuality. Last Friday we were told we had to bring in our beds from airing, had to scrub the floor, dust and wash windows, all in one hour and fifteen minutes. We made it! I was so happy to think we had accomplished the almost impossible. To express my gratitude to the fellows I opened the wonderful box of candy sent from the church. In one of your letters you said I should open a certain box. Not being certain which one you meant I opened the candy. There was plenty for all 35 of us on the first floor of the barracks. (There are 65 in the barracks two floors.)

Everybody is certainly taking care of me in writing letters. Marcy wrote three this last week and her sister is writing me. I've asked Ellen to drop Marcy a note. Is that OK, proper and everything? Darn it, I wish you could know Marcy. She is honestly very exceptional. She sends me all the Wesleyan news. She also sent me three pictures of herself in childhood days. Wow! They are really funny. I haven't written her as much as I'd like to because of lack of time. I try to write her at least once a week, and so far have done that. She is very wonderful and I'm enjoying becoming more acquainted with her via mail.

Mother only!

Christmas is coming! I got paid $22 Thursday and get

paid again the end of this month, I'm sending a mail order check in my next letter. Would you take care of my shopping? The roses for Marcy sound swell. Also how about perfume or stockings for Ellen? Would Daddy like a symphony to play on the church recorder? How about adding money and my name to something for Joanne and Frank. It's pretty difficult to say exactly what to get, so you decide what's best. I have lots of money, over forty dollars. Since our pay is in cash sending a little home is the best bet. I'm sending only ten dollars. Anymore needed will be sent at a moment's notice.

OK Uncensored

I was so sorry to hear about Aldo Fontana (a Gallipolis friend, two or three years older, who was killed in action). Things like that really bring the war to the front with a bang. I'll bet Aldo was a good soldier.

Your letters are very welcome. You write exactly what my appetite calls for. Mrs. Robinson sounds very nice. You, Mother, are really working at that, aren't you. I got the Mu Murmers (the OWU Delta Tau Delta News Letter), but wasn't very impressed by it. I hope the Messiah goes well. I'll bet it does. I'd love to hear you sing once in public, Daddy. I mean an honest, real performance. I have never heard an actual performance, did you realize that? Of course, I already know my Dad is tops in music so I don't see why it matters.

For the first time in many, many years I will miss the annual Christmas festival. For how long have I heard or participated in them anyhow? I'll be there in spirit. Then also, I'll get a first hand account of what it contains when I make the phone call.

I could have gone into town last night but decided on catching up here. Don Gothard, Kenny Morgan, Bob Rahn and several others still are supposed to hear from me. Don got my Address from the Gallipolis Tribune. It was nice to hear from him, as it was the others.

Church was again nice this morning. I have had time for thought while drilling, etc., and I'm beginning to wonder if I'm not evading the most important job in the world when it comes to the ministry. Thursday evening we stood in line two hours waiting for more fatigue clothing and several of us fellows had a real theological discussion. Time will tell, and since I have time, I expect to be told.

Whatever you do, don't worry about me. If you check on stories of awful work, etc., in the army, you'll find they come from fellows who have never experienced anything rustic. Lots of fellows like to draw on parents' sympathy by tales of woe. At times, it's plenty tough, but it's nothing dangerous or that the ordinary boy can't handle.

I met another Wesleyan man this week. Also I'm making some grand friends in the barracks. There are some fine fellows in my squad. Really reverent, clean, and outstanding men.

December 14, 1943

My, but I enjoyed the Messiah program you sent. What a grand idea it was to put it on. I do wish I could have heard it. So many of the numbers are familiar to me, since we practiced a long time on them at Wesleyan.

Today it is raining. It's a cold and dismal rain. The army is very considerate and we are doing most of our work inside. This morning we went into gas chambers with gas masks. Then we went in without gas masks. You should have seen the tears run down our faces, for the gas was tear gas. It really makes you sob, no matter how tough you think you are.

This noon we had chicken. What a meal! I had three

enormous pieces. I'm sure I'm gaining weight even though I haven't been weighed since Fort Hayes. This is the first time I've had a chance to dash off a letter during the noon period. As you can see from my writing, I'm really dashing it off. By the way, how do you like the stationery? It cost only $1.00.

I haven't had a chance to get the mail order, but I'll send it Wed. or Thurs. That's a joke when you asked if I needed money. Also, we get paid again Dec. 30, so my only problem is how to keep it safely, not on having enough.

Thursday we go on a long hike. We've had two already, but this one is going to be exceptional. We carry full field packs plus rifles and gas masks. Altogether it doesn't weigh much over 40 pounds. I've gotten so used to it that it feels about like ten pounds.

I better stop. This is too messy anyhow. The Messiah program really impressed me.

P. S. Could you stick my basketball gym shoes and a supporter in a box sometime? That's all I'll need. I might get a chance sometime to use them. Thanks.

December 20, 1943

I cleaned my rifle until it glistened, and now I am at the service club waiting for a Christmas program to begin. It's great to have this evening off as I really didn't write all I wanted to yesterday. Also I got two letters from you this evening which I want to answer.

I got a lovely card from Mrs. Brown with a crisp new dollar in it. What a lovely thought. I certainly appreciate it. The mail also brought a card from Eileen. And, Mr. and Mrs. Feely gave me a year subscription to the Readers Digest. Marcy informed me she is sending the new book on Ohio Wesleyan written by one of our history profs. What a swell Christmas I am having! Did I tell you I got your box?

Yum, yum mmmm! I managed to have it around for two days before we completely blitzed it. Mother, I and many other fellows send thanks, and we all agree you are the best of cooks!!!!!!

The day in Columbus yesterday was fine. I finally didn't hear the musical program. I was all ready to go when I got in a basketball game in the U.S.O. gymnasium. I played with another Ohio boy, from Bellevue. We had a grand, grand time. It was wonderful to get back on a basketball court. Since I'm hearing this program tonight and am going to hear one Christmas eve, I'll still get to hear my favorite Christmas melodies.

The Christmas spirit is absolutely pouring out of me. Honestly, it's terrifically wonderful to be alive. I love Christmas and all that it means. I think of home a lot. Not in a sad way, but in a happy sense, because I feel I'm doing my part to preserve homes and happiness such as we have always enjoyed. Also, I have a great faith in the future. My ramblings are coming forth because of beautiful background music which seems to bring out the sentimental in me.

I have been relieved of my corporal position. This gives me more time to myself. I enjoyed the work, but am glad to have the honor (?) passed around as it should be.

Thank you so much for taking care of my shopping. Thanks for the "Upper Room." I haven't had one since being in the army, but I will certainly get into the habit of reading it again starting in January.

Tomorrow night we go on a thrilling night problem. We will be out half the night taking a route which we will plan by map and compass. The stars are beautiful here at night. I've never seen such beautiful skies as we have here in Georgia. No doubt the environment has something to do with my new appreciation, since it's the same sky that was, and is, in Ohio.

The program looks fine and I know it was a success. Please give my regards to everyone, and again, have a wonderful Christmas. (How does Johnny Lupton look? (A Gallipolis classmate who had a Christmas furlough.)) Don't forget to listen for a telephone call Saturday eve. In case I don't make it count on hearing from me early Sunday afternoon.

December 22, 1943

I just got your air mail letter. Really, I don't plan to answer each one immediately, but It is required by "Uncle Sam" that each of us hand in a letter home before 9 p.m. tonight. A mother wrote the Major because she had never heard from her son. The Major was raving mad. Wow. So here I am writing a required letter. Forgive the briefness, but I'm on special detail tonight which starts right now. Merry Christmas. Merry Christmas.

P.S. I saw Merrill right after I mailed the last letter. He expects to leave any day now.

December 25, 1943

What a glorious Christmas I am enjoying! First of all, thank you for all the fine gifts. I opened them this morning at about 11:30. All the other fellows had cheated and opened their gifts before today, so practically the whole barracks enjoyed with me the thrill of opening presents on Christmas. All the gifts were so welcome!

We were on our own time starting at 5:30 Friday (yesterday). I did all my washing to make sure today and tomorrow would be filled with nothing but leisure. At 11:30 p.m. about ten of us fellows went to church. The service was lovely. It was a communion service held in candle light. We were there two hours and enjoyed every minute of it. (At one point I dozed asleep, but was awakened by a buddy's elbow in my ribs.) I got to bed at 2 a.m.. Nevertheless, this morning I arose for breakfast. But after breakfast I went back to bed and slept until 11 o'clock. Then I arose and opened your gifts.

Today it seems every single man wants to call home. I doubt very much if I'll even get near a phone booth. I hope I can make connections tomorrow.

We had our Christmas meal today at 2:30 (it is now around 5 p.m.). What a meal it was. Oh! Our officers ate with us and the company commander even offered a prayer before we ate. I'm sure I can't remember all we had, but I'll try to list the menu: turkey, mashed potatoes, gravy, peas, cranberries, bread, butter, olives, celery, coffee, lemonade, pumpkin pie, dressing, fruit salad, ginger snaps, ice cream. Darn it, as you can see by my order of listing, I can't remember exactly all we did have. Anyhow, we had fruit on the table and even had tablecloths. (Home sweet home!!) Also, each man had ten miniature Hershey chocolate bars and a pack of cigarettes. I gave my cigarettes away, but, of course, ate all the chocolates. We get no meal this evening. If I can eat any breakfast tomorrow, I'll be surprised.

I enjoyed the letter of the 21st telling of Ellen fixing the tree, etc. I got a big kick out of Ellen wearing my old pants. I wish she would confiscate all my old clothing. If I keep putting on weight at such a awful rate I'll never be able to wear any of my clothes.

Thanks again for taking care of my shopping. I did miss the pleasure and joy of giving this Christmas. I made up for it a little by sharing all your food. (It's all gone already.) Also thank you a lot for sending Marcy the flowers. If only a small group of us fellows had been intimate enough to share the joy of giving, Christmas would have been more real. Giving is so much of Christmas. Nevertheless, today is very real to me. I'm enjoying it immensely. Also I'm sure this Christmas we fellows have been celebrating it for what it really means more than ever. I think the exchanging of gifts may tend to hide the real celebration.

When does Ellen's vacation end? Has she ever dropped Marcy that note? I'll bet she'll be thrilled to sing with the Cincinnati Symphony. I'm writing this in the music room of the service men's club. All the fellows are appreciators of good music who are in here. Some of them are superior musicians. I can tell by their expressions as they lean forward with a crescendo, etc. Really, all types of fellows are in the army. And in the A.S.T.P. the men are mostly superior. I'm glad you are enjoying the company picture. The man on my left plays the bass violin. He's a nice fellow, went to Northwestern for a semester.

Thursday night I had guard duty. This is perhaps the most important job a soldier has during basic. I walked my post from 12 midnight until 2 a.m. We sleep all night in the guard house in case of any emergency in which the guards on duty need our help.

Last week was harder than the first two weeks. Next week will be harder. Merrill (Niday) said the fourth week is the hardest week. It's nice we have this little vacation to rest up. The tough part is the very strenuous bayonet drill. We had six hours of bayonet work this week. We have 12 hours next week. Burrrr. It's nasty but necessary.

I can't get over all the wonderful gifts. The sewing kit was a "must" which you conveniently filled. Also the razor blades, shaving cream, hankies, chess board, shine cloths, and candy, were all very happily received.

Ellen's thoughtful gifts of socks, tie and nuts, were appreciated. Honestly, it seems you just read my mind as to what I wanted. Did you ask other soldiers what they would want or what? The sweater and cookies from Grandmother were swell. All the boys envy me with my gift from Joanne and Frank. Trousers and shirt exactly the right size and really perfect. Now I have three complete O.D. uniforms compared to the other fellows two. Just call me a plutocrat! (Or is it aristocrat?) The camphor ice came immediately into use when I burned my finger a little on the furnace door.

Marcy gave me an interesting volume on Ohio Wesleyan. I read a little in it last night and it is interesting. You can see my Christmas has really been full.

I guess I'll draw this to a close. Gee, I hope you all had a wonderful, wonderful Christmas! I'm so glad the Christmas program went well. I knew it would. Tonight I'm going to the big musical here at camp with 300 male voices and an orchestra of 65 members.

December 29, 1943

This will be a puzzle to read. I grabbed the nearest paper around and this was it. This is from the small notebook in which I keep all notes from demonstrations and lectures.

The phone call was swell. It took four hours to complete it. Every time the phone attendant called out a name I jumped a mile. When finally my name was called, I could hardly believe it. I enjoyed hearing your voices immensely.

I'm writing this during the noon rest. We have to go out on the field in just a minute. (Woops, in fact right now.)

Here it is after ten o'clock. All lights are out at ten except the ones in the toilet. I'm writing this now sitting in the bathroom (on what?) with a delicious popcorn ball in one hand. The box came today and I am already on the last ball. I still have the apples to eat. All the fellows who shared the box send their thanks, too.

Today was another hard one. This morning we dug machine gun emplacements. Three of us dug a hole five feet square and four and a half feet deep in less than two hours. We also camouflaged it during this period. This afternoon we had two more hours of bayonet drill plus two hours of first aid. We are now going over a long course similar to an obstacle course carrying our bayonets on rifles. It's really tough.

Yesterday we hiked twelve miles. Also we pitched tents and dug fox holes. It rained all morning, but this didn't slow us up a bit. You can see this week is getting plenty tough.

Tonight I had K.P. (kitchen police) as I have tomorrow also. As soon as I got off I tore down to the gym to try out for the regimental basketball team. The shoes arrived conveniently on time. The regiment team has already been picked but they needed three more men. A regiment consists of 4000 men so my chances were pretty slim. Only 40 guys tried out, but I still didn't make it. All the three men picked had had college experience. The captain in charge commented on my playing. I was pretty hot getting ten points in about five minutes.

Merrill has been assigned to a college in New York. He leaves Friday sometime. He was hoping for Ohio U., but that was building dreams. It certainly has been nice having him around.

Marcy wrote a lovely thank you letter. Mrs. White must have really fixed things up nicely. Thank you so much for taking care of it for me. Marcy was honestly thrilled.

Thank you again for the box and everything this past yuletide season. Also I hope I can call you again sometime. It was lots of fun. I better sign off as K.P. will be hard tomorrow. Also tomorrow night we have another night problem.

January 2, 1944

Here I sit robed in sin. Starting today I and 12 other fellows spend all our free time for the next four days in the barracks. Yesterday we had our usual big inspection. For some reason the Tech Sergeant decided there was dirt on one of the heels of my shoes. So, I'm confined for four days. I honestly don't quite see that I was at fault, but nevertheless I guess it means I'll have to shine harder the next time. Sometimes I think they get a fellow just to keep the others on their toes.

Next week I get to be a squad leader for the third time. This makes up in part for my slipping up on the shoes. Being squad leader is now a more respectful position, so I accept it gladly. Last week was a tough one. We went over a bayonet obstacle course, which seemed like a nightmare. It is about two hundred yards long and filled with everything from barbed ditches to high walls. Keeping one eye on the sharp bayonet and the other on the barbed ditches really gets you mixed up. We all made it in good order, but were pretty well exhausted. Also, during the week we dug two fox holes a piece and a machine gun emplacement. Thursday night we had another night problem. With the help of luminous compasses we came out fine.

I still enjoy all of the training. You can really feel your muscles and endurance building up. Just picture doing exercise in the out of doors at least 9 hours every day and you can see why a person's body can't help but develop favorably. Some of the training sounds pretty terrible, such as sticking dummies (with bayonets). As I always said, I'll never develop a hate for the enemy; nevertheless, if it ever becomes necessary for me to put to practice what I've learned to save myself, I can do it. I certainly hope it never becomes absolutely necessary. (Sometimes I do get awfully impatient to go to the front though.)

I was sorry to hear of Ellen's flu. Has she recovered completely? Several of the fellows have bad coughs, etc. We put up cubicles (tent halves between our beds) every night to keep the germs from spreading. Many have been on sick call, but so far I've been lucky. (I'm knocking on wood.)

Time out for chow! Yum. Yum. Sunday afternoon or evening, we eat cold meats, peanut butter. It's just like raiding the ice box, almost.

This morning I got out for church. It was a lovely service. The nicest thing about the service was the chaplain's lovely wife and two little children were in the audience. It was good to see a nice family again. I'm enclosing the program.

I got a nice letter from Eileen. She said she had visited you. If I ever get lots of time I may answer it. I also am getting the regular Y News Letter, which we started last summer. It's very nice. Dean Somerville (OWU dean) wrote me a nice note. I sent him a Christmas card.

I sent you a letter containing my new year's resolutions. Would you mind saving them until next year? The Y. F. (Youth Fellowship) started a tradition with me in that respect. I think it's a grand idea. I kept most of my last year's resolutions. I didn't keep the one in which I resolved to pick a profession, darn it. Next year I better keep it, or else. What with a lot of uncertainties in this year, I had a lot of resolutions to make.

Did I tell you Merrill was assigned to a Catholic School in the Southwest corner of New York? It's not far from home and a pretty nice set up. Of course, he was hoping for Ohio U. When my time comes if I get out of the South I'll be happy. (I'm happy now, but being closer to home would certainly be lots better.) Just think, next

Wednesday the 5th, I'll have been in the army 8 whole weeks. It hardly seems possible. Also it's hard to believe that 4 weeks of basic are over already. Probably it won't be more than ten weeks before I am once more cracking books. (I'm not sure whether to be happy or not over this prospect.)

It was great that so many of the fellows could be home for Christmas. What is Gwinn doing in the service? It seems Wendell ought to be about ready to go on the water, or has he already? (John Gwinn and Wendell Lloyd were Ellen's high school classmates.) Some of our cadre (non-coms) are leaving us to go overseas. This spring is sure to see an immense movement across the water.

I've started reading the "Upper Room" on schedule. Also we get a booklet put out by the Service Men's Christian League which is very interesting. Its name is "Link." It contains stories, discussion topics, jokes, Bible readings, etc. I'll send you a copy sometime. By the way, I'm sending my watch sometime soon. It quit working the second week we were here. As soon as I get to the post office I'll mail it.

We got paid again Friday. I get $24.85 every month what with bonds, etc., taken out. I still accumulate too much money to have around. (I may send home another money order. I have 40 dollars on my person now.) Are they sending you my bonds? You should have two $25 ones now.

I hope no one else has caught the flu. Don't forget to keep well and don't work too hard.

January 5, 1944

I'm sneaking another note during the noon hour. Yesterday a Major General inspected our area. He was very pleased and proclaimed our company the best in the regiment. And, to top things off, our captain said our platoon was the best in the company. That makes us about the best in the regiment, which includes 64 platoons. (Boy, are we good!) Of course, others claim the same thing.

Monday night we had a 5-hour night problem (7 to 12). Since I'm the squad leader I had to lead my squad taking all compass readings and orienting the map. Our problem was to travel about a mile through enemy territory. Machine guns, mortars, rifles were all firing about us constantly. It was the most thrilling experience we've had yet. Our squad hit the small hole in the enemy lines exactly. The only catastrophe occurred when three of our men failed to keep up and got lost. I went back and found them, and we finally came together at the designated spot. It was all very exciting.

At Christmas time I got a card from Edith (Edith Swartz, my landlady at OWU), saying food was following. Still no food! Mail certainly pulls funny tricks sometimes.

Today is the day Ellen leaves, isn't it? Every day at some period I live part of the day at home. imagining what's going on, etc. Boy, am I ever looking forward to that week or so in the future when I can be at home again. By the way, has Merrill gotten his furlough yet? Let me know if he does.

I'm back in the "Upper Room" habit . Also I've almost completed the new "Readers Digest." Finally I'm getting to do necessary reading. It's time to fall out. This afternoon we have three hours of field fortifications. This means plenty of digging and hard work.

January 9, 1944

This has been a most exciting week. In fact, it seems that each week becomes more exciting. A big factor in our increasing interest is that as each week passes we fellows become better and better acquainted. Already many, many lasting friendships have been made.

Before I start relating this week's experiences I want to catch up on replying to your swell letters. I certainly was sorry to hear of Mr. McCormick's death (longtime member of the church and my former Sunday school teacher). Also I was sorry to hear of Fred's queer antics at his sister's funeral. Is he all right now? Your article, Daddy, was tops! It presented everything perfectly. I hope someday I may be able to put forth such good thoughts in such a fine style on different subjects. Several of the former basketball players in the barracks read it. They agree two games a week are grueling.

Thursday morning we played football. I haven't had so much fun in years. My extra ten pounds helps a lot. Our whole platoon played (80 on a team). I carried the ball back on a kick off for almost a touchdown. During the game I got about a dozen tackles. On the last tackle I made, I forgot that I didn't have any equipment and I laid a guy as hard as I could. The result was that I was knocked out. Bang!! What a sensation that was! For a period of an hour or so, all my thoughts were completely jumbled. I went to the doctor and I was told to rest for the remainder of the day. The next morning the doc checked me again and allowed me to go on duty. All I suffered was a slight headache. I gained the experience of being knocked out. I've always felt cheated in that respect, but not anymore.

I'm enclosing a clipping, which caused a little comment in the barracks. Isn't it a coincidence? I wonder if the man's middle name is Walter? Some Sunday I plan to see him. A couple of the fellows are calling me chaplain now.

I saw Norm Scrimshaw (president of Delta Tau Delta while I was attending OWU) again last night. He left today for Camp Howze, Texas where he will join the 103rd Infantry. I heard from Bard today (Bard Battelle, a roommate at OWU). He is in Augusta, Georgia. He's in the signal corps division of the air corp. His basic is only 6 weeks and very soft compared to ours. He has it tough in that he's in with older men all of whom are tough in language, etc. He expects to be shipped to Patterson Field this week, or perhaps overseas. The later is only a slight possibility, but must be taken into consideration.

This evening I had charge of the whole barracks for two hours. All the noncoms had to leave, so I was put in charge. I handed out passes, etc., and it was fun.

This morning we hiked 10 miles in a slow drizzle. The mud gets terrible here. A ten or twelve mile hike is nothing to us now. When we go 15 miles we begin to cuss. This afternoon our whole battalion paraded before the major. It's fun to be part of 1000 massed, marching men - even if it was still in a drizzle and slimy mud.

Aside from more tactics and four hours of machine gun, we haven't done much new this week. Next week we day-fire rifles. (That is, we merely learn how to sight, etc. Real bullets come later.)

Only a week from next Saturday (two weeks from tonight), and we go out on the range for our first two weeks of bivouac. Time is certainly flying.

Your candy was deeelicious. I can still taste the last piece. Edith's box arrived and it was nice too. Of course, not up to your standards. Has the watch arrived yet?

January 16, 1944

Right now I should be in church in town. Another fellow and I had planned to spend all day in Columbus. Just as we were about to leave, in walked the 1st Sergeant asking for Westerman and two other fellows. He explained that the regular C. Q. (charge of quarters) was ill and one of us had to take his place. We flipped a coin and here I am. The job isn't much. I merely sit here in the company headquarters building just in case anything comes up. It's permissible to write letters, so I'm not bad off. I do hate to miss church and town though.

The 22nd we start on our two weeks on the shooting range. We hike the twenty miles from here to there. While we're there, we will live in four-man tents. We will shoot rifles, machine guns, mortars, bazookas, and throw hand grenades. We are required to attain certain scores to enable us to pass basic. This past week we've been learning all the positions, how to sight, and all preliminary work to real shooting. The two weeks on range will go fast and will be interesting.

This past week has been cold. Yesterday was the coldest it has been yet. Brrrr. I do hope it warms up before the 22nd. We won't have any heat in our tents. We do have plenty of warm clothing though. Someone swiped my gloves, but I bought similar ones for $2.50. (Pretty expensive, eh wot?)

Did I tell you I heard from Bard last week? He has been in Augusta, Georgia, which is on the other side of the state. He's finishing his 6 weeks of training aqnd is expecting to go back to Patterson Field. I think I wrote you about that already. I also heard from Manning (Manning Weatherholt,a friend from Gallipolis) this week. He seems to have given up the college idea. Too bad. I think it definitely is a mistake if he doesn't start his college career right away. Kenny also wrote me. His letters are very interesting. College is doing wonders for him. At least it seems that way via mail. Bob Rahn is still awaiting his navy call. He is counting on visiting Wesleyan next week.

Last night when I was cleaning my rifle, I forgot to remove a finger while closing the bolt. Today I can't hold this pen exactly right. (Ah, another good excuse to fall into the bad writing rut.) Our rifles are beauts.

They are worth almost $90., so we care for them very

carefully. In fact, before we apply for passes our rifles have to be glistening. It takes at least 30 minutes to clean it well. Sometimes after rainy days we spend two hours on them.

I just learned that a man will relieve me at 4 o'clock. Whoopee!! Maybe I'll get a chance to attend a Y.F (Youth Fellowship) meeting in town. I've only been in town one other evening, so I feel I ought to go in again before going on the range. Columbus isn't too appealing. I'm told that it has a swell Methodist Church, and I'd like to check it out. Also I want to pick up a flashlight.

Things sound OK at home. I'm glad Merrill got his furlough. Did he really get a chance at O.C.S. (Officer Candidates' School)? I certainly wouldn't have passed that up. Merrill said he would drop me a line. It will be interesting to hear directly from him how difficult these A.S.T.P. courses are. Some say they are demons, others say they're just snaps. Merrill should know definitely.

Only 8 weeks from now I'll probably know when and where I'll be going back to school. The prospect of school doesn't thrill me too much. I look at it as a period during which I'll work hard studying, but it is really a period of rest and comfort before the real thing comes. Overseas is what beckons me.

I managed to read, "Here is Your War," by Ernie Pyle. Thanks so much for sending it to me. I enjoyed it a lot. I felt very close to all his stories. We are acquainted already by this training with the conditions and tactics he described. I like the compliment he paid the infantry.

Your comparing me with Pyle blew me up so much that I've started a sort of book. Marcy has been insisting that I write a type of record of events too. So, with all this encouragement I've started. So far all I have is about 1000 words. Starting ten weeks late offers a problem. It will probably never result in much, if anything. Finding time and energy is the big problem.

I enjoyed Grandmother's letter. We really have a stalwart background on all sides. Wouldn't it be lucky if I were sent to Michigan.

I hope everything continues so well at home. Keep away from the colds. Did Tom and Alice (Uncle Tom and Aunt Alice Pryor) get down? It would be nice having them in Columbus.

January 16 enclosure of a church bulletin with the following written on the back:

This bulletin is a little late, but still interesting. The services are well conducted. One phase which I didn't particularly enjoy was the taking of attendance by a show of hands right in the middle of a service. This wasn't done Christmas, but usually it's done every Sunday.

Did you read about January 1st being national prayer day? Well, that day we were in the field being instructed in hand-to-hand fighting (dirty fighting). We were interrupted by a whistle, and we all assembled about a chaplain for a few moments of prayer. It was very impressive to see 1000 soldiers all on their knees in prayer. It certainly made a person think, especially when we stopped dirty fighting for prayer and then continued dirty fighting. War is really trying.

As a whole our religious life is pretty well taken care of here in camp. Chaplains often drop in the barracks for brief visits.

January 19, 1944

Here's a note in the middle of the week instead of the usual time. Since we're leaving for the range Saturday and I don't know how much time we'll have to write, etc., I thought I had better drop a line now.

I don't want to discourage myself and you, but usually only about 10% of the fellows get furloughs after basic. Merrill was lucky. I surely hope I am too. I would really love to get a box while on bivouac. It would be especially nice if I got it while there so I wouldn't have to carry the contents out. The weather has turned very beautiful yesterday and today. Here's hoping it remains that way. We have been wearing our long underwear ever since basic began. We're taking our woolen pants and shirts along just in case.

A very incoherent paragraph! Tsk .Tsk.

I had a nice surprise in the form of a letter from Charlotte Lloyd and Jo Wells. (two Gallipolis girls who had been in the flute section with me in the high school band.) It was nice to hear from them. I'll answer when I get time.

The whole barracks seems to be sick. Everyone is going to bed early, and all complain of headaches, fevers, etc. I too feel a little groggy, but it's nothing to complain about. Chronic fatigue is the big trouble this evening, no doubt.

So Farley is a lieutenant? (Again my opinion of lieutenants is lowered, air corps "lieuys," that is.) Really, that is fine. I hope he keeps going ahead. I wonder sometimes though, when men such as he (education, etc.) are commissioned and fellows like Norm Scrimshaw are privates in the infantry.

Today was spent actually firing carbines. We hiked only three miles to a range. I spent the morning in the pits and the afternoon shooting. Although we were just practicing, I shot "expert" scores. I hope my luck is as good on the real range with bigger weapons.

Well, I guess I too will turn in a little early to cure this fagged out feeling. It's swell to hear from home so often. I feel as if I were right home with you with every letter.

January 21, 1944

Yesterday I thought surely I was dreaming when I found out we could sleep till noon. Yes, the whole company snoozed all morning, and then most of us were set free not having to return till Monday morning. So yesterday afternoon, a gang of us had a bang-up game of basketball, followed by a hearty meal at the service club., and then a relaxing movie. And, this morning another late snooze, plus chapel, plus an afternoon of a little football and a lot of relaxation. The weekend has been restful and nice.

Your letter came this noon. Daddy, your talk on "Why You Sing as You Do" sounded interesting and fun. I'll bet the Rotary really enjoyed it. By the way, I wish you could tell me why I sing as I do. This morning in chapel I noticed a forced sound in my voice. It's hard to get a natural, easy tone. I wish I could sing just half as well as you do, Daddy. My range seems to be getting smaller, too. Maybe I'm not using it enough. How about some professional advice?

It's nice of Mrs. Feely to send candy. I must write them and thank her for her kindness. Probably it will arrive tomorrow. The Readers Digest is such a nice gift, too. I'm glad Joanne and Joey arrived home safely.

I saw the movie "Music for Millions." It wasn't the moving picture it could have been. The music was too good for the plot. The two didn't coincide. The Messiah was fine, as it always is. Clair De Lune was lovely, too. I wish Jose Iturbi would be happy just being a musician. When a man tries to spread his talents too widely, none of them get the proper notice, not even when he's a great musician such as Iturbi seems to be.

What do you know?!!! Marcy just phone me. It was wonderful talking with her again. I phoned her last week and certainly didn't expect a return so quickly. A phone call to me is complicated. The call goes into battalion, and a runner comes down here expecting to find me. Luckily I was here tonight.

I think I will phone you next weekend if it's possible. Would you mind being roused from bed Monday morning? If I don't phone, you'll know I wasn't able to. I'd like just to say "hello" again, just for the fun of it.

It's getting late, so I'll leave you once more.

January 25, 1944

Finally I am getting a chance to write. From Saturday noon on is a continuous story of busyness. We left at 2 o'clock Saturday. The whole battalion marched together. One thousand men in two single files made a line 2 1/2 miles long. We carried heavy packs. Here's what was in them: 2 blankets, tent half, 5 tent pegs, tent pole and rope, raincoat, toilet articles, cartridge belt, full canteen, bayonet, rifle, heavy steel helmet with helmet liner, overcoat over pack, and many other little things. Our whole load weighed about 60 pounds.

We hiked all afternoon. During our march we were attacked by three P-39's (fighter planes). Three times they came over. They didn't actually fire bullets, but their maneuvers were thrilling. Also, we had three gas attacks. Walking fast in a gas mask is really something. The breathing is difficult, but of course it's better than not breathing at all. Of the three simulated attacks, one was using real tear gas. We are never in actual danger. All is just simulated.

Saturday night we pitched pup tents and ate C rations. We woke up at 4 a. m., rolled packs and were on our way again. The night was swell. It reminded me so much of Beaver Lodge. The hike Sunday morning was really strenuous. We force marched all the way, and it was dark all the way for we arrived at our destination around 5 o'clock.

If this doesn't make sense it's because I'm really worn out. As soon as I got here Sunday, I started K. P. (kitchen police) which lasted until Monday noon. When I wasn't on K. P. , I was on the range. We are on the range every day from 7:15 until 6 p. m. Now tonight I am on guard from 10 until 12. Any free time we have we clean our rifles. We shoot at least 60 rounds every day, so our rifles get filthy. (I go on guard in about 15 minutes.)

Maybe I never explained about K. P., guard duty, etc. We take turns at these jobs by company roster. It just happens that my turn comes up on both K. P. and guard this week. Whew! Ho hum, etc.!!

So far all I have done on the "book" is the introduction, and that smells. I'm looking forward to receiving the watch. It will be nice to know what time it is again. The interesting comments about Merrill excite me. Only 6 more weeks and I'll probably be assigned. Gee, I hope it is close enough so you could visit.

The flu really didn't grab hold. Four fellows stayed back. Four more couldn't stand the hike and were finally taken back. The rest of us are feeling swell.

This life is tops. I'm in a tent with the sergeant, two corporals and another trainee. It's nice, but we do a lot of errands for the N. C. O's. Crowded conditions got us in here. Of course we have no running water, lights or any of that stuff. I'm writing now by candle light. You should see all these tents. There are over 200 (1000 men, 5 men in a tent.). Last night I took a quick plunge in a creek. Brrrrr. It was good to feel clean again. (Notice the past tense.)

Tomorrow we shoot for record. I haven't been doing so well in practice. I hope I can do better tomorrow, although I'll still be behind in sleep, darn it. Our rifles are superb. They shoot accurately at 500 yards. I got five straight bull's eyes at 500 yards.

I expect the corporal of the guard any minute, but I'll write until he comes and then quit.

The real experience will be our two weeks of tactical bivouac. I'm looking forward to it. These two weeks are also swell, but the tactical work will be even more thrilling.

I just got back from guard. I must hit bed pronto.

January 30, 1944

For some reason I'm getting more mail than I ever have. This week Bob, Scrimshaw, Merrill, Don Gothard, Ellen, Marcy, Mrs. Tanner and you have all written me. Bob wrote to tell me that he has finally received his navy call. Feb. 7th is the date, and Notre Dame is the school. Isn't he lucky?! "Scrim" is hoping to get office work, but at present is a rifleman in a rifle squad. Merrill finds his work easy and is enjoying life a lot. He plans definitely to go into the air corp. Don G., the boy who goes with Charlotte Lloyd, wrote me about Gallipolis since he was just home on furlough. Ellen and Marcy are both fine. Mrs. Tanner sent a nice picture of Mark in uniform. I have a lot of correspondence to catch up on.

Today I slept until 10 o'clock (luxury). I should have arisen at 8, but since I am in the non-com's tent, the man awakening trainees didn't come here. Usually we do sleep late on Sundays, but since we just moved here there was work to do.

Perhaps I didn't tell you that the battalion changed camping sites. We moved yesterday. This site is lovelier, having many more pines and less sand.

We have not been living on "C" rations. Only three meals have been made up of rations. The kitchen staff is with us, so we still have excellent food prepared for us. Rations are excellent food anyhow. What looks like "dog food" is really good when warmed up. You would honestly be surprised.

This afternoon I took my second bath during this bivouac. The stream was icy but today is warm. I even washed my hair. After the bath I went to church (a natural sequence, eh wot?). The sermon was the best yet. After church we had a wonderful bull session. In the tent was a Jew, Catholic and several Protestants. We were present to find out about each other's religions. The idea was formulated by our sergeant. The discussion was swell. For the first time, I actually feel I know the differences between the three groups.

Our non-coms are really fine. I didn't realize it until now. Sergeant is the solid New England type. He has his degree in geology. He had well-founded arguments for God through his studies. Our two corporals both have junior ratings, one from Purdue, the other Kansas. One majored in history and English, the other agricultural chemistry. Good trio, huh? They're fine men to be under.

Did I write that I shot "sharpshooter?" It's the same rating Mark made. "Expert" is above it and I was hoping for "expert." Six fellows made expert, but I was lucky to get sharpshooter. The rifle is a superb weapon. It's accurate perfectly at 500 yards.

Your day dreams are my daydreams, too. Wouldn't Michigan be swell! But Georgia Tech won't be bad. (I'm expecting the worst just in case.) Wherever I go, 12 weeks will probably be the longest period I'll be there. Three months of school is about all I can hope for. Many are dropped after two or three weeks. You know me and math.

Overseas is what I'm looking forward to. It will come sometime, I'm sure, and it will be a great experience. All the non-coms in this company had overseas physicals Saturday. They're pretty excited to think that they might be going soon.

A man told me today of an A. S. T. P. man who got an 18 day furlough. I'll be satisfied with a three day pass. It will be great to be home again sometime. It's surprising how much we all enjoy this life though. There's nothing like living together with a swell bunch of fellows, especially in the great out of doors. Just so the weather stays nice.

Please excuse the hurried scribbling. This is by candlelight.

February 6, 1944

Ho hum and stretch! We got up at 3:30 a. m. this morning to start our long trek back. What with 14 miles behind me and also a lot of work straightening things up in the barracks, I am now one weary soldier. The hike wasn't too tough. Rain dampened our spirits for the first hour or so. It soon turned out to be a cool and perfect day for hiking. Our loads weren't so heavy this time, so we kept a faster pace. We were in the barracks about noon. We didn't actually start until 5:30 a. m.

The last part of the week was very interesting. We shot grenade launchers, which had enough kick to practically knock you flat on the ground. Also we fired mortars. I fired a mortar five times. One mortar shell costs $18.75. Just think, I alone used up five bonds in ten minutes. Probably

$2,000 worth of ammunition was used in that one afternoon of practice. Wow! No wonder wars cost a lot of money.

Of particular interest was the mental conditioning course which we took Saturday morning. You crawl for about seventy-five yards under barbed wire, over small logs, in and out trenches. All during this machine gun bullets are whizzing over your head only 21 inches. (So said the instructor. I think they are higher) Also dynamite explodes around you making a very loud noise, but definitely! This part of training is probably the most publicized of all the training. It isn't bad at all. You do feel like keeping close to the ground though.

Saturday afternoon we had demonstrations of some of the army's weapons, which we didn't have a chance to operate ourselves. The rest of the days were filled with rifle squad firing, tactics, anti-aircraft firing with rifles, and other things.

I've been watching the news on A.S.T.P. If it does close I'll try to slip in on the training angle. "Corporal Westerman" would sound pretty good. If I can't do that I think I'll try transferring to transportation or the 7th Armored Division. Then again, I wouldn't mind much at all staying in the infantry. These are just spur of the minute ideas, but I'll probably follow closely to these plans, if A.S.T.P. closes.

Your note about Joy Werner possibly visiting here interested me. (Joy was the daughter of Rev. Werner, the senior pastor at Grace Church in Dayton.) I still haven't even talked to a woman, except across a counter, for going on eleven weeks. Isn't that a record? Where in Georgia is she going to school?

It seems every time I write I don't have your letters with me. Consequently I probably don't answer any of the questions you ask. Next letter pop all the questions you have and I'll make sure to give you the dope.

We get tomorrow off after we scrub the barracks thoroughly. I have two weeks' dirty clothing to wash. Nevertheless, I plan to go into Columbus in the evening and perhaps call you if the lines aren't too busy. After all, it has been almost fourteen weeks since I've seen you and I've only called once.

All of us fellows are really getting close now. It will actually be tough to break our swell platoon up in a month or so. Some of the men here are very nearly the best I've had the opportunity to know. Did I ever tell you we have a fellow from Spooner (Wisconsin)? And, another buddy comes from about six miles from Brutus (Michigan). Small world!

Bang!!! All during my writing I've had a hunch someone was around that I knew. I've been looking up after every sentence. Now, the man appears. Bob Kuetcher from Wesleyan, and a rival for Marcy's affections, is the fellow. Gee, it's swell to see him.

Well, I surely hope to be taking to you tomorrow at about this time. I'll keep you posted on anything new about A.S.T.P.

February 13, 1944

I wrote a note immediately after phoning you, and then failed to mail it. Such perfect phone connections made it almost exactly like a visit at home. I was so excited that I walked out without paying for the call. Luckily one of my friends paid it for me. It cost only $1.56 for those five minutes. Isn't that reasonable?

This morning I am again in town, probably for the last time. We are going out for bivouac tomorrow. The weather is cold; so it promises to be an unusual experience, darn it. All my equipment is in top shape, and all of my clothes clean and ready to keep me warm.

Did you get the pralines I sent? That is my Valentine gift to you both. Also I want to send lots of love to the best parents in the world. It was certainly great talking to you on the phone. If I ever actually get a furlough I'll probably be overcome with excitement seeing you again.

Valentine's day presented a problem as to what to send Marcy. A dollar box of candy was finally my gift. Realizing its shortcomings, I'm attempting a phone call to her this morning. It may not get through, but if it does, it will be a nice way to send Valentine greetings. She wrote a cute poem for me which must have taken considerable time. Candy would be a poor exchange.

Although Marcy writes regularly (about twice a week) it is strictly on a friendship basis. In fact sometimes I have to tie a string on my finger to remember to write her. With only a month's real acquaintance nothing would develop naturally. I want to keep in contact with her for she is swell and maybe after the war I might get to know her better. So never worry about me "breaking my heart" or anything like that. But she is great!

We had another game of football, CRASH! CRASH! I bumped my knee and had to limp for two days, but it's O. K. now. When I get back to college I may want to play. Ten extra pounds seems to make a lot of difference.

This week we have been studying aircraft identification and tank identification. We also had a five hour night problem with an actual tear gas attack. We have been having extra large doses of calisthenics. Our meals have been extra super. During bivouac we lose a little weight and I think they are preparing us for it. During range bivouac I lost five pounds. I have it back now, bouncing the scales around 172 with uniform.

No further news about A.S.T.P. has been given. I think I'll probably get in school a couple of weeks before final action is taken. On the way this morning I talked with an infantryman with three years experience. They really get around: Alaska, Aleutians, and now Fort Benning. Any life in the army is bound to be exciting, The man had had three years of college.

Did I tell you 17 men have dropped out of our platoon since the beginning? If you miss more than five consecutive days, you are automatically set back in your training. We began with 65 and now have 48, an unusual percentage. Measles, flu, ankles, etc., have been the cause. If you miss only one day of bivouac you are set back. That's where a lot of fellows were lost.

Your food has been coming and it is swell as usual. That fudge with the taffy taste was really super. Wow!

I haven't been writing too regularly. Pressure is being put on us so that we won't slack up now. I owe Mrs. Tanner a letter. Also Kenny. Be the diplomat for me if it's necessary, Thanks.

There is continual griping in the army. So much that we all do it not meaning it and not realizing it. If i ever sound disgusted in my letters, disregard it because it's S. O. P. in the army. ("S. O. P." means "standard operating procedures.")

Next time I write will be from a pup tent. Four of us are going to pitch our pup tents together making a warmer arrangement. We each carry half a tent. Four will make two tents. I'll be seeing you from a tent or foxhole. (Ahem)

February 17,1944 (Post card)

Here we are in the middle of our first week. So far weather has been bad. It has rained every day and night. At present we are limited to post cards. I'll write a letter later. Four of us are living in a double pup tent. It's as warm as toast and lots of fun. Although we haven't washed or brushed our teeth since Sunday, we are very comfortable. Sunday we get to march back to camp for the day.

February 18, 1944

I don't know where to start. The most logical place is where I left you Sunday. We started our hike out here early Monday morning. It rained most of the way and was pouring when we arrived at our destination about 2 o'clock.

Pitching tents, etc., was a tough job in the rain.

As could be expected that night was pretty damp. Tuesday morn the sun was out long enough to dry things pretty well. During the day we practiced attacking different positions, and then went on the defensive. Tuesday night it rained more. In fact, it has rained a little every day so far.

All our time is spent practicing tactics and maneuvers. We have had two night problems. Wednesday night we hiked for four hours in the pitch black with rain pouring. That was an experience I'll never forget! We had to hold on to each others' rifles to stick together. Often ten of us would fall all at once. The terrain was very difficult and sloppy. Mud over our ankles was not uncommon. Last night we hiked four more hours, but it was pleasant compared to Wednesday.

When we have night problems we get the next morning off. Usually the time is spent cleaning our rifles. The sun is out this morning and the weather is perfect. It's exactly like spring. Several of us have heard robins. As yet we haven't been able to see one.

This morning I finally relented and brushed my teeth and washed my face. For five days I didn't use water except to drink. In fact, none of us did. The rain has kept us clean.

We don't receive packages here. But, one of the fellows on KP brought me your box. It was delicious! We still haven't quite finished the nuts.

I'm glad you liked the pralines. It was a meager gift to express valentine sentiments. March 4th, Jewel's wedding! That's swell. March 6th, Joey's birthday! It hardly seems possible. March 5th, basic over! Ah!!

Rumors are already coming about going to school. Someone said we were going to Wisconsin. Well only a couple of weeks and I'll know if I go and where I go.

Sunday we get to march to camp for a good shower. I'll try to drop you another note then. We have a thirty hour problem which ends next week. That will be interesting.

So sorry to hear about Ambrose and Marybelle! (a church couple from Dayton who were getting a divorce.) Speaking of Dayton folks, I got a nice letter from Joy Werner which I answered.

February 20, 1944

We hiked in early this morning. I changed clothing, showered, shaved and shampooed. Needless to say, I feel like a new person. I'm writing from the Service Club. This is rather a hurried note for in short time we start back out.

Next week all of our work will be done at night. We sleep in the day time only, for seven days. It will be a very interesting week. If only the weather takes a change for the better, everything will be fine.

It will really be wonderful to have Joanne and Joey at home. Boy, I wish I could be there too. Certainly Ellen will come to see Joanne and Joey anyhow. There is no chance for me to be there at all. But I'll be there in spirit.

The news about the watch was startling. That certainly is swell of you! I didn't tell you, but two days after I got my watch back I broke the crystal and lost the second hand. It still runs OK. I never expected such a large gift. I'll really cherish it. I appreciate so much Doug's and all of your thoughtfulness.

You are taking care of me! Thanks for sending Ted my letters. I've wanted to write him, but haven't got around to it.

You have probably heard the news about A. S. T. P. It was announced to us officially yesterday. All they said was that it was dissolving all except a small portion which would remain in operation. So, it's very definite that we won't get to college. I'm not disappointed, but I know you will be. It's very exciting waiting for further news as to what will be done with us. Of course all types of rumors are being spread. Maybe we will get to college even yet. But expect anything, as I am.

I still have a craving for the air corps glory. Having gone through the weather conditions which we have without experiencing any ear trouble, I wonder if maybe I couldn't make it. Do you think it might be a good idea to have ready two or three letters of recommendation just in case I want to transfer to a specialized division which requires them? At present we're all just sitting tight to see what develops. I won't do anything rash. Anyhow, you can't in the army.

I got a swell letter from Bard. He's now at Patterson Field going to more school. He is attached to a crew which will build radio stations. He is very happy over his good luck and I too am happy for him.

I also got a nice letter from Mother Crandall from the Delt House. Everybody certainly is nice to us soldiers.

February 22, 1944

I just got your splendid letter, Daddy. Both you and Mother write exactly what I want to hear. Of course, any word from home is welcome.

Yesterday we started our day at 5:30 a. m. and never closed our eyes until 8:30 a. m. this morning. That's 27 hours without sleep. We had tactics during the day and a 15 mile hike at night. We started the march at 10:30 p. m. and ended it at 4:30 a. m. We ate breakfast and took off on a simulated attack through thick woods. It's really surprising how much you can take when you're trained for it. We went to bed at 8:30 a. m. this morning. I got up for lunch at 12:30. I plan to go back to sleep after I finish this and after I clean my rifle. Work starts in earnest again tomorrow noon when we begin another big jaunt which will continue all night.

Last night I was a connecting file. I kept the rear guard in touch with the main body. The strain on the eyes is a lot. We wear hankies on our rifles as guides. I hope we get a moon for the next night work.

With the A.S.T.P. closing I would like to get in as a non-com. The only hitch is that non-coms were formerly needed here at Benning to train the A.S.T.P. Now that there is no more A.S.T.P. there will be a surplus of non-coms. The main reason I would enjoy being an "n.c.o." is so I would get a chance to see just how much I like instructing. (The teacher angle.)

It is sure we will have good care taken of us. Our lieutenant tells us that our basic is actually as hard, if not tougher in some respects, as his officer candidate training. If we should remain in the infantry we ought to get some type of rating or special recognition.

I have to make myself think about the future, for really I'm content to just drift with whatever wave the army has to offer. I'm positive everything will turn out swell. One disappointment is the elimination of the furlough possibility. Since furloughs were given from the colleges, chances are now very remote.

We haven't had rain this week yet. It has been cloudy all the time so we're keeping our fingers crossed.

Maybe during the period of waiting after training I'll get a chance to go over to Macon, Georgia (3 hour trip) to visit Joy Werner. She tossed an invitation my way and I and about 10 others would like very much to take advantage of it.

It won't be long before Joey and Joanne will be home. That is wonderful! I'm going to attempt to find a birthday present for him.

Well, so long for awhile. My yawns are getting so big that I can't see to write. (Big mouth!)

February 27, 1944

Here it is Sunday morning and I am actually prepared to go to church in a real church. Since we've been camping so much I haven't been to church for five Sundays and then, I haven't been in church with a mixed congregation s i n c e leaving home. So here I am in Columbus, Georgia, waiting for the time to pass until church. Three of us are going together.

This last week of bivouac was swell. One of the things I learned from it was that the human can adjust himself to almost any condition. During our last problem (supposed to be 33 hours but was actually 40), it rained off and on. One night it rained enough so that we were soaking wet all night. It didn't bother me in the least. We are in top shape now. Our intermittent wettings and cold and hot weather were enough to put any average man down with a cold. All of us came through without a sniffle. We lived on C rations during the last problem. They are very good, hot or cold. After this bivouacking period I feel sure I could handle everything actual combat conditions would have to offer.

No more A. S. T. P. news has come our way. We have the 14th week scheduled now. I have a sneaking feeling that our basic will be extended to 17 weeks. At any rate, I'm riding the wave. As soon as our future is outlined for us, If I don't like it I'll try for the air corps. We may get good breaks though.

I got the nicest letter from Lucille Harris in Dayton. Buddy Knepper is a Captain and Squadron Commander, overseas, of course. Bob Harris is a Top Sergeant overseas. Charlie is a Private of the year in Kentucky someplace. Charles Whistler is just graduating in engineering at Purdue and is slated for the army. I guess he was deferred. Susie is quite the belle of Fairview High School, and Peggy Knepper is in the WACS. I am enclosing the picture Lucille sent. You keep it. Isn't it fascinating to see how childhood ambitions have developed in our Dayton neighborhood, especially in Buddy's case.

This coming week will be pretty strenuous. We have a four mile forced march to be completed in forty minutes, with full equipment. Also, we have a twenty mile hike Wednesday. Then, too, we have physical tests, 32 push ups, etc. When I came in the army I could do only 18 push ups. Now I can just about do the required 32.

I got your delicious cake and candy bars yesterday. They were excellent. The watch hasn't come, but I am anxiously watching the mail.

Marcy is working very hard on the yearbook. In fact she is giving up her vacation to get the copy in. She's carrying too much work.

I imagine you have seen Kenny by now. Give him a hearty "hello" for me. I hope he can work on Manning fast. Don't you think Manning should start this semester. I definitely do.

I got a swell long letter from Ellen. I have the best sisters in the world, absolutely!! And I didn't even send any valentine greetings. I hope they'll forgive it.

Nine men from our battalion will be chosen for O. C. S. (officers' candidate school). One of the necessary requirements is four years of R. O. T. C. (Hmmmm)

In our problem I was captured. Cuss. I was on reconnaissance patrol to find out information about an enemy machine gun. It was a daytime patrol. I sneaked past several outposts, but finally I was spotted. I was too aggressive. Prisoners got exchanged every eight hours and I got caught just before the exchange, so I didn't lose out on anything

Being back in the barracks is just plain luxury. Isn't it funny how your standards change? On bivouac our tents were heaven compared to foxholes. Fox hole were swell compared to nothing. Now barracks which were looked at as holes in civilian life are the last word in comfort.

I'm still excited about Joanne's visit. Also I'm glad she's coming later for that increases any possibility of me happening to drop in during her visit. But since we are in the unsettled conditions that we are in I'm almost positive no furloughs will be in order for us.

I better head for church. The two other fellows have decided to wait for their phone calls. It will be exciting to worship in church again.

I still weigh 170 so I didn't lose much this bivouac.

March 2, 1944

I got the wonderful watch. It is absolutely the most perfect watch I can imagine. I am so happy to have it. Thanks a million!! I showed it to a few of the fellows and before I knew it the whole barracks was around to look at it. One of the boy's father has a watch just like it, and he says his dad says it is the best. Man alive, I am surprised and grateful. Thanks again.

Your box also came night before last. The peanuts added in the popcorn balls made them excellent. Needless to say, about eight fellows send congratulations again on your cooking. I chime in even more emphatically, of course.

I am widening my correspondences. Susy Whistler (from Dayton) wrote a very interesting letter. Also Joy (Werner from Dayton) has written twice. Including Marcy, my life with the opposite sex is very complete now. Chuck Whistler wrote a nice note too. I think he would like to meet Ellen again. (Who wouldn't?)

Still no news about A.S.T.P. Everything is closed now to us including air corp. Probably in a week or so everything will be changed and we will be able to tell where we're headed. I do hope some type of furlough is included in the plans.

Yesterday we took our big 20 miler. It wasn't hard at all. Today we have more physical tests and the four miles in 40 minutes grind. Tomorrow we have mental tests, or tests to see what we have learned. Saturday comes the big parade. And Sunday I am a fireman again. Cuss.

I went to a Lenten service last night and it was lovely. The service in town was a disappointment. But last night's was very worshipful and fine. I hope I may attend all these services.

Our platoon is having a party next Tuesday. We four squad leaders are planning it. We have a fine lodge, Cherokee Lodge, with piano, etc., for the evening. Also we have chartered a bus to get us there and back. Our meal is a three course one with fried chicken. We are not furnishing any beer or licquor and the lodge does not sell it. Many of the fellows will bring it in, though. The whole thing is costing us $2.50 each which isn't bad considering that one platoon paid $5.00 a piece.

Finish later.

(I was going after some dry cleaning, but I'll go later.) I went after all.

Now it's after lunch and I just got your letter. I too have an infinite faith that whatever comes will be all right. Since so far everything we've heard has been rumor, who knows? We might get excellent assignments. This noon also brought a nice note from Joanne. A cute, darling picture of Joey was included.

So this will get to you this week I'll mail it right now. I must get some air mail stamps. It's much nicer to get "fresh" letters.

(Some letters missing here between March 2 and 12)

These letters probably reported the news that my next place of "residence" would be Alexandria, Louisiana and Camp Livingston where the 86th Black Hawk Infantry Division was located.

March 12, 1944

Did you read the article in the February "Readers Digest" entitled "Jungle Fighting?" In it there is a reference to Col. George Bush. Is this our Col. Bush? I immediately supposed it to be. Also in the March "Digest," Dr. Holzer's (a Gallipolis physician) name is mentioned in a "Friends of the Land" article. Don't we know a number of influential people though.

The M1 rifle you mentioned is the same weapon we use. It is really a masterpiece. It's a real pleasure, believe it or not, to care for it. We are able, of course, to tear it down completely and reassemble it in record time.

I realize now that I have left out a lot of details about our training in my letters to you. At any rate, we are able to make minor repairs and breakdown completely the light machine gun, the Browning automatic rifle, and the M1 rifle. Also we could take care of the 60 mm mortar. The B. A. R. (Browning automatic rifle) is one of my favorites. It can shoot 550 rounds a minute. Wow! A reasonable, safe firing rate is 125 rounds a minute.

All this last week we have been going into the B. A. R. more intricately. We fired it and I shot sharpshooter scores. It's a honey. It weighs 20 pounds being twice as heavy as the M1.

It's remarkable how a pack and a rifle don't affect us at

all now. It takes an awful grind to really wear us out now. The difference is really quite remarkable. It's funny, but just the day I got your letter we had been commenting on how much more we could take than at the beginning of training.

All of us fellows had let our hair grow out, so today we got it clipped short again. I figure by furlough time it will be grown out again.

This morning Bob, Jack and several others and I went to church. It was a lovely service with the chapel packed. A civilian visiting preacher spoke a short word and the chaplain gave the sermon. The preacher was much better than the chaplain.

The watch continues to be perfect. I haven't wound it yet nor have I moved the hands since setting it. It is perfect. All the time buddies want to know how much, where, etc.

We are still leaving this week for Louisiana ("Oh Suzanna" etc.) The more rumors we hear the better Camp Livingston sounds. It's sure to be a good place. I'll let you know immediately all about it. (May not be until Sunday, though.) Latest rumor is that we will be there for 13 months. (Ho Ho) Could be true, and the monger actually believed it.

Remember how you used to spit between your teeth, Daddy? Well I just performed the trick from the drinking fountain on my buddies. Result, all over my own letter: "Crime doesn't pay."

Well, I guess I'll sign off for this evening.

March 14, 1944

Your nice letter came this evening. I'm glad you like the picture, and do probe into the box for some of it is interesting.

Today we did nothing but lie around. But, this afternoon we were informed that our troop train was delayed and we would remain here for perhaps a week or more. Since the time of departure is uncertain no furloughs will be issued. (Cuss!!) Tomorrow training will begin again so that we won't become slack. I'm sure though that they won't give us a hard schedule.

Last night after a big inspection by our Major we hitchhiked a ride into town in our captain's big Olds. (Hot dogs!) We played basketball for almost three hours, Then this afternoon again four of us played four officers in the sports arena. We licked the socks off them, and were they surprised. Ho-Ho. These last two days have been full of playing.

It is possible that some of the A. S. T. P. will become non-coms. It depends on the openings in the units they go to. Maybe we'll be lucky, but possibly not, too. I'm enclosing the 86th's insignia. The B. H. stands for Black Hawk. You may keep it.

I plan to call you sometime during Joanne's visit. When would be the best time? Could I call when Ellen was there too? Ellen wrote a fine letter all about her Dayton visit. She did have fun.

Floyd Mussard (Ohio Wesleyan) wrote and he sends you his regards. He is now in the air corps reserves. They are even shelving air corp men because of a surplus.

Do have a grand time during Joanne's visit.

March 19, 1944

I can just picture the house now. What a hub-bub 608 must be! Joey surely has advanced in his actions since I saw him. Playing behind the steering wheel and banging the piano sound like a three year-old child's activities. I'll bet you're all having a grand time.

When is Ellen going to be home? What a reunion that will be. I'd give anything to see her melt when she sees

Joey. How long has it been since she has seen Joanne? Way over a year, hasn't it? I'd certainly like to be there!

This should be our last night in Georgia. Yet, we've spent "last nights" here before. At any rate, all is in readiness for the trip. A nice long trip will be a treat. I'm going to read my "Ohio Wesleyan" book. We're rising at four a. m. Ho hum.

It's interesting to hear about fellows' reactions to furloughs. One boy who was on a convalescing furlough came back four days early because home was boring. Since everyone is in the war effort, I do feel right at home in my place in an army camp. I have never been the least bit homesick, but, of course, a trip home sound mighty inviting. I figure that at least by the end of May I'll get a visit there.

I have seen two shows this week, "Lady in the Dark" and "It Happened Tomorrow." They were both entertaining. This morning eight of us went to chapel. It was packed and a different chaplain gave an excellent Lenten sermon. We did enjoy the service. It will be interesting to meet the new chaplain at Camp Livingston.

Your candy and nut cake came early this week. It was delicious! Packages come quickly and safely. I may have forgotten to thank you at sometime, but I'm sure all have arrived here. I may be sending another smaller box in a couple of weeks. I have some Benning literature you may be interested in.

Have a good time during the visit. Does Joey dampen his pants? I've forgotten the age when that ceases. I'll be writing from La., I hope.

COMPANY L
and COMPANY M
343 INFANTRY, 86TH DIVISION
A.P.O. 450

CAMP LIVINGSTON, LOUISIANA

March 22-September 12, 1944

March 22, 1944

After 30 hours of train ride here we are at Camp Livingston. The train ride was a delightful surprise, going through New Orleans, etc., as is the camp itself. Instead of regular barracks, we live in six men hutments. They are much more private and very cute. (Look something like tourist cabins.)

In my hut are two young medics and two older men. They are all O. K. and I know we'll get along fine. One of the medics, I've found out already, is a devout church goer and is against liquor. I'm sorry our old platoon is so split up, but it does enable us to make new friends and meet new personalities. Anyhow, all of our old platoon is within a half mile walk in one direction or the other. So, we'll still keep in contact with each other.

Since we didn't arrive until 2 a. m. things are still unsettled. My address is permanent though: Co. L, 343 Inf., 86th Division, APO 450, Camp Livingston, La.

How is Joey behaving? I'll bet every person in town wants to come and see him.

It is now pouring outside. Hmmm, I'm finding that the roof leaks a little too. So far, I see only one spot and that's just a small "drip."

It was thrilling to see New Orleans and that vicinity. We took a round about route to get here. We went up to Birmingham and then back south. At first when we started north rumors began flying again about going to a camp in the North. (I'd like to read o/c Postmaster sometime.)

Not knowing exactly what the score is yet, I'll write

tomorrow or the next day.

March 26, 1944

I just came from a lovely church service. It was the best I have attended since Gallipolis. The chaplain is such an excellent man. He is a real preacher; none of this catering to army likes. There are two protestant services, and I'm going back at 11 o'clock to check on the other chaplain. Also this morning I signed up for the chapel choir. Since I'm pretty well settled I can get into things easier now.

How are things at home now? Still so lively? I haven't got any mail from Marcy for almost two weeks, nor from you for over a week. I shouldn't have told people to wait for my new address. No doubt Monday will bring lots of news. Anyhow I can imagine pretty well what the house is like now. I can just see Joey banging the piano. I can picture Joanne tearing downstairs if Joey squeals when she is away from him. Or does she get that far away from him? If I remember correctly Ellie should be visiting at home this weekend or next. Don't forget to agree on a time when you'll all be there so I may call.

After having a chance to orient myself, I find Camp Livingston to be one swell place. Two blocks from my place are library, guest house, service club, theater, post exchange, bowling alley, and chapel. How's that for being ideally located? Our non-coms are swell fellows. They are young, decent and full of fun. The food is even better than at Benning. In fact it is perfect. It's the best I've eaten, except, of course, at home.

Speaking of home (ah!), I'm sure to get a furlough by June. I'm secretly hoping to get it around Ellie's graduation. Seven percent of the company is always on furlough. You'll know when I get mine because of a wire for money.

Our chances for ratings are no good. There are enough old men left in the company so that if any vacancies do arise they will take care of them. A private's life is fine, so I don't mind. And yet, there is always a slim chance.

Yesterday we fired two courses. The first one was called "Salerno." You walk along a path and surprise targets pop up. The other course was firing at transition targets. I shocked myself and shot "possibles" (perfect scores) on both courses. It must have been my day.

The weather is lovely here. I'll bet spring is beginning to get in the swing at home.

Where is Mark (Mark Tanner from Gallipolis) in Texas? I thought I saw Alfred Ingerick (Gallipolis) here. Could you find out if he is here?

I hope you're having a grand time !!!

April 1, 1944

Here it is April Fool's Day! "Look, your shoe is untied!" So far, very few jokes have been pulled. In fact, I forgot all about the day until one fellow attempted a "fooler" on one of the buddies in this hut. And, today is Nibby's birthday, approximately anyhow. Isn't his age eight years now? Still he is lively and full of pep. He's a real puppy at heart. Give him a couple of extra pets and wish him a late "happy birthday" for me.

I have certainly been enjoying your descriptive letters all about Joey's visit. I honestly feel as if I had been right there. I was at the station seeing Ellen in and it seems I was there to see Joey and Joanne leave. I'll bet Joey caused a riot at the pot-luck dinner. You surely have been keeping me posted. Each letter is like a short visit home. Daddy, your letter about the post-war planning was very heartening. I have re-read it several times. When we soldiers realize that sound post-war planning is being done at home it makes us more anxious to do the job well. It's a grand idea sending out those letters.

Tomorrow is Palm Sunday, and I'm on 24 hour guard. Curse! Well, Easter I'll surely be able to go. By the way, Mother, would you be so kind as to take care of some lovely flowers for Marcy again? I would appreciate it a lot. A corsage would be the thing. I'd do it myself, but a trip to town is impossible this week. I hope this reaches you in plenty of time. Thanks! Her address: Marcine Percy, Monnett Hall, Delaware, Ohio. Send me the bill if you like.

Four days last week we spent in the field. We ran some night problems and also had some interesting problems during the day. It got cold in the night. It was surprising how cold it got, especially when the days are so hot. It also rained, so we had a taste of all types of weather. I meant to write from there, but we didn't have time.

I like my hut mates more and more. They are swell guys. All have been in the army 14 months. Each Sunday the whole hut goes to church in force.

The A. P. 0. number means almost nothing. Probably after four or five months I might go over, but not before then. Forty old men are leaving next week.

The prospect of the furlough is plenty thrilling. We get seven days at home plus traveling time. The end of May is my period, I hope.

Have a grand Easter!!!

April 2, 1944

Guard duty was easy so I have time to write again. I got PX (post exchange) guard. I just stood around keeping order from 5:00 to 10:00 p. m. Then I was off today at 2:00 p. m. until 5:00 p. m. I was happy to have free time during the church hours. The church service was lovely. I did miss the choir. If there had been one the service would have resembled one of the services at home pretty closely.

This afternoon I started "0/C Postmaster." I think it is unfair to ridicule some natural army problems. The army is above the optimum size and a lot of conflicting orders, etc. are bound to result. I should read the whole thing before forming an opinion. So many ignorant fellows tend to slam some army tactics that I am prejudiced against any unfavorable remarks about the army. Maybe right after church was the wrong time to begin a humorous book. It's probably very good.

Your candy, nuts and candied puffed wheat came today. (We have one mail call on Sundays.) It is swell and the box is melting away quickly.

How do you like this fancy stationery? Camp Livingston is said to be the most beautiful camp in the U. S. It is lovely! Tall pines are all about. Swamps with Cypress trees are also prevalent. We lose sight of the beauty of the swamps when we have to wade through them Grrr.

I finally wrote Ellen today. I am a poor correspondent with my wonderful sisters. Don't you think the Syracuse job offers more for Ellen? I also wrote Kenny Morgan and Don Gothard today. For almost the first time I am ahead in my correspondence. What a wonderful feeling. Oh, yes! I must write Joanne and Frank. (There goes the wonderful feeling.)

I'm glad the five fellows have been given a second chance. Surely they should have it.

April 9 we change uniforms and go into light khakis. The days are warm enough for them. Still the nights are chilly.

Do have a glorious Easter! When in church I feel as if I were right at home. In fact, sometimes I shove the hymnbook a little toward one side as if I were sharing it with one of you.

April 2 Letter to Ellen

For a brother who realizes that his sisters are about the most perfect women on earth I certainly am an awful correspondent. I do count on Mother sending on my letters to you, though. Each letter home is meant for the whole family.

Today is Palm Sunday! The rain is drizzling down, but still the Easter spirit is about. I just returned from a lovely chapel service. Our chaplains are swell and the whole program reminded me quite a bit of a Palm Sunday at home. Probably just about now you are preparing for your chapel. (Our service was at 9 a.m.) I know it will be lovely. Is your choir doing the "Palms?"

I am on 24 hour guard duty. The guard started last night at 5 p.m. I was Stationed at the P.X. (Post Exchange) from 5 until 10. Then I was relieved until 2 p.m. this afternoon when I go back on duty for three more hours. It's a soft duty for I do have a lot of time off. I'm glad hours were such that I could go to church.

Mother wrote about your offer from Syracuse. Which will it be? Syracuse or Cincinnati? Going on for your masters and then also having teaching experience is a mighty tempting offer, I'll bet. Yet that $2000 smackers a year from Cinci sounds good too. Which does Wes like better? The Syracuse job would be my choice.

I slipped up on phoning home. I had planned to call when you were all there. We didn't have any free time during that period so my hands were tied. Anyhow, it shouldn't be too long before I'll be talking to you personally. At least by the end of May I should get home. We get seven days at home plus travel time. That will be a glorious week. I'll want to spend part of the time at Wesleyan if college is still in session then.

How does it feel to be in that last semester? I'll bet

there is a sort of continual feeling of merriment. I'd like to visit Western again. No doubt I would go nuts though. I honestly haven't said a word to any women, except for across a counter, for almost five months. Isn't that a miraculous feat? I can hardly believe it myself. The fact never bothers me unless I stop and think about it. I must start attending service club dances, etc.

I told Marcy in one of my letters that I hadn't written you in a long time. She pronto suggested I do it immediately. She thinks a lot of you and enjoys hearing from you. I appreciate your correspondence with her. Although I never got to know Marcy very well she is a grand person and maybe someday I'll know that she is more than that. She writes regularly and I hope continues to do so. I'm afraid some of my letters aren't too conducive to answers. Nevertheless, she writes back and that's what counts.

So you saw Bob Owens and Jean Hickson! That must have been a surprise. Your whole Dayton trip sounded swell. Bard wrote that he had seen you. He said you and Wes made a handsome couple. Who wouln't think so.

Bard should be in the South Seas by now. He's on a mission to build a radio station, and he flew there. He should return in a couple of months. Isn't that thrilling!

Your visit home sounded fun. Mother wrote very descriptive letters and I felt as if I were right there with you. Didn't you love Joey!!! And wasn't it swell to see Joanne again!! Gee, we certainly have a family to be proud of.

I enjoy the jokes you send. In fact, one usually goes up on a bulletin board and the whole company enjoys it. Army life has so many laughs that you can't help but stay happy.

I almost forgot! How about sending Mother flowers for Easter. I'll be happy to split the cost with you. I hope this reaches you in time.

Have a happy, happy Easter.

April 7, 1944

Here I am four letters behind you. The mail comes very quickly, in fact, more often than I can answer back. The fine Easter box has come and gone. The cookies weren't dry at all and were excellent. Thanks a lot! Also thank you for checking up on Al and Mark. That was certainly Al's double I saw.

This evening along with your two letters I got a neat little photo booklet from Joanne. The pictures of you, Mother, are super! It was a thrill to see your face again. Ellen and Joey are keen too. It's grand to have the photos and I do appreciate them. I'm going to lend them to Marcy. She's heard so much about you, Ellen and Joey, that she would enjoy seeing the pictures.

My goodness, so Morris, Swanson, and Loren Thomas are all in the services. Will there be anybody left in Gallipolis? Surely the war can't last much longer with such all out efforts. I was surprised to hear about Floyd. He had written that he might go soon, but I wasn't expecting it so soon.

Thank you so much for taking care of the flowers. I do appreciate it. I know Marcy will too.

This morning we had a fifteen mile hike. This afternoon we sort of recuperated from the grind. This evening I went to a Good Friday service at the chapel. Tomorrow morning we have a regimental parade which will be an immense affair. I wish you could see it. We are a snappy outfit.

Easter we change uniforms to khakies. There is going to be a large sunrise service which is sure to be thrilling and impressive. I would rather be at home, of course, but our service will be nice. The music sounds swell, Daddy. "No

Shadows Yonder" is still my favorite. I've been humming it all day.

Do my letters ever sound pretty incoherent and confusing? Sometimes I write after an all night hike or something similar and I can hardly gather my thoughts. I'm afraid pretty often my letters are apt to sound nutty. Tell me if they do.

I'll write again Sunday. Lights are going out now. Taps are sounding too. They are beautiful.

April 9, 1944

Wuxtree! Wuxtree! The rumors are flying! Rumor #1 - By the end of April all furloughs will be completed. #2 - In six or eight weeks the entire division is going over the "pond." Believe it or not. Probably not. Just to play safe, how about sending some money? I think, furloughs are apt to come sooner than I expected. We get paid tomorrow, but a little extra wouldn't hurt. Ten or fifteen dollars will be sufficient. Ask the post office what way to send it.

I just returned from the Sunrise Service. It was lovely, but it lacked the touch Daddy would have added. I'm enclosing the bulletin. We were all dressed up in our summer khakies. Our battalion marched to church. It wasn't compulsory, but a large number of fellows turned out. There must have been 2500 or so there.

I don't know if I told you, but we have a basketball court right outside our hut. Jack Sarvis is in a neighboring company, and we play together almost every evening. Yesterday he and I took on four guys for the fun of it, and we licked them ten points. Jack is 6' 4" and pretty terrific. We really have fun.

I volunteered for heavy machine gun training. For a period of a week I go to school (?) to be trained in this weapon. It's water cooled and an arsenal in itself. Then I may be transferred to a heavy weapons company. It's more interesting to be a specialist in a big weapon such as this.

I think these rumors are pretty well founded. There is an immense movement going overseas. Bard and Floyd are witnesses of this. I hope the furlough isn't too soon. A week ago I got my head shaved and I look pretty terrible.

I hope everything goes well today at home. I'll be thinking of you all day.

P. S. What do you suggest on visiting Wesleyan during the furlough? Would the car be available for a one day's visit?

April 10, 1944

This is just a note to confirm one of the rumors I wrote you about. Tonight thirty-one fellows left on furlough. Probably two weeks from tonight I'll be happily choo-chooing home. I think our tentative furlough date is April 24th. There are approximately 65 fellows eligible for furloughs in the company. Half left tonight. The other half leave when they get back, which should be in about two weeks.

It seems entirely too good to be true. I'll believe it when I see you and not before. Perhaps 20 or 25 dollars would be safer. I may want to get a couple of things for the trip. I'm certainly glad I wasn't in the batch that left tonight. A buddy has my furlough bag and I'm not prepared for a trip home. In two weeks I should be ready. (And by that time maybe I'll have enough hair on my head so it won't look like my face.!)

I think I'll attempt coming by way of Huntington. I'll check train connections this weekend. No doubt I'll end up calling you at the last minute from Hamden or some out of the way place.

Tonight I'm back on guard again. With so many

fellows leaving, some of us had to do double duty. It's a special guard watching the prisoners' stockade. We stand up in little guard houses with search lights just like in prisons. My shift begins in an hour. We're on two, off four, for 24 hours.

The communion service sounded very original and impressive. I was glad too to get all the news about the fellows. Too bad about Mark and Merrill's illness. I hope it isn't serious.

Grandmother (Wuerfel) sent a lovely Easter box of cookies and eggs. It was swell of her, and I do appreciate it.

Marcy has her last class Friday at 2:30 p. m. I do want to spend most of my time at home; but then I want to see Marcy and Wesleyan for an afternoon and evening too. Would Saturday be the time? I absolutely want to be at home Sunday for church. Maybe, Mother, you and I could drive to Delaware together? And maybe Daddy could find business(?) in Columbus so we could make it a threesome? Well we'll figure that out later. All I know is that I am coming home in less than a month. Whoopee!!! I wish I could see Ellen too! Just think, 22 weeks tonight (or tomorrow night) since I've been home. It will truly be wonderful to see you again.

Here I am off guard and feeling like writing more. Today we got a captain for a company commander. I was disappointed when we got the news that our 1st lieutenant, who is a swell man, was going to be replaced. But now we find that the captain is also swell, so all is fine. This company is now almost completely made up of former A. S. T. P. men, so it's really an outfit to belong to. I'm very well satisfied.

I can't help but keep thinking about the furlough. I was just wondering if it would be at all proper to ask Marcy to visit home over Saturday and Sunday, that is if Ellen were there. The big thing is that I want to be home every minute possible, and yet I would like to see Marcy. It probably is too unconventional. I would like your opinion though.

When we fellows get news of going home we seem to forget that you also are in the war and that gas, food, etc., is rationed. It will, honestly, be heaven just to be at home going no place except Gallipolis. So don't vary any standards or go to any trouble just for me. As I said before, being home is the big objective

I'm hopped up over this furlough idea. I better calm down. Two weeks (or more?) is quite a while.

P. S. Marcy probably wouldn't accept, but if she did you'd love her. But then again maybe you wouldn't. Twenty weeks of knowing a girl via mail could possibly give me the wrong opinion.

April 12, 1944

This is another note to say expect me anytime. The suspense is terrific! Every night they call a list of about ten men. The names aren't taken in alphabetical order, so I haven't any idea at all when my turn might be. Tomorrow ten more men leave, names to be given tomorrow evening. It's a lot of fun. With so much to look forward to the days fly by and every chore we do is a pleasure.

The swell bulletin and letter came this morning. I am glad, Mother, that Ellen arranged for the flowers. I wrote her suggesting it, and she did do the job well. Thank you so much for getting Marcy the flowers. She too enjoyed hers immensely. I got two letters from her today. One written just after she got the flowers, another written in the evening. She did appreciate them.

The church decorations sounded perfect. Where did you get the white choir curtain? Say "hello" to Franklin Greene for me. We are old buddies from way back in chemistry class. I think he'll make a good janitor.

I wish I could tell you when and where I was coming. I think I'll probably be arriving home around the 22nd or 21st. That's just a guess though. I have to wear cottons while in this district, but I will change over when I get in the North.

The fellow with my furlough bag comes back tonight. Also probably by tomorrow I'll have your money, so I will be prepared just in case.

General McNair, commander of the army ground forces, is supposed to be in this area tomorrow. We have really been preparing for him. Scrub-a-dub-dub!!!

Well, I hope to see you soon!

P. S. Even if your money doesn't arrive before my turn comes I have enough to make it, so don't worry.

April 14, 1944

Your letter with money order came this morning. $25 is "pulenty!" Also the medic who borrowed my bag has returned. Now all I need is the furlough. I am expecting it Wednesday. Of course it may come sooner or a day or so later. It's too bad I don't know definitely.

I certainly am writing you a lot. It's just that every letter you get you'll know I'm coming a day later. I'll write daily. The first day you miss a letter from me you'll know I'll be around pronto.

The Major General spoke to all the non-coms this evening. His big points were: we have one more shipment of men leaving the 86th this month. After that the division will remain intact for a five month training period plus one month of maneuvers. So perhaps the longer my furlough is delayed the less apt I am to be on this next list. I would really rather go overseas pretty soon after my furlough, but it looks as if I'll be around for quite a while. Yet even Major Generals have been known to make faulty statements. Or plans have been changed after being announced.

I just wrote you about this since news is so scarce when I write often. Usually I forget statements like that regardless who makes them. After all, this is the army.

In thinking it over, I believe it would probably be much better to visit Marcy in Delaware. The excitement of the furlough news made me get big ideas. If I go by Columbus I'll see her, Kenny and other just for that day and then zoom home. You no doubt have written are writing the same advice. You would enjoy meeting her, though.

Can Ellen be home maybe? Since I don't know when I'll be there it does make arrangements difficult.

You can see I'm still hopped up over coming home. It's possible something might cancel furloughs, but I doubt it. Fifty-six men are gone now on furlough.

The machine gun continues to be interesting. Hope to see you soon.

April 15, 1944

This afternoon we changed our living quarters to correspond with our positions in our squads. Now I'm in a hut with a former Benning buddy, three other Ohio men, and our sergeant. Only the sergeant smokes and we are sure to get along swell in all ways.

This evening I visited Alexandria for the first time. The town is nicer than Columbus, Georgia, but is still the typical war time army town. We saw a show, "Hy Rookie," ate a meal and came back early. Also I got the money order cashed.

A letter from Kenny was waiting for me. He says that the V-5 (Naval air corp) is leaving Wesleyan. This complicates their excellent (?) financial standing and seems to complicate several things at school. Also in his letter was a note from one of his girl friends, a nice Gamma Phi pledge whom Marcy wrote me about.

I got definite news about the furlough so will stop writing daily. We are firing the heavy machine gun Thursday, the 20th. Only after firing will we get our furloughs. So probably Friday night, or Saturday, I'll be starting home. It will take around thirty hours for the trip, I think.

Kenny wrote that Floyd was still at Jefferson Barracks after returning from the disembarkation group from which only one left (or sumpin'). Anyhow he still seems to be here in the States which is fine. Bard is in the South Pacific someplace.

Tomorrow a big group of us are planning on church. More and more I like this group.

April 18, 1944

It was nice talking to you last night. Of course it will be much nicer talking to you and seeing you at the same time. It took only an hour for the call to go through. I had to reverse the call since I didn't have any change.

Just as I hung up the receiver rain started pouring down out of a clear sky. I didn't get too wet coming back to the hut. In the hurry of it all I lost my pen. Curse! It was the cheap red one I got for selling magazines in Dayton. I'll have to buy another one soon. Perhaps at home would be the best place.

I meant to tell you last night that we are allowed only seven days at home plus traveling time. I'll probably get two or maybe three days for traveling. I wrote Marcy last night after calling you to ask her to visit that (?) Sunday. I'm afraid it was a poor letter. Maybe she'll come anyhow.

As I told you last night quite a few men are changing companies. So far I'm still in Company L. We finish firing Friday and then I may be switched to M company. This move would delay my furlough. Since it's probable I called last night to tell you. But, I still have slim hopes of going home this weekend and transferring, etc., when I get back. Time will tell.

- I'll finish this after mail call this evening-

This afternoon was a soft one. We had one hour of creeping and crawling and three hours of training films. This evening I went to choir practice. We   sang hymns for two hours. It was an enjoyable evening. I got a ride back from chapel in a jeep.

Well news is scarce so I think I'll get to bed early. I hope everything is going swell in Gallipolis. Hope I see you soon.

(FURLOUGH AT LAST!) April 20 - May 1, 1945

CHAPTER THREE

M COMPANY

M COMPANY

May 2, 1944

First of all, Daddy, I hope you had a wonderful birthday. Just as the train pulled out Ellen and I both woke up to the fact that we had forgotten to even say "Happy Birthday." Happy Birthday and may you have many, many more.

The whole trip was perfect. J. T. (John Thomas Russell from Gallipolis) and I had a chair car all the way. We slept at least two-thirds of the trip. I've never had such an enjoyable train ride.

It was raining upon our arrival. We caught a taxi after lunch and were in camp at two o'clock. I got my stuff and moved right away the two blocks down here to M Company.

It's nice being in heavy weapons for the training will be of a different nature and I won't have to repeat so much.

I bought a pen at the P. X. and it seems to be a fine one.

Thank you so much for the superb week. The

furlough could not have been better in any way. Thanks again and again for everything. Home cooked meals, sleeping late, driving again, and best of all your fellowship. Everything was positively perfect.

Seven letters and two boxes were waiting for me. It was interesting reading them all.

I must close now. I'm not quite adjusted in my new situation. There is more straightening to be done.

I'm not suffering any after-furlough effects. The glory of the week will last until the next one I'm sure.

May 4, 1944

This morning we woke up at 4:45 a. m. to go to the range. We were to fire the M1 and the carbine. I rolled out sleepily and had breakfast. Then I found out that I had already fired this particular M1 problem; so, I could just wait in my hut until noon when the carbine problem begins. So here I am writing you at ten o'clock in the morning after sleeping for 12 hours. What a life!

I do feel sorry for the men who are firing the M1 problem. It has been raining pitchforks all morning. Yet, it will probably be raining this afternoon too. I can't get over this being told to just wait in my hut until noon. My. My! "This ain't the army!"

Quite a few men from a Tanks Destroyer outfit have transferred into our Division. Now we don't have our little elite group of ASTPs and Air Corps. In fact, I'm now in a hut with three "T.D.s" and a heavy weapons staff sergeant. They are all good fellows, but I think they may be shipped out to another camp soon. A heavy weapons company so far seems to be a fine set-up. Our training will differ from the rifle company's, so I won't be at all bored in the next few months. We won't spend so much time on night problems, and that's a nice change. More of our time will be used on the weapons themselves.

Yesterday I was on K. P. It's S.O.P. for a man back from furlough to be on K. P. the next day. I guess they think it sort of eases a person back into army routine. Our kitchen is well run and the food is good. It isn't quite as fancy as "L" company's, but it's still good.

The trip back certainly was fun. Ellen and I had such a good visit between Huntington and Cincinnati. At Cincy, J.T and I caught our train pronto and found luxurious seats in a chair car. At St. Louis we got in an older car, but a colored porter whispered to us that he had a couple of better seats for us. We followed him and, sure enough, we got another chair car. With such comfort we slept at least two-thirds of the trip. At St. Louis the Mississippi was very high. In fact, at one place we went through three inches of water. Another two feet and we would have been delayed.

I saw Jack Sarvis last night. He thinks he will be changed to this company too!! He also had a wonderful furlough, and we had a grand time comparing notes. J. T. is a short distance from me. Only about a block. He seems to be working in fine already. Jack told me that Bob Tomalka got gypped out of his office work. When he returned from his furlough his job was gone. He is now in Headquarters Company, which isn't a bad deal.

Three letters from you, one from Marcy, one from Dr. Shaw(an OWU professor), and one from Joy Werner were all waiting for me. It was fun reading them all at once. I answered Joy's last night as it was written April 17th. She said Bard was in Australia, but I don't believe she really knows.

This company has an excellent day room. In it is a small library, ping pong table, pool table, radio, and coke machine. Last night I beat five fellows in ping pong. The games were close and fun.

I am still kicking myself for forgetting your birthday Monday, Daddy. And Marcy's April 18th. What an absent minded person I am!

I am so very happy having Marcy wear my pin. The whole furlough was just as I had hoped it would be.

I'll probably get a letter from you today, but I'll send this on anyhow. "L" company is next door, so I just check on my mail there; and there is no delay forwarding it to "M" company.

The rain has let up considerably. Maybe it will stop this afternoon.

Insert: Description of HEAVY MACHINE GUNNER (MOS 605)

"Loads, aims, and fires a heavy machine gun from a car or tank or from the ground. Assists in carrying and setting up guns for ground firing; estimates range and sets sights accordingly; adjusts aim for the proper lead of moving target; field-strips the weapon to replace worn or damaged parts and reduce stoppages, and performs detailed stripping to clean properly and maintain the weapon. May fire the light or caliber .50 machine gun. May be required to drive a scout car or tank and may operate a radio. Must be thoroughly familiar with the characteristics, nomenclature, and tactical employment of the caliber .30 machine gun. Must be trained in firing a machine gun from a mobile or immobile position at a fixed or moving target. Must be trained in recognizing and rapidly reducing ordinary stoppages. Must be capable of making rapid and accurate range estimates. Must be trained to perform the duties of any member of the gun crew."

May 7, 1944

What a beautiful Sunday morning this is! It's cool, the sky is a solid mass of deep blue, and the sun is shining with all its might. My but it is lovely., And I don't have a thing to do today but go to church and play basketball.

Last night I looked for "Packy." He was on a three day pass, but now I know where he lives. I got a postcard from Jim Hader, the brother Delt, with his address. I'm going over to see him this morning before church. I mostly just lounged around last night. I even volunteered to clean a machine gun I was feeling so good. I played some ping pong and pool in the day room.

Marcy has written that she doesn't want to date. It makes me happy, and then again I know it isn't fair to her. I wrote her explaining that I'd like to have her go out with other fellows because of the war, etc. She seems rather positive that she doesn't want to. I haven't got her reactions yet to my suggestions. I know she will look at the problem correctly and settle it herself. It does thrill me to know that she would like to wait for me. She means so much to me and my plans for a happy future.

Yesterday we fired the machine guns on a transition course. I qualified for it was pretty easy. That gun is certainly a honey. So accurate and powerful.

A notice is on the bulletin board saying that two percent of the company may volunteer for paratroops. Hmmm! It's mighty tempting. For body building there is no better branch. For good pay paratroops is best. For safe excitement paratroops is tops. If I volunteer it would mean a delay of overseas duty of several more months. It is really safer than you can imagine. No one is ever killed in a jump. Only once in a while are any bones broken. And in combat even though you are let down behind enemy lines what's the difference? It's the same whether you attack the enemy from the front or the rear. Write your ideas on this subject to me. A lot of silly ideas are floating around about paratroops, just as there are about submarines. Submarines have the lowest death rate in this war, as do probably the paratroops.

I think I'll stop now and finish after church. I know this service won't be as nice as last Sunday's, but I'll enjoy it.

Here I am again. I went to church in the 341st chapel with "Hade." It was swell seeing him again. After that I ran over to the 342nd chapel where I had promised to meet Tomalka. So I've been to church twice. Bob and I had dinner at Headquarters Company where he is stationed. It was a good meal with chicken and all the trimmings

I had a most unusual experience this morning. "Hade" and I went to the regular protestant service. It was communion and of course we participated. When they passed out the drink I noticed immediately that it was yellow instead of the usual purple. I wondered and then remembered Marcy telling of a communion service where lemonade was served. So I drank it down and soon found out that it wasn't lemonade. After church "Hade" asked me if I had ever had wine before for communion in a Protestant service. I told him I had never had wine before. So when I went to the Lutheran service with Bob Tomalka I didn't take communion. I guess the chaplain was Catholic, Lutheran, or something. It's a cinch he wasn't Methodist. I was and am pretty disgusted.

Well Mother, you are still protesting against "Mothers' Day." And I still think it's a grand idea. Uncles, aunts, sisters etc., aren't to a son or daughter what their mother or father is. I guess I will have to conform with your request though. The PX has no cards or nice gifts and I won't be able to go to town this week. Anyhow you know that I love you and know that you're the most wonderful mother that could ever be.

Too bad that Bob lost so much money. That was a silly place to hide it. I have written Kenny thanking him for his assistance. I surely appreciated it. Coach Beattie should make an excellent coach. Glad to see they have him signed up.

Am going for a game of basketball. See you again later.

May 10, 1944

My, here it is Wednesday already. Daddy should be just finishing choir practice, and I'll bet Mother is occupied at home doing something useful as always. It's fun to sit and think of what you are doing.

Last night I saw a show of a most unusual sort. Its title is "Between Two Worlds." I recommend it because of its unusualness and because of its thought stimulating abilities for the masses. All of the fellows left commenting, and not the poo, poo, sort of comments. You see, the show deals with heaven and hell, judgment day, etc. See it if you can and tell me what you think.

This evening I volunteered to help load machine gun belts. It was a bigger job than I thought. We just finished at 9 o'clock. I am enjoying the heavy weapons work. At present I am second gunner, The position holds no rank except that I am ahead of five other men in our seven man squad. Only the first gunner gets a corporal's rating. Perhaps I'll lose my position, and there's little chance of getting no. 1. I am enjoying it though.

Congratulations John Lloyd! That is fine. Gosh, but I was sorry to hear about Jim Gatewood. (Two Gallipolis men. Lloyd received a promotion and Gatewood was killed in action.) Two different types of glory!

Last night I finally met Packy McFarland again. He had just been on a three day pass to New Orleans. He was thrilled with the city and encouraged me to visit if I could get the chance. I shall sometime.

Marcy is writing plentifully. I'm glad for it helps acclimate me to the fact that she isn't close by.

Tomorrow morning we get up earlier than usual to do some firing. So I must turn in quickly.

Mother, I hope Mothers' Day is happy for you. I'll be thinking of you more than ever then. The chaplain says this Sunday is devoted to you. Hmmm, don't get impatient. I think it's wonderful and proper.

P. S. Name, serial number, blood type, P. for Protestant on bracelet. W. S. Westerman, Jr., 15121772, 0,P.

The reason we're busier now is because our training period began Monday. So now we're back on full schedule.

May 13, 1944

Dear Daddy, (Normally letters are addressed "Dear Folks.")

This must be a surprise for you getting a letter from me just to you. There is no special reason for it except that it is a little more "man to man."

This week we started on schedule for a 13 week training period. Being in heavy weapons, a lot of the lessons are new and interesting. I'm enjoying the machine gun work a lot. Thursday I fired 375 round by myself. That is quite a few bullets for one man to fire in one day. We were running firing problems.

Company M is definitely "on the ball." The non-coms are fine fellows and there is very little strict unnecessary disciplinary actions. Then also there are a lot of Wesleyan men around (5). My whole set-up here is a nice one. Chances are still very slim for getting any stripes. I am second gunner, but only the first gunners get corporal ratings. Being in a nice company, having friends all around, living in a fine camp, all this makes me well situated and happy.

Perhaps I don't know when I'm really well-off. But I would like to transfer to the paratroopers. Openings are now available for men in the paratroopers. It would mean fifty dollars more a month that I could send home for college and civilian plans. Also it would mean a chance to get a really strong body. By joining up I could do more for the war effort and also more for post-war efforts. I honestly would like to do it.

The outfit may be a little more dangerous, but a machine gun nest seems to me to be more of a target for the enemy than one of 500 or more paratroopers floating through the air. Already you and Mother have told me to do what is better or best. I favor the paratroop deal. Yet I wouldn't want to do it if I thought Mother might worry excessively. That's the reason I'm writing you. Do you think she would worry too much?

If I should fail in the training I would be placed in a replacement center for overseas, practically the same thing I'm in now. I'm pretty confident I could handle it.

The weather is getting pretty hot. There is a breeze most of the time, so it isn't bad. I'm on KP tomorrow. Working in the kitchen on

Mothers' Day seems very appropriate. This evening several of us are going to visit Alexandria again.

May 15, 1944

I have decided to pass up the paratroop deal. I am too happily situated right here. Also I believe I can work in those correspondence courses here whereas it would be impossible to do it there. So, send the school work as soon as you get it. Those extra hours would be well worth the extra money "paras" would offer.

Yesterday I was very appropriately on KP. What is better than to stay in the kitchen on Mothers' Day? It would have been more fun breaking dishes for you, Mother. But we did have fun in the mess hall. We talked at least a full hour about our mothers. We were off duty at 5 o'clock.

I'm sending this before we fall out for morning drill call. Tonight we have a short problem, so I won't be able to write then. I'll finish this at noon after mail call. I might as well continue writing until the whistle blows.

The pop corn balls are super!! The heat seemed to affect the pickles a little. When I pulled out the jar rubber, juice flew everywhere. The pickles tasted peculiar, but were fair anyhow.

I saw a most enjoyable show. Quite a few good shows have been coming and I've been taking advantage of them. This one was "Once Upon a Time." Really most remarkable! You must see it. The whole story is built around a boy and a caterpillar. The clever author should be given a medal.

Better stop.

Here it is noon. This morning work was soft. All we did was sit. Two hours of first aid, one hour of map reading and an hour of drill to keep us awake. This afternoon we have two hours of bayonet and two more hours of first aid.

I'll close since I'll probably hear from you this evening or tomorrow.

Oh, yes, Saturday eve four of us visited Alexandria. It is a nicer town than I expected. We got on a wrong bus and rode through the residential section. I sent some roses to Marcy to arrive there the 18th, one month late for her birthday.

May 19, 1944

This training schedule is certainly radical. Some days we'll work very hard; other days are snaps. This morning we went through a patch of woods filled with mustard gas. After that we were allowed to return to camp to scrub and decontaminate all our clothing. I did my work fast, so here it is only 10:30 a.m. and I haven't anything to do until 11:30.

Tuesday we had a nine-mile forced march. The heat was pretty terrific, but we clocked off the nine miles in the allotted two hours. Yesterday we went fifteen miles in four-and-a -half hours. But we started that hike at 5 a. m. so it was cool and delightful. We eat lots of salt (salt tablets) and the heat doesn't even bother me, really. Of course hotter days are coming.

I have forgotten all about the paratroop training. This outfit is too swell to leave unless something very unusual should present itself. J. T. Russell left here yesterday to go to Camp Howze, Texas. He will be back in Gallipolis in a week or so. His Uncle "Barky" died and he's getting an emergency furlough for the funeral. "Barky" was the nearest thing he had to a father. I'm sorry to see "Russ" leave. He'll still be in the infantry too.

Did I thank you for the pictures? They are swell! I'm sorry now that I didn't take more. Bob Tomalka took three rolls while on furlough. Do send the better ones to Marcy. She'll enjoy them too.

Thanks for the advice about Marcy, Mother. She is dating now, and that makes me feel better. During the war the fellows don't consider a pin a "touch me not" sign, so she may continue to have fun.

Also, Daddy, thank you for the advice on the paratroops. I had decided in favor of your opinions before my letter reached you. But I appreciate your sound opinions. By the way, keep me posted on conference events. Even though I'm far away, conference outcomes certainly mean a lot to me, as everything which affects you and Mother interests me and is important to me.

I'm glad you enjoyed the flowers. Ellen was

responsible more than I. I'll probably hear from you this noon so I'll sign off.

May 21, 1944

Here I am again. Am I writing too often? This is just a note anyhow to answer your last letter. First of all, Mother, I'm in Company "M" now, not "L." (Do I hear you saying, "Did I write "L"?") I get the letters just as soon, but it's better to put "M."

It's now Saturday afternoon and I have completed all my shoe-shinings, washings, etc. It's a pleasure just to sit back and catch up on correspondence. Bob, Jack and I are going in town for church in the morning if weather permits. Right now it is drizzling a little. We hope to go to a youth meeting in the evening. I spend less money during the week in this company so I can afford a bi-weekly splurge in town.

Have you heard anything more about schoolwork I can do here at camp? I am interested and would like to get started. Our outfit is getting a little more strict, but we still have leisure which I could use more profitably.

By the way, this is a big favor to ask of you, but do I still have that little radio up in my room? Could it be fixed inexpensively and sent down here? If it costs too much it wouldn't be worthwhile for its apt to get rough treatment. Several of the fellows have radios in their huts. We have none and would enjoy one a lot. Will you investigate? Thanks a lot.

I was surprised to hear that Don has shipped already. I expect to sail in December. (That's strictly off the record!) I have read a little about the "Memphis Belle." The picture sounds thrilling.

Enclosed is a note about a queer, unusual man in our company. He is only 19, but looks at least 30. I couldn't help writing you about him.

Wish I could be in church with you tomorrow.

Enclosure:

Curious Persons I have Met

Character Sketch

"Cue Ball"

The prize character of Company "M" is Charlie.... Charlie is 19 and already married and divorced. He's one of those "short in stature but mighty in muscle" fellows. He seems to know all about life. Both the rugged and cultural aspects have been ventured upon by him.

When first you see Charlie you tend to brand him as the "east side" or pug type. His nickname is not original, but appropriate, and was derived from the remarkable similarity of his head and a cue ball. Maybe pool or billiards played a part in his re-christening, but certainly his shaved head holds priority in reasoning.

When it comes to pool, craps, holding your liquor, knowing the "right" women, "Cue Ball" is tops. And as for language, you can honestly say that he speaks a language of his own, but definitely. He isn't limited to these few aptitudes. As a mechanic he rates with the best of them. Twice he has refused T/5 ratings with, "Them stripes limit your freedom."

The most amazing thing about Charlie is his ability in the field of fine arts. As a piano player, he is extraordinary. Such numbers as "None but the Lonely Heart." and "Holiday for Strings," are his favorites. The light fantastic numbers with a light fantastic touch seem to be his specialty.

Picture a rough tattooed man seated daintily at a piano picking out beautiful little tunes and you have the scene so often seen in our day room. "Tough but oh so gentle," really describes "Cue Ball." He places himself on the little stool about 24 inches from the piano, thus it's necessary for him to play with his arms straight. It's a picture one will never forget.

Such cracks as, "Get the hair out of your eyes, maestro," don't phase Charlie in the least. He has a mind of his own, and it is an unusual mind.. At any rate, his mind has developed an unusual combination of pleasures.

May 23, 1944

I got the food yesterday with your nice letter. The cookies and nuts were fine and we enjoyed them immensely. Also in yesterday's mail I got some material from Ohio University. The mail man was good to me.

The wonderful weekend I had planned took a peculiar twist. Saturday eve I was eating chow when my name was called for stockade guard. So I went on guard instead of my other plans, naturally. The shift was to be only 24 hours. At the end of our period no one came to relieve us, so we were on duty for 48 hours. I stood guard 16 hours and was glad when we got off. Sunday night there was a terrific storm. The lights around the stockade went off for about two seconds. We thought we were going to have some real excitement.

I'm turning my little carbine rifle in for a 45 caliber pistol. Pretty soon I'll be carrying a B.B. gun. Our training is getting more and more interesting. We're learning about range cards, etc. Now I know how to fire on targets 1500 yards away. It's complicated and fun.

I wanted to drop a line to you to let you know the cookies arrived and have left.

A couple of fellows are arguing about a technical point on the machine gun. Excuse the quick exit, but I want to get in on it.

May 24, 1944

Dear Daddy,

When I read Mother's two letters this noon all I could do was exclaim, "For Heaven's sake!!!" I certainly was surprised. Still am for that matter. But if you are even more healthy now and you are feeling better and fine, I guess it's O. K. I can just see how swamped your room must be with flowers and guests. How does it feel to be on the receiving end of a sick call for a change? Is it true that an appendix operation isn't so difficult now? For some reason

I'm always a little hesitant of any operations. Must have been the ether I didn't like when my tonsils were removed.

Our squad leader and 1st gunner say to tell you they hope you are well soon. They are both fine fellows and it is a pleasure to work under them and with them. We all live in the same hut now so we discuss all our family news freely. I just moved to this hut last night. All the fellows are swell "Joes."

In thirty minutes we are going out on a four hour scouting and patrolling mission. We have been working hard this week. I hope this weekend is free for church and other weekend pleasures.

Today we fired the 45 caliber pistol. As second machine gunner, this is my official weapon. It is very nice to have on hikes or during close order drill. It's an accurate weapon, but different to shoot. After this war I should be qualified to teach riflery in summer camps. Assembling and disassembling weapons is second nature to me now. It's nice to keep after war plans in mind.

I hope you are enjoying your rest period. Probably people are keeping you pretty busy. If you get some free time, drop me a note telling me all about your operation. Gee whiz, I thought you had had your appendix out. You certainly can't tell what the next day will bring, or the next letter.

I have to camouflage my face (blacken it with coal). I'll write again soon. If this night problem is interesting I'll write about it.

May 26, 1944

I'm so glad to hear that you're getting well quickly and easily, Daddy. I'll never forget how surprised I was to hear that you were in the hospital.

I find myself all out of stationery, so forgive the notebook paper.

That night problem we had Wednesday wasn't much. It was similar to those we had during basic. We got in at 12:30 a. m. and then we got up Thursday morning at 4:00 a. m. I'm still sleepy even after 10 good hours of rest last night. Yesterday we drove 30 miles to a range and fired our guns at distances of 1200 and 1500 yards. I fired 1000 rounds. Our group of forty fired 30,000 rounds. We had eight guns and all of them were steaming all day. It was quite an experience. One machine gun got so hot that a water plug blew out and steam shot 10 feet into the air.

Today I am on a trash detail. We ride a truck and haul trash. I stuck my neck out when I told the 1st sergeant I had had classes on malaria control. That's how they singled us out. "Has anyone had malaria control?" Me- "Yeah." "O.K., you help out on trash detail."

Next week on Tuesday we are going on bivouac for three or four days. My letters will slow down in numbers then. I am returning an Institute bulletin and keeping the one you marked, Mother. I'm not sure which course I'll take, but I hope to have time to fill out the blanks and decide tomorrow sometime.

Keep me posted all about Daddy. Get well quickly, Daddy, but enjoy your rest.

P. S. How much is wrong with the radio? I can afford to pay the bill easily.

Later-

Here it is about 4 o'clock. We worked hard this afternoon. Four of us loaded and unloaded a truck load of coal. I guess "trash detail" includes about everything.

Tomorrow morning we have a full field inspection. So tonight I scrub all my equipment and we also clean up the barracks. I do hope I get this Sunday off. I'm starved for a free weekend, especially after this week which has been more strenuous than usual.

That's fine, Mother, that you are not worrying about sleeping alone. That's a real accomplishment. Is Nibby still a good guard?

May 28, 1944 (A Get Well Card)

Dear Daddy,

How's everything? You will be going home real soon, won't you? I got into town today and attended both a church service and a Youth Fellowship. Enclosed is a bulletin. I'll bet our congregation really missed you.

Ellen will be home this week. That is swell! Aren't you proud of her excellent record. Gee, I certainly am. Ever so often I realize how terribly fortunate I am to be a member of a most wonderful family.

I'll write a letter tomorrow or Tuesday. Get well fast!!!

May 29, 1944

This is just a note, darn it. I'd like to write more, but recently all my attention has been going to a fast talking machine gun. Did I tell you I have been advanced to the first gunner position? Probably in two weeks or more I'll be a P.F.C. which means four dollars more a month.

At present I'm a little tired and maybe I shouldn't write in this state of mind. So I'll make it short.

Yesterday our visit to town was fine. We attended both church and Youth Fellowship. Both were good and uplifting. Enclosed is the bulletin which I meant to send yesterday. I am glad to hear that you are recovering quickly, Daddy. Also Ellen's homecoming sounds swell. This week should be an interesting one at home.

The weather is pretty warm. I seem to sweat easily here. Still the heat doesn't bother me at all as it used to. More power to the adjustments the human body can make.

Tomorrow I practice domesticity, or sumpin', on K.P. I'm really lucky for the company is going on a strenuous difficult attack problem. I'll get out of more than half of it.

Today we learned to fire blindly enclosed in canvass. There isn't a thing we can't do with our machine guns. It's a super weapon. Our platoon Tech Sergeant complimented me on my firing today. (Big Head!!)

I better sign off until later this week. The "baby" needs more attention before firing it tomorrow. We're proud of our gun. It's the fastest of the company's eight mainly because of real good care.

What's Ellen decided to do? Camp, at present, isn't it?

I do hope everything is going smoothly at home now.

May 30, 1944

K.P. was fun today. Really it was ten hours of singing and laughing with the secondary job of washing dishes. This evening we were dismissed, and without going out to finish the 24 hour problem with the company. Pretty smooth, eh wot? Probably we'll have K. P. again tomorrow to make up for it. Suits me.

With the extra time this evening I filled out my application for "U. S. A. I." I'd like to take the Sophomore

English Literature class. I don't exactly understand what kind of money order to make out. We get paid tomorrow and I can afford it easily if you'll tell me what the procedure is. I plan to get the application O.K.'d by the C. O. tomorrow or the next day.

Enclosed is an interesting letter the Readers Digest is sending to all service men. A real service and real advertising, don't you think?

Guess what. Struble from Cincinnati, one of my former hut-mates in Company "L," attempted suicide by slashing his wrists. I'm pretty sure I know "Strub" better than that. I think he's trying everything for a medical discharge. I don't believe he has any intention of going through with it. At least I hope this is the case. I'm sure he couldn't be that despondent, or whatever the word is.

How are things at home now? Has Ellen arrived yet? Is Daddy getting all healed? Is Mother working real hard? No doubt a nice newsy letter will come tomorrow.

I'm going to bed early tonight just in case I get awakened around 3:00 a. m. to get in on the tail end of that dawn attack. "Nothing is certain in the army except uncertainty." This seems to have been especially true this last week or so.

A new order has come through. 86th Division men are eligible for furloughs every four moths now. Hot dogs! This means I ought to be disrupting regular events again sometime in September. If the next months pass as fast as this first one has, it will be no time at all before I'll be seeing you again.

Have you seen J.T. around for his uncle's funeral?

June 1, 1944

Whee! At last I'm started on the long ladder of advancement the army has to offer. If I'm extremely lucky maybe I'll get to step up a wrung every six or seven months. All kidding aside, I am happy to have the PFC stripe. It means four dollars more a month. That's fifty more each year for post-war plans. So, call me PFC from here on. Eleven stripes were given out this month.

Mother, your post-war suggestions got me all excited. 'Course, you can't count on anything definite from the government as to college money. But if it does come through maybe I could work out something exciting and worthwhile like that. School and camps still appeal to me and I believe finally I've reached definite conclusions. Post-war is bound to have a lot of happy surprises and disappointments for everyone.

Gee, it's good to hear that you are around home again, Daddy. Your whole experience sounds so interesting. Dr. Holzer is "on the ball" combining business and a visit as he did. Your total expenses are certainly reasonable. That's swell.

The improvements on the house sound fine. At last the long needed toilet downstairs!

This evening our squad leader left on furlough. Next in seniority comes me, so for the next ten days I get to be acting squad leader. The big joke about it is that actually there are only three in our squad who go on the field. Three other members are drivers and another one a cook. So my temporary responsibilities will be small. Also our machine gun went to ordnance today for repairs. No gun cleaning for a few days. Hot dogs!

I phoned Marcy this evening long distance. It took only one hour. She hadn't received any mail from me for ten days so I thought I had better call. I had been writing all along, but for some reason my letters were held up. She said she had gotten several Wednesday. She has asked several times if I would visit in Lima a couple days next furlough. That will be O.K., won't it?

Did I tell you we get furloughs approximately every four months now? Our squad leader had just had one in the last of February. So I'm hoping to be home again in September sometime. No doubt that will be my last one before overseas.

June 4, 1944

"Magna cum laude," that's absolutely wonderful!!! Last night when I read your letter and looked at the graduation bulletin I almost felt like crying. I have been showing all my buddies the "Ellen Sylvia Westerman, magna cum laude" all day. Ever so often I get set back when some dumb nuts ask me what that means. I can't help but look back and see that really it's a natural outcome of preceding events, but still it thrills me. I am so very happy for you, Ellen. The Westerman family has certainly made a wonderful showing so far. Now I do want to try to keep up the record when it comes time to open the books again.

It's good to know that you are recuperating quickly, Daddy. It's good to be getting so much good news from home.

Yesterday afternoon several of us came into town for a show and some shopping. We went back early to camp. This morning Bob Tomalka and I came back to town for church and for the excellent youth meeting this evening. The service this morning was interesting indeed. Have you ever heard of W. L. Stidger? Well this morning during the time for the sermon he told us all about his exploits and what a fine man he is. I was surprised at his speaking technique. A lot of people seemed to think him wonderful. I didn't enjoy him, even if he has written fifty books (about which he doesn't brag, so says he).

The deeee-licious cup cakes were wonderful. Second

gunner Faria says, "These are the best cup cakes I've ever tasted." First gunner Westerman seconds the motion. They were good!!

Have you ever received any news about Bard? I wrote a month ago, but haven't heard any news. Did you reply to his mother's letter? Floyd is finally over. At any rate his mother got letters from him on a transport. I'm almost certain now that I will have another chance to be home before going over.

A group of us are applying for weekend passes for next Friday 'till Monday morning. I don't want to pass up the chance to visit New Orleans. Since we don't know exactly when maneuvers will start, we figure we better take advantage of the opportunity now. Of course, as always, there ara a lot of "ifs."

Bob Tomalka and I have been talking about camp work. Bob was valedictorian at LaCrosse. He is really fine. Maybe someday we'll go into business together. Who knows what the future will bring?

So long until Tuesday or Wednesday.

June 7, 1944

Hello again! Is it hot in Ohio too? Our steel helmets keep us from getting sunburned in the face. But you should see the backs of our hands. Another month, and so far as hands are concerned, we will pass for colored folks. The weather hasn't been that unbearable. There is always a slight breeze to keep it pretty nice. Last night it was actually cool enough for blankets. I don't think the south will be so bad this summer.

Enclosed is a picture of Jack Sarvis, Dick Arentson and Bob Tamalka. We got it snapped at a cheap joint last wekend. Pretty humorous, eh wot?!

It was good to get your letter, Daddy. And you really sound as if you were feeling fine and the ordeal of the operation wasn't too bad. You mentioned my 45 pistol. It is a rotten weapon unless the opponent is within 30 to 40 yards. Its accuracy is punk. It has been said by quite a few army men, and I agree with them, that the pistol 45 cal. is the poorest weapon owned by the army. Of course it is meant for close combat mostly. As for the machine gun, in my estimation it's the last word. It must be cared for properly and won't fire properly with too much rough treatment, but it is a beaut.

I sent in the check. Thanks a lot. At present I wonder if there will be time to do the work, but it's worth the try. Weekends I could find more time to do more creative work, I believe. This week I am especially busy since I'm acting squad leader, But that job will end soon.

Have you written Marcy, Mother, sending her those pictures? I told her you were going to, but she hasn't acknowledged it as yet. She mailed me a couple more snapshots of herself which are good per usual.

Did I tell you that Sunday Bob and I sang in the Vesper Choir at church? Gosh, it was fun. We liked it so much we're going to try to make it a weekly practice. We are invited to a church youth meeting this Thursday night, but, of course, it is pretty much an impossibility.

Retreat is in a half hour and I must clean my pistol. Tonight we have a problem. We had one this morning and finished it at 2:30. So, we've had an hour or so free this afternoon.

Ellen, how does it feel to be home again? I admire Wes immensely for his steps with the Negro church. He is one to stand up for and act upon his convictions.

June 11, 1944

This letter is being written under very dangerous circumstances, and I want you to appreciate that fact. I'm on K.P. again (Sunday, too, Hmmm) and I should be looking industrious. Instead I'm just looking for the mess sergeant. Until he appears I'll continue to write. He really wouldn't do anything, though.

Last night Bob and I went into town and attended a nice U. S. O. dance. We even danced. We didn't go to New Orleans because of an inspection Friday and another one Saturday morning. We worked pretty hard and didn't feel like traveling during the weekend.

Your letter of the 8th came today. So you know Stidger? After I returned from hearing him, I read an article by him in "Link." It was a good article. I think he is a better writer than speaker. I should have asked him if he knew you or the Brashares.

It is fun to hear about Ellen. You must be tearing the place up, Ellen. That candy was delicious. We got it yesterday. Of course it's all gone now.

Good news! The length of furloughs has been extended to 10 days at home instead of seven. And I am expecting it in early September. Whee!!

Since I'm endangering my PFC stripe by writing now, maybe I had better quit. I'll try to rush off a longer note tomorrow or the next night.

We have a fifteen mile hike tomorrow starting at 4:00 a.m. Ho. Hummm.

June 12, 1944

I am enjoying all the happy news from home. The letters from home play such an important part in army life. I wonder how the navy gets along while they're at sea.

Speaking of letters, I'm trying to renew some acquaintances via mail. Yes, finally I have written Mark and Tommy. I would like to hear what they are doing first hand from them. Then, too, they are buddies whose friendship is worth keeping at least in part for a long time.

This evening our corporal squad leader came back from furlough. So now I'm relieved of the extra duties, which were never too "extra" anyhow. He had a fine furlough. We were all sorry for him because word of a three-day extension for him (in accordance with the new ten-days at home business) just missed him. Probably if he had been home four or five more hours he would have received the telegram. Tough luck!

This morning we had breakfast at 4 a. m. and were on our way for the hike at 5:00. We took it slow and finished the fifteen miles by 10:00 a.m.

This afternoon we had a three hour problem which involved a lot of double-timing with guns. So tonight I'm tired a little bit. I'm not losing weight in this hot weather. I drink lots of water at Daddy's advice. The nights are cool so we don't lose any sleep either.

After being home for a long weekend while an old flame was also home from the air corps, Marcy is beginning to wonder just how much she likes me. Hmmmm! Strange enough I'm not worried a bit. Not that I'm overconfident, but rather that I think everything will turn out O. K. or as it should be.

Tell Joanne that I sewed on my stripes myself. It costs ten cents apiece at the PX and that's too much. Rather than ability it's stinginess in me that makes me do it.

Our commanding officer leaves for overseas Wednesday. I hope our next one is as good. I was glad to hear that J.T. got home. Did he have long there? How is Heber? (Heber was J.T.'s brother.) Does Heber have a rating?

'Bout time for taps.

June 15, 1944

This is really a hurried note. In ten minutes we start on a three-day problem. I wanted to acknowledge your last letter and Ellen's swell letter, which I received yesterday.

Last night I fired one of two machine guns selected to fire demonstration for the officers of this regiment. The Major General commander of this division was there. It was such fun putting on the show. We got several compliments from important officers.

Daddy, I hope you have a pleasant Fathers' Day. I wish I could be there personally, but I'll be there in spirit as usual.

We are going to dig emplacements today. I'll write again Sunday.

June 17, 1944

We are all ready to return to camp. In fact we have been waiting for two hours for our trucks. It's 30 miles to camp, so we aren't walking it.

Amazing enough the mosquitoes aren't bad! The jiggers are disgusting though. Between sentences I'm itching and scratching vigorously. The weather has been warm but O. K. for bivouacking. We are equipped with excellent mosquito nets, so all we do is put up the nets and not our tents.

During the three days here I've fired about 3000 rounds. We've really been keeping the guns hot. Most of our work has been firing on villages, mock villages. It's interesting and fun.

I'll be glad to get back to camp. If possible I'm going

to church in town tomorrow. It's rumored that we are coming back in the field Wednesday for ten days. If so, this is a weekend to be taken advantage of.

The demonstration problem we fired Wednesday night for the officers was similar to our village problem here. We fire down a street while riflemen run in the buildings on the side of the street. As long as the riflemen keep out of our sector, they're safe. It's still a little dangerous though.

Yesterday one of the men in the second platoon killed a diamond back rattler. It was young with only three rattles. It reminded me of the good ol' days when Daddy and I helped kill the old rattler with seven rattles.

The latest - there will be no maneuvers. Or we will go on several two week excursions but no real maneuvers. Time will tell! Announcements of drastic schedule changes come down all the time, but it's not very often that we change with them.

Yesterday we had a chance to fire the flamethrower. It's a rugged weapon throwing a solid sheet of flame for some fifty yards. It's used mostly against pill boxes and cement emplacements.

We got mail while here. My allotment was two letters from Marcy. She got the snapshots and enjoyed the letter. She leaves, or has to be at camp, the 28th.

Now I am writing from the U. S. O. in town. The surroundings are quite different from the place where I was writing this morning. We got back in camp at 1:30. By 3:30 we had the guns and equipment all clean again. So after chow I came into town by myself to meet Bob here at the U. S. O. He won't be here for an hour so I'll catch up on letters.

June 21, 1944

Hello again! Today we are preparing for our ten day

jaunt in the wilds which starts this evening. I have everything in order so now I can write a last civilized letter. (Meaning the last one on stationery.)

The swell popcorn, caramels and fudge came yesterday morning. All of it was in fine shape, not melted or anything. As usual it's all gone now. And the whole hut sends "thanks." I got plenty; in fact, I stuffed myself.

Did I acknowledge your good letter, Ellen? I don't recall when last I wrote home. I think it was Saturday eve. Your bicycle riding and bridge playing with the old girl buddies sounds fun. Gosh, it won't be long before you're all wives. It doesn't seem but just a little while ago that Mother was telling you to wear your scarf to high school.

The weather continues to be warm. And today is the first day of summer, isn't it. Wow! I wonder what's in store for us. It's not uncommon for me to down four or five root beers in ten minutes. We sweat continually. I don't remember my forehead being dry for at least twelve days.

I got a long letter from Bob Rahn yesterday. He loves being an ensign, but can't get used to it. His position is being an executive officer on a landing craft. He has 25 men under him to train and take care of. At this moment he is on a two week cruise getting some additional training. His address is Washington, D. C., Solomons Branch. Maybe someday I'll be on his landing craft. If he's ever in New Orleans we're going to get together for sure.

Everything must be humming at home now. Is Bible School done? Has Ellen done all her packing? How is the painting coming, and are the steps finished? I can just picture all the hub-bub around there.

I'm going to ask you to keep the repaired radio at home. At least until some of these rumors die down. Anyhow it seems we will be

doing a lot of field work such as these coming ten days.

I hope it didn't cost too much. I'll probably ask for you to send it on, anyhow, soon. But keep it for now, please.

We won't be working too hard these next ten days. We are an enemy detail for rifle companies who are really the ones running the problem. Also I understand our camping area is near a town, which means we might have running water, etc.

Sunday Jack and I enjoyed church and the youth meeting again in town. The sermon was excellent, "You Can't Go Home Again." I think you have read the book.

Of interest to Ellen - Bob Rahn said he had met many people who know of Wes or of Ellen, and also a lot who know Wes and Ellen. I guess by now one name brings on the other even to the most casual acquaintances. At any rate, he said he had run into an unusual number of people knowing of the two of you. Small world!

If I had my way I would go overseas right away and get into the European theatre. Rumor has it that maybe in two months we might be sailing. I hope this is the case. However, probably we will end up in the Pacific and won't leave the U. S. for four months. It is pretty sure I'll get a furlough before going over anyhow.

I'll pause for noon mail call since a letter from you is due.

Just as I expected your nice big letter came this morning. I think I have answered most of your questions. The food is fine, although sometimes this warm weather cuts down on your appetite.

It is good to hear of your improvement, Daddy. By the way, have you made any arrangements for fishing this summer? Several of us were talking just the other night about fishing. We did have some good times.

Gosh, so you are leaving tomorrow already, Ellen. That means this won't reach you at home.

I appreciate the folks questions and interest in the

army men's doings. Say "hello" for me to all who ask.

I'll write again from the field.

June 23, 1944

Here it is our second day in the field already. And today is the day Ellen leaves, isn't it? I am happy to have her use as much of my stuff as she can. She doesn't need to worry about caring for it either. It's perfectly swell to have her use it, and use it hard.

What a surprise to read about the two weddings. What next? Joe Thompson (Gallipolis) is a fairly nice fellow. I always thought he had several possibilities. Earl Prose (Gallipolis) is really a good guy. He will always work hard to be a good husband. Probably both events will last, but the news of them is surprising.

This evening along with your letter came two V-Mail letters from Floyd Mussard. He is in New Guinea. One letter was written May 29th, the other June 8th. Aside from terribly hot weather, he doesn't mind his situation so much. His second letter was to notify me of a change of address since he had been assigned to a "Troop Carrier Wing."

Being in the field this time is almost delightful. For once in my army life, I'm almost suffering from too much sleep. We are acting as an enemy detail. At 8 o'clock every morning we leave our bivouac area in trucks. It takes an hour for us to reach the enemy area. As soon as we reach the dangerous (?) area, a patrol is sent out to locate the enemy's position. When we locate them we just lie down and sleep until the appointed attacking time. Then we fire blanks for 30 minutes and hop in the trucks and return. We are always back here by 4 o'clock. It's a soft life. The rifle companies who we harass are the ones having the hard time. So far, the bugs haven't even been too bad.

One hour on one of those hard tables! That is

something. Did you actually fall asleep on one of those boards, Daddy? It must have been hot there. As I look back it seems to me that hot weather made me more worn out up north than down here. Isn't "Corky" an officer? What is his rating? Where is Wayne stationed now?

It's a nice coincidence that the radio didn't cost you money when I realized it wasn't such a good idea to send it here.

How much do you weigh now, Daddy? I'm losing a little in the warm weather. About 160 or 165 is my speed now. Is the house quiet without Ellen? What are Joanne's and Frank's plans for a vacation?

June 27, 1944

What a pleasant surprise that must have been to learn about the coverage on the operation. $72 is a reasonable sum for health and happiness certainly.

I too agree about prayer, family background and experiences holding us together in spirit. Especially since my furlough I have felt actually right at home all the time. In fact, I think my next furlough will come very naturally since I feel as if I'm home so much of the time now.

Speaking of the next furlough, it is very probable that I will have my next furlough before Sept. 1. Marcy will be in Long Island until Sept. 1. How would it be for us to take a jaunt together to see Joanne? Marcy is only four hours train ride from New York and with the additional three days to my furlough it seems a swell time could be worked out. I would be satisfied to see her one evening only. Since this furlough will be the last before overseas, I'd love to see Joanne, Frank and Joey too. What do you think about it? Of course there is a chance I won't get another furlough, and when, and if, it does come it won't be for seven or eight weeks or maybe more. But it doesn't hurt to make sketches

I guess.

I appreciate the clippings, and my they have been interesting! Keep it up.

Yesterday I had K.P. The work wasn't hard since there are no dishes. There were lots of pots and pans though. Today I don't do a thing all day except stand two hours of guard at one of the gates. Gosh, this is a soft life out here. It's actually like a vacation.

The wild razor back hogs around here offer some rare comedy. Every night one gets in somebody's tent. Then there is a lot of excitement. Did I tell you one stole my lunch right out of my pack last week when I was on patrol? I had left my pack on the ground   when I moved out. When I returned the pack was moved twenty feet, the lunch was gone further than that.

The nights are cool. In fact, the last two nights I've used my blanket. Also I've been sleeping without mosquito netting. Even the jiggers aren't around. It seems to be a super camping period. What with field showers only 500 yards away, the set-up here is fine!

Did I tell you I got two V-mail letters from Floyd? Sometimes I forget what I have written. Floyd's in New Guinea.

Bob Rahn is at the same base as Bob Wolfe. I wonder if by some chance they have met? Maybe!!?

Just now a chubby pal from Pennsylvania was looking through a group of pictures I have. He will pay a dollar for one of Ellen. Hmm! Of course I won't sell it, but it does prove once again how beautiful Ellen is. I'll bet she has a swell time at camp this summer. Maybe if she pulls the right strings she can get even a more important position for summer after this one. Or does next June seem to fill all her plans?

We are suppose to return to camp this Saturday. A

new camp rule just came out. For the summer season we aren't required to wear our steel helmets except when the situation is tactical. This is nice for we won't get so hot. Instead we wear only our helmet liners which are of cardboard and very light.

How is the house coming? Is it almost finished? Are you having any chance to pick up some sun tan?

I'll write again soon.

P. S. The pine needle is one of several thousand which make the floor of our tent as soft as a mattress, almost.

June 28, 1944

Last night I got a delightful letter from Joanne describing Joey's differences in behavior from last year at this time. I certainly did enjoy reading it. I almost felt as if I were bouncing him on my knee. What an intelligent nephew I have! (Proud Uncle Scott!) I hope the opportunity to see him again will come soon.

A group of us had a ball game after supper. It went into ten innings and finally we lost 21 to 19. It was lots of fun. It reminded me of the good ol' summers at Beaver Lodge. In fact a lot of this army life reminds me of "just camping."

Bob Tomalka is out here too. He is on night shift so I hardly ever see him. Last evening he and a medic whom we had met at the Methodist church in town and I got together for a discussion. We talked for over two hours without half realizing it. It was the kind of talking Bob Rahn and I used to enjoy so much. Mostly theology, life, and post-war plans were our topics. The medic is a fine fellow and we want to become better friends. Did I tell you that Bob Tomalka's birthday is the 9th of July? I must send a V-mail letter to Bard right away. Also, I want to send a card to Donny, Marcy's brother. (Bard and Donny have birthdays on the

10th of July.)

Speaking of the 10th, don't forget you have given me birthday presents all year long and I'm not expecting any more, and I mean it. My watch is still king of all watches. When we were setting up our tents I was pounding a tent peg in with a shovel. I was talking at the same time. All of a sudden I missed the stake and hit my watch full in the face. Results? Not a thing happened. Only by tilting the watch in the sun are you able to detect little cracks in the non-breakable crystal. It is truly a magnificent watch, but I must be more careful in the future.

The Children's Day program sounded so very sweet. I could just hear them singing especially the "That Cause Can Neither be Lost nor Stayed." I bet you were wondering what to do for a minute with such a terrific combination as a Campbell and Brown. Whew!

I can think of nothing else right now so I'll dust the machine gun once more and snooze for awhile. I am out in the wilds again today just waiting for the enemy. They aren't due for a couple of hours yet.

P. S. It's evening and we're back in the bivouac area. A "Digest" came in the mail tonight so I've got lots of nice reading. It's thundering and may rain. The ground needs it but we don't.

July 1, 1944

Although I would love to keep any news of a furlough strictly to myself and surprise you someday in the future, I think it is wiser to keep you posted. Today Larry Seigel informed me that his name was on the furlough list for July 16th. The significance of this is that Larry and I both left together last time April 22nd. In other words - whoopee!! But - almost a dozen men in our company had furloughs last April 22nd. So it is safe to count on a furlough for me at least by the second week of August, and more probably before. Naturally, the sooner I see you the sooner I'll see the other side, which will also make me happy. There is always the possibility of something else coming up. But it does look excitingly definite that I'll be seeing you again within a month or six weeks. And it would be wonderful if we could fix up a visit to Westfield with a side excursion by me to Long Island.

Yesterday I got a beautiful Delt ring from Marcy. It's a swell ring and one to be proud to wear. It is sterling silver with the Delt crescent, etc., attached on the face.

We were to have gone into camp today. Instead we will remain another 24 hours. For this reason the stationery is still not stationery. By Monday we should be back on a normal more difficult schedule.

I got a fine six page letter from Tommy Robinson yesterday. He is well situated and has a rating equivalent to a buck sergeant. Best of all, he definitely is planning on college again after the war. Phys ed. will be his major. He likes Michigan a lot because he thinks Wesleyan may not be included in the government pay program. That's a new angle, which I hadn't thought of. I like Wesleyan a lot because of the fraternity, the "Y," and the other ties. But if it isn't on the "free" list I'll choose another, naturally.

About money to finance a jaunt to New York, starting now I shall pinch pennies. What with penny pinching and perhaps cashing in one bond it could easily be financed. Starting next month I'm taking out an additional ten dollar bond.

I enjoyed your letter yesterday, Daddy. I'm especially happy to know that you are now 100% back in shape. The whole Children's Day program and the vacation school plans and completion were interesting. I shared your news with a pre-theology pal. It's surprising how many fellows are out here who are planning on the ministry. I know of four, all of whom I have met only in the last week. They are swell fellows too, naturally.

Your letter came today, Mother. I'm looking forward with eagerness to the box. You did have a busy and varied day.

We have to help some other fellows break tents so I'll close hurriedly.

July 4, 1944

We're celebrating the 4th by starting out on another "field trip," this time for only three days, though. We got back here in camp Sunday night about 1:30. Yesterday morning we cleaned our equipment. Now this noon we are going out on an attack problem until Thursday night. I won't get another chance to write until Friday so I'm rushing this off now.

Your doughnuts arrived Sunday at a mail call we had just before coming back in camp. So I had a lot of fun. There were six of us in the truck and with much adieu I unwrapped the box and together we devoured the contents while bumping along the road. I'm saving the apple juice for sometime when I can get ice. Thanks a lot. The donuts were deeelicious.

Last night I took in a show, for a change. It was "Home in Indiana," all about horses and county fair sulky races. I enjoyed it thoroughly. You would too, I believe. It reminded me of the days in Dayton when Daddy and I used to watch the races.

Did I tell you my squad leader hurt his hand severely while setting off a parachute flare? He has been in the hospital for three days. I'm in charge until he returns, which I hope will be very soon.

It seems quite certain now that the last week of this month or the first week of August we are going to leave camp for a condensed period of maneuvers someplace. I hope this won't interfere with furloughs. News is certainly queer around here. One day one thing, the next day something else.

Are you doing anything special for the 4th? Gee, it's a beautiful day here. I hope it's the same at home. Is it still so terribly hot? How's Nibby? I haven't heard much about him lately.

I hate to cut this visit so short, but chow is just about ready and I'll have to run.

P. S. A round-trip ticket to New York via Columbus costs only $36.00 from here. Just something along that favorite topic of furlough.

July 5, 1944

Last night, all night, we dug our machine gun emplacements and fox holes. A full moon made the work more enjoyable. Today we sleep, for tonight we will attack the same positions we dug last night. Since I'm not sleepy now, I'd like to talk to you about some amazing observations I've made during this intimate army life.

My topic is vocation, or life work. When I first arrived at Benning I was surprised and somewhat comforted to notice through discussion that almost all the fellows my age were still wondering what to do after the war. Some had decided once, but dropped their ideas. Others had two years of college behind them but were unsettled still. Only a few seemed to be positive of their goals. This was particularly amazing to me since we were an ASTP outfit - a group of intelligent men.

Choosing your life's job has always seemed to me to be the most important thing you do on this earth. Now I find it disheartening to learn that this choice is too often made through "flip of the coin" thinking, rather than the deep serious thoughts that are due it.

A few interesting examples: a husky Russian once told me while we were on guard together that he was going to be a doctor. Reason - "My parents have always wanted me to be a preacher, lawyer or doctor. It's always been between those three professions. I like doctoring best." Money was his chief motive, that is besides his parents who had already motivated him plenty.

Larry Siegel of Cleveland also likes being a doctor. His uncle runs a wealthy hospital and has promised him a position. Larry even hinted that being a doctor wasn't his dish at all. But, that position with his uncle was worth it???

Natural abilities seem to be recognized by the fellows as a vocation motivator only in sports. At least three have decided on coaching because of their aptitude in physical prowess. Then there are men with wonderful leadership and speaking ability, as natural and worth using as any physical abilities, who will choose the meat business because they know of a set-up they can work into.

All this makes me wonder. And as I try to gather my thoughts I find conclusions and results are difficult to draw from these observations.

Some questions come to my mind - Is the job made for the man, or is it a case of re-making the man for the job? Should you work to exist or should you work to live?

To clarify the first question I will enlarge upon it. When the time for the "choice" comes, a type of mature person will be making it. His heredity and environment will have caused him to be the type he is. Will his choice be determined by his background, his abilities, his interests, his life; or will he be jerked from his place by a lust for money, limelight, and earthly rather than spiritual and mental desires? In other words, 18 to 20 years shapes a man for a position. Why let something unreal pull a man out of character in one year or six months of dreamy thinking.

Really the second question: "Should you work to exist or work to live?" is answered by the elongations (?) on the first. Let your life work be work you do from love, work you do because it is your life. Don't allow your work to be "sweat for the off hours." If you work with one eye on the clock and the other on the paycheck, no part of your life will be really useful or happy. So, work to live, not to exist.

And that's why I find it disheartening to see men picking vocations just because of money, etc. , not as if their work was their ambition, but rather the frivolities their work would allow.

And at this point I'm ready to scrap all I've written. For after a moment of clear thinking I realize all my conclusions have been drawn in an unfair period. What does any soldier want most - a weekend pass, a furlough, any amount of fun with the least possible work. No doubt these erstwhile desires have been carried over somewhat into post-war plans. Ten to one, a year after the war most of us younger fellows change vocation ideas.

Yet there are fellows who don't get "prodigal son" ideas during this war. Take "doc" for instance. He had two years of pre-med. Then he came into the army as a medic. Now he has discarded the medical profession in favor of another position "in which I can do more good and be of more help." Yes, now he wants to be a preacher.

If all of us would think always in a "service" frame of mind, more of us would choose the proper profession, for after all we are here to be God's servants.

It's fun to try to think seriously ever so often. I was in the mood today. Since no open ears were about, I decided to take my mood out on you. Certainly the least used, of all the parts of the body, by the army is the brain. That is, the brain actively, instead of passively.

Your nice long letter came just as we left to come out

here. I did enjoy sharing Ellen's experiences. My but she is having a fine time. Her future looks almost blinding, it's so bright. And a Bishop for a father-in-law to be. That is wonderful!

The ice cream social sounded delicious and successful. Wish I could have been there. What a shame about Janet's husband. I do hope he is only "missing" and will be found soon.

It's funny, but I do enjoy camping. I have to keep it a secret, sort of, or the buddies would gang me. Naturally, I gripe with them to keep them comfort, but I still enjoy it and look forward to more of it after the war.

This is certainly enough. I'll save it till we get back in camp tomorrow. Then I'll answer your next letter and send it all at once.

July 6, 1944

Hello again, or still. Your letter of the 2nd came this noon. The clippings and the bulletin were welcome and interesting. Daddy is certainly back on full schedule with a sermon and funeral in one Sunday again.

I'm all excited about this coming weekend. I have a two-day pass which starts Friday, tomorrow, at 5:30 p. m. and ends Monday at 6 a. m. The set-up is ideal for a jaunt to New Orleans, I'm going to run over to Bob's company this evening to see if he wants to make plans like that. If he can't, I think we will just sleep in the U. S. O. at Alexandria and save money and take it easy. A lovely base ball, which is most welcomed, and a box of delicious cake cookies came from Joanne this evening. I must send her my thanks fast. The trip to New Orleans may be too impractical. ('Scuse the jumbled paragraph.)

Our war-bond drive is going full sway. Our company is running a close second. The winner gets $100 for the company fund. The company is backing it 100%. Jerry Vagos, who sleeps in this hut, purchased a $1000 bond. Whew! I wonder if you could do a favor for me. What with the possibility of a furlough in the middle of August, I want to save money towards that. So could you cash in one of my other bonds and send me $18.75 for a new bond. It doesn't sound patriotic, but all of us are purchasing more bonds and that's the only way I can manage it. Of course it isn't absolutely necessary. In fact you could send the money and I would buy it for you, or are you buying bonds in Gallipolis? Skip it or send it. It would be appreciated and would help that drive. The contest lasts until August 1st.

We didn't get too much sleep last night. The problem was interesting but pretty hard. This evening I'm sleepy. I do want to see Bob before I turn in. So I'll cut this short to see what we can work out. I'll write again a note tomorrow to let you know what we do.

July 8, 1944

What a fascinating time I am having! Goodness, but New Orleans is a thrilling spot, so very rich in history, beauty and spots for servicemen. This is the most exciting weekend I could possibly have, unless, of course, I were heading home. Bob isn't with me. He has his two day pass for next weekend. Rather than forfeit my pass I decided to come ahead by myself. Sure enough at the bus station I met two pals heading here. Together we have been having one grand time!

We boarded a bus last night at 8:30. Arrived here to get a nice dormitory bed in a hotel for $1.50 at 3 a. m. This morning we took a two hour tour all over the city. Now after more looking around we're lounging in a servicemen's home, a building re-made for us. It's just like a house with lots of mothers running about. It use to be Gen.

Beauregard's home.

This evening we are taking a boat excursion on the river. Tomorrow morning we will go to some interesting church and then head back for camp.

And now I must tell you about my interesting furlough adventures. I was going to keep it a secret but I guess I should tell you. When I came back to camp from the field there was my name on the list for July 27th. Whee, says I. Then an hour later I looked at the list again and I had been crossed out in favor of a staff sergeant. Why I don't know. But, this means that probably my name will be among the first in the August list. But, the trouble is that it is now known thnat we are leaving camp for short maneuvers the end of this month. This means possibly no August furloughs will be given. So now I'm in the guessing stage again. It was fun being so excited for awhile anyhow. And now I'll have the pleasure of being excited again. If all goes well I should be running up the steps the first week in August. I think my name was eliminated because I'm acting squad leader. Our squad leader seems to be under the weather for awhile.

There are lots of French sailors around. Gosh, this is exciting. If we can squeeze in a trip to Lake Ponchartrain tomorrow we will. What a life!

P. S. The cake was delicious! Bob got a big piece and sends his thanks. It came Friday morning and by Friday evening it had vanished.

July 10, 1944

This has been an extraordinarily happy birthday. Five letters plus your keen toilet bag have livened it up too. My but that kit is swell.

The only difference between yours and the best they sell

in the stores is that yours is better. And all the added articles, wow!! The surprise of the gift plus its superness is all really great. Thanks a million . And I certainly can use it.

My eyes are blinking on me, hence this scribbling. We got the 9:30 p. m. bus back to Alexandria from New Orleans. We arrived in Alex at 4:30 a. m. So I got back in camp at 5:30 a. m. just in time to go on an attack problem with the company. I didn't sleep much on the bus and this eve my head is noggin', or I mean noddin'.

The five letters today were, one from you, one from Joanne, two from Marcy, one from Marcy's sister, Jan, and also a card from Mrs. Morgan. Gee, everyone timed the mail perfectly.

It was swell to learn that Janet's husband is known now to be safe. Hallelujah!!

Today the official announcement of a month's maneuvers during August was made. Also it was mentioned that after maneuvers we would have a change of address. Naturally all the rumormongers grabbed that statement. Aleutians, New Guinea, France, Camp Atterbury, Indiana, take your pick. Three for 5 cents, seven for ten cents. Also some say we will be occupation troops. I hope not. I'm still hoping to have that furlough soon. If I'm lucky I may get it right during maneuvers which would mean dodging a lot of field work. General opinion seems to be that furloughs will be given during maneuvers.

Marcy is having a wonderful time at camp. One letter the little girls are absolutely angels. Next note they're devils. Already, she has been kept up all night by poor little asthma victims. I can't help but snicker at some of her reactions. She is a queen.

Sunday I went to a Methodist church. In the afternoon we swam at the municipal pool and then went out to Lake Pontchartrain. At the lake guess who I met.

Don Gothard!! We got to talk for a half hour as I was just leaving for my bus. Don is really a fine fellow. He still holds his standards for no smoking, etc.

I haven't had a chance to write Joanne yet. Maybe I can do it tomorrow

I guess I had really better turn in. Thanks again for the lovely birthday. Let's do hope for the next one at home, maybe.

July 15, 1944

Thanks so very much for the money order and the extra five. Wow! I must confess that I had ulterior motives, or sumpin', when I asked for the bond money. When I wrote asking for the $18.75 I was under the impression I was getting the furlough July 27th. I wanted to surprise you completely. The only way I figured I could get money without you realizing it was for a furlough was by asking for it by the bond angle. Now that the 27th business was called off and since I told you already of the actual furlough chances, I confess!! In spite of the New Orleans jaunt, I probably will have enough to tide me over till next month. If I do I'll put the money into a bond as I told you I would before when I was thinking of surprising you and using the money for furlough. Thanks for the cash again, though.

This has been one of those topsy-turvy weeks. Up one morning at four, night problems next night, sleep all day next day, etc. Today I am on stockade guard. We are relieved tonight, so I'll get a chance to go to church in town tomorrow, Being on guard today was a nice break for we miss a fifteen mile hike. It seems that often I'm lucky like that.

I enjoyed your added comments and the clipping on vocational choices. I would like to go into it much farther someday in connection with a guidance program for my high school, if I ever end up being a principal. Contrary with guidance opportunities, I've been thinking recently of elementary work. A position such as Ben Evans (elementary principal in Gallipolis) has offers plenty of chances for an immense amount of good work. And, too, there is opportunity for guidance of a different sort in grade school. I'll have to give more thought to the subject.

The other night I argued two hours for Dewey. As far as convincing any pro-Roosevelters, I didn't succeed. In fact my opponents would say I lost the argument. But they didn't convince me of anything either. I'm still 100% for Dewey. That "horse in the middle of the stream" business is going to win out for Roosevelt I'm afraid. Also the fact that Roosevelt seems to be pals with the other big shots of other countries has the people thinking he must be back in. It will be interesting to watch. Probably it would be better if elections were cancelled during the war, but since the pros and cons are already disrupting the peoples' war thinking, I think we should switch. Next election (presidential) I'll get to vote. Goody!

I've been enjoying all of the things in the toilet kit. The dark glasses are fine. All the fellows use them and I hadn't bought any. The money belt will come in handy since my other one wore out long ago.

Joanne and Frank wrote a nice letter inviting me to visit on furlough. Also Frank worked out a fine train schedule. Connections are fine and for only $36 I can make New York via Ohio. I want to be at home at least six of the ten days. At present Marcy's only free time is on Sunday. If necessary maybe I'll have to split the six days into three at home, then to New York, then three more at home. I'm not worrying over any plans. I wouldn't be too disappointed if the New York deal didn't work out. I could stand it too if I didn't get a furlough even. I do want to get overseas. But naturally I want a whole lot to see you all again first. It's almost positive I'll get to anyhow.

Gee, it must be hot at home. I'm surprised how it doesn't get excessively hot here. Inhabitants of Lousiana say it won't get any hotter here too. The South isn't so bad in the summer after all.

New Orleans was a wonderful trip. I shall never forget it! If we should happen to be here for a longer period after August than we expect, I'd like to visit Dallas, Texas. I've never been in Texas. Dallas is a trip about as long as New Orleans. Norm Scrimshaw is stationed at Dallas, so maybe a get-together could be worked out too.

How was John Cunningham? (A Gallipolis classmate.) I haven't heard any definite news about him for a long time. Ann has one more year, hasn't she?

Wednesday we ran a proficiency test with our machine guns. Umpires were all around grading us and asking questions. Our platoon did fairly well. We hit 21 out of 24 targets during one phase of the test. Another time a surprise enemy machine gun nest fired blanks at us. In about five seconds we were firing and hitting them. (The occupants of the nest were safe in a fox hole.) We don't know our grade yet. I think it was good.

Yesterday morning I fired six rounds with the well known bazooka, or rocket launcher. Also I threw two real live hand grenades. Ever so often we work with other weapons than our own. It's good training and helps keep the training varied.

That's about all the news. I hope Nibby gets to run again soon. All those canned plums sound delicious. Be sure they are on a furlough menu. The middle of August is still the period I expect to see you.

P. S. Are you still feeling so swell, Daddy? I'll bet the operation is history already.

July 18, 1944

This afternoon we are going to the field again for a short period. I really enjoy living in the field more than in garrison, except for the difficulty in corresponding, So I'll write now and then not again till Saturday or Sunday.

Sunday we spent in town. Really, it's getting so that we almost live all day Sunday in the nice Methodist church. I'm enclosing a bulletin. In the afternoon we had the opportunity to see "Song of Bernadette." It was a wonderful picture and I enjoyed it immensely. Yesterday, Monday, I was on K.P. We had fun eating up all Sunday's leftovers, including chicken. Then in the evening five of us put the kayo on a large watermelon. Yum Yum.

Speaking of food, Grandmother sent a wonderful large box of cake and cookies. Also I got a nice birthday card with a note. Naturally the food was tops. (I learned a long time ago it was born in the Wuerfel family to be ace cooks.) What with all the eats my stomach was bulging last night. Still is a little for that matter.

I got another letter from Tommy yesterday. Do you remember Col. Carlson of Carlson's Raiders and "Gung Ho" fame? Well, he has been wounded and is now in the same hospital in San Diego where Tommy works. And the best is - Tommy has administered a blood transfusion to him, and has talked with him. Pretty exciting! He says Carlson has thrilling tales. I guess so.

I am satisfied to just wait for my furlough. If it doesn't come till September, swell. If it comes earlier, swell, too. I still think it will come second week or so of August. So the painting is completed. There will be changes to look for. I'm anxious to see those new church steps too.

Wasn't it fine of Frank to spend so muuch time working out time tables. I know now exactly the best connections. I really appreciate his work. Gosh, I hope I may see Ellen too. There are so many, many things I'd like to do and see. Just being home is great though.

How's the heat now? Pretty warm here now. Whew!

July 19, 1944

Here we are back already. But we go out again tomorrow to stay until Saturday. Your nice long letter was waiting this evening so I thought I would answer right away.

I don't understand about Manning (Wetherholt, from Gallipolis) joining the Delts. We were inactivated about a month after I left which meant we can't pledge or initiate any more fellows until we get re-activated. It may be that the remaining Delts have seen to it that we are active again. I hope so! I hope you didn't sell Mrs. Wetherholt on Manning's joining the Phi Delts or one of the other fraternities with Delt in it. No doubt we are re-activated now and I just didn't know about it. It certainly would be swell if Manning did pledge Delt!!

All the interesting news was welcome. I do hope Bill Betz will be found I'm glad to hear that Bill Jones is commissioned for duty in the navy. He'll probably feel better about it all now.

Although I know my furlough won't be until August, I'll be very happy to have the surplus. Heavens, I won't need so much though! Expect quite a bit back. I want at least five days with you at home. Six if possible. Two days of visiting in New York will be grand. We shall see how it all works out.

Don't you plan on taking any vacation at all? If you are sacrificing vacation money for my furlough., please don't. I won't need to touch the $18.75 till furlough. That plus my August pay will be sufficient. I wouldn't need the $50 at all. I'd love to see you plan on a couple of weeks at Ted's. (Ted Wuerfel's Camp Beaver Lodge at Burt Lake,

Michigan.) Couldn't it be worked out? I'll bet it is fun around home relaxing, but the change of scenery would be nice.

I'm looking forward to your sermon, Daddy. Last time I was home I wanted to ask you if I couldn't have the sermon every Sunday. I realize that would tax you and Myrtle (the church secretary) too much. Do send one ever so often though. Your are the best. And I say that with the experience of hearing many other preachers.

Gee, for some reason this election business is thrilling me. Man alive, I hope Dewey gets it. The one big edge Roosevelt had over Dewey in my mind was his conferences with the other big-wigs. In this weeks "Post" there is a good editorial taking from Roosevelt that edge. So many people seem to be pro-Republican. I think there is a fine chance for Dewey.

Faria, my second gunner, has volunteered for the paratroopers. I'll hate to see him go.

Our problem yesterday and last night was per usual. We (meaning the battalion) set up a defensive position. Faria and I dug all night on our machine gun emplacement. The earth was just like rock. About 2 a. m. we had a real thunder shower. After that it was easier digging.

I'll write Sunday again.

July 24, 1944

Everything is buzzing again as once again we load jeeps with our squad equipment for another jaunt in the field. Saturday night we finished up last week's escapades. Now today we are going out until Thursday. "Busy little bees."

The high-light of last week's field work was Saturday when we got to ride in the M-4 Sherman tank. After we got acquainted with the huge vehicle (34 tons) we ran a battalion problem with 19 tanks supporting us. It was quite thrilling. Now I understand that these next three days we are going to run our entire regiment with a tank battalion which includes12 companies and 60 tanks. This will be the biggest problem I've ever participated in. Of course next month on maneuvers probably the whole division will partake. We leave for that month period a week from today.

Yesterday Jack, Packy and I went to town. We were too late for church in the morning but we went in the evening and heard an excellent talk by a Lt. Col. chaplain on "After the War, What?" It was a real inspiration.

Everyone is excited around here. Five hundred men are leaving this regiment on P. O. E. list. Packy (whose picture is enclosed in the other envelope) is going. Also, many of the men I took basic with are on the list. Riflemen are supposed to be the only ones included. Yet it's possible I may go since I have had so much rifle training. But I'll forecast that I won't be on this list but a later one. I would like to go now since so many of my friends are going, but then again since it's indefinite whether or not they'll get furloughs first, I'd rather wait and go after my furlough. It is nothing to worry about. Those listed won't be going for a couple of weeks anyhow. By the end of this week I'll know for sure.

I'm still counting on that furlough and I think you are safe in expecting me second week or so of August. Gosh but your paragraph on fixing up my room made me anxious to see you all again. Actually though it has been only twelve weeks this morning since I left home last time.

Along with Packy's and my picture we had taken last night I'm enclosing the bond and a picture of our machine gun. Our company is made up of both weapons pictured-eight machine guns and eight mortars.

Marcy writes that she will be able to get 48 hours off. Also she would like to meet me in New York. Perhaps it would be grand if Joanne would write her inviting her to spend the one evening at her house. I'm sure she would accept and would love to do it.

All the news is so very heartening!! We mustn't be too optimistic, but it's a cinch that everything looks wonderful. I'm expecting to be home for good Christmas after this next one. Want to bet?! I'm glad to have the prospect of going over soon, since one of the few nice things about war is the opportunity to see foreign countries. Everything is sure to work out for the best I'm sure. In fact there is no doubt in my mind that it will.

Isn't it a coincidence that we both were impressed by the same "Post" editorial. I'm trying to keep up on the election news. It is exciting and I would like so very much to see Dewey get in. The news of plans for a 6-6 system in our city schools is interesting. We are behind being an 8-4 set-up. More recreation facilities are definitely needed.

So you had a visit with John. Swell! I've always liked "Cutty." I'm glad he was kept in the air corp. He'll make a fine navigator.

I shouldn't have even mentioned that P. O. E. list business. At least I shouldn't have said it was possible I would be on it. Actually there is very little chance of me going. I'm rated as a machine gunner and have been for over six weeks. Only riflemen are going. However you will be interested in knowing that so many of my friends are listed.

The other day while riding in a jeep in a convoy I thought I saw Mrs. Mostz (spelling?) in their Buick. I didn't see the license plate. They aren't riding around in Louisiana are they?

Enforcing of a curfew rule sounds good. Gallipolis could use it I'm sure. The poorer girls probably are the offenders.

Well I'll sign off now. Did you forget the sermon you

were sending? See you again via mail Thursday at least.

P. S. I want to thank Grandmother in a letter myself this weekend if possible.

July 26, 1944

Gosh, how I do enjoy work in the field. These last three days have been swell.   Honestly, this out-door life agrees with me 100%. Just call me field soldier. The only disagreeable thing of our little jaunt was an animal, or bug, called the tick. (Remember Wisconsin?!)   I extracted about six and brushed off twice that number. However I'll take the ticks willingly for outdoor life.

This afternoon twenty-one of us came into camp a day early. We are going to try for the "Expert Infantryman Badge."   The tests last two full days starting tomorrow morning early. Bayonet course, compass course, first-aid problems, field sanitation questions, a series of strenuous exercises and many other things make up the grind. It will be quite difficult. It has to be for every man passing the test will receive the badge plus five dollars extra every month. Even though I haven't done ten push-ups since Ft. Benning and have only handled a rifle and bayonet once, I'm going to try for it. I have too much Scotch in me to pass up the chance for the extra money. (By the way, how much Scotch do I have in me?) I don't expect to pass it. Only about 10% do.   Even our officers failed.   But, "nothing ventured, nothing gained."

You'll be glad to know that our company is not sending any men on this present P. O. E. list.   There are enough present riflemen so that former riflemen do not have to go. I expected this to be. Rumors now have it though that any men not having been on maneuvers before, will not get furloughs until after August. So perhaps it will be Sept. before I see you. At any rate I'm saving the money order until I definitely know.

This is being whisked off at 90 m.p.h. I hope my sentences are not too incoherent.

Finally my two literature books arrived. They seem very interesting. Since they came while we were in the field I read 150 pages of the one novel which I must complete. Its name is "Pendennis" by Thackerey. So far it's good.

While we were in the field a farmer with a luscious load of water melons came by. Needless to say we cornered him. Three of us bought four melons, two for .30 a piece, and two for .50 a piece. And were they good!!! Ripe all the way, and they even tasted cool. What a life! I'm looking forward now to maneuvers. In the field you eat more, sleep more, have more freedom, but work harder. It's a pleasing exchange.

Although I would have been happy to go overseas on this list of riflemen, it will please me more to wait a while longer and go as a machinegunner. Gee. I will miss my buddies, though. Still, Jack and Bob will be here as they aren't in rifle companies.

I don't suppose it would hurt for Joanne to go ahead on the invitation to Marcy since still I might be home in August. Whenever it is it will be wonderful seeing you all. I have even more things to talk about this trip.

Perhaps what I like about the field is that you have more privacy. Not that I'm becoming an isolationist, but the woods offer a swell setting for long, long thoughts for after war plans. I don't like to day dream too much either, but the more certain a man's goal, the sooner he's going to get there

I must dash a note off to Marcy. I know I'll be too tired to write tomorrow or Friday. (My muscles ache just thinking of 35 push-ups.)

Probably I missed your letter today for they had mail

call in the field tonight. I'll write again next chance.

July 31, 1944

I'm going to catch up on correspondence, or else, today! So here it is 8:15 a.m. and already I'm starting to wield the pen. I'm not sacrificing church for I plan to go in this evening if possible.

Your two letters came Thursday. And they were so interesting as usual. The "Bijou" sounds swell, but I won't ask you to forward it since it would probably get soiled in the field. Naturally Marcy looked nice! Hmmm. I'm so glad to know that D.T.D. is active again. Manning wrote me and spoke of two other pledges. I am happy to get that news, too. At last the Gwinn-Clark duo has come to a positive end. I guess it really ended quite some time ago. But, it's nice that both are finding people more meant for them. Eloise's captain sounds interesting. I'd like to meet him. Dinner with "Monty" is no little experience.

I too saw "Song of the Open Road" about six weeks ago. I agree parts of it were all right, but other parts stunk. I think too much of the acting was given to the girl, especially since I read it was her first movie.

The more votes the democrats lose the better. I'd really like to see Dewey in. Statements about the man make him sound like a second Abraham Lincoln. I like the way Mrs. Dewey claims that people don't realize that persons in the public eye are really just like other people, not supermen.

Our corporal returned yesterday from the hospital none the worse except for some scars on his fingers. He was in a whole month. It's grand having him back. Did I ever tell you about him? His name is Bob Gleason from the east side of Chicago. He is Italian and went half-way through high school. It's quite remarkable how much he knows for the amount of education he has. Being from the east side he says "toid" for third, etc. We kid him about it.

A good fellow!!

Now there are three southerners, two Louisianans, one Texan, and three northerners, one Chicagoan, a Rhode Islander and me, in the hut. It's most alarming and dismaying to talk to the southerners about negroes. I had heard there was a problem, but never realized it was so terrible. They still think of the negro strictly in slave terms. Should they vote? "No, No, never!" We get in hot arguments almost coming to blows. It makes me happy to see how much all the northern buddies stick up for negroes. It's an issue bound to come up more strongly after the war

Yes we use picks when digging gun emplacements. Sometimes the ground is soft, but other times it's hard as rock. A gun emplacement is five feet in the front, five feet deep, and six feet long. There is a "T" which is dug only six inches below the surface of the ground and on that rests the machine gun. Two of us can dig it in two or three hours sometimes. Other times it may take all night. If we have time we improve it digging a trench from the rear and adding ammunition shelves. It's pretty slick looking.

Furlough news is scarce. Another list came out yesterday with furloughs up to August 7th. I expected to be on it but wasn't. We are going in the field Monday for a month. Probably I'll get mine on the next list which may mean around the 10th or 14th of August. No furloughs will be given after the 18th as they want everybody here the end of the month when we change camps. So if I'm not on the next list it means not until September, which might be better. I'm not worried, but of course I'm very, very anxious to get home!!

The "expert infantryman badge" tests weren't too awful. They were strenuous though. I almost got lost on the night compass course, but finally, luckily, I came in on the right stake. We will find out who made it in a week or so.

I had KP yesterday. In the evening the cook wanted to get out early. So we served chow at 4 o'clock and by 5 o'clock we were out of the kitchen. Whew! Usually 7:30 is the closing hour. Not bad.

I owe letters to Mark, Floyd, Kenny, Manning, Tommy, and Marcy. Quite a correspondence, eh wot? It's lots of fun hearing from all of my old chums. Floyd is quite happily situated in New Guinea. Overseas must be nicer than most folks expect.

Next letter will come from the field.

August 1, 1944

What a life! Yesterday we drove 90 miles. The convoy was immense since the entire division moved out. I figured that there must have been at least 250 jeeps, 250 two-and-a-half ton trucks, and 100 trucks of other types. The 90 miles took about four hours which isn't bad time for such a parade.

Our spot is lovely. Faria (he hasn't gone to the paratroops yet) and I have a swell location for our tent. It's right between two trees so we don't need to use tent poles. This morning I built a little wash stand for our helmets. Another day and this place will be just like home. (Almost!) Last night was delightfully cool after a nice rain washed everything. We don't mind Louisiana rains for just a short time after it rains everything is dry.

We are told that we'll get to keep our locations for ten days or so. After that we'll be on the move making camp as we fight (?). For now we'll be running problems right from here which is nice.

I don't know as yet how mail service is going to be here.

Now it's evening. It was morning when I was writing the other side. The day has been vigorous but nice. But, I find out that tomorrow we are leaving this lovely area. It will be for a period of three days and then we will return here.

As I was saying about the mail - service is apt to be very poor here. You probably won't hear from me more than once a week. Likewise, we'll be lucky if we have mail call twice a week. I'll write as often as I can though.

I don't like to wear out the furlough theme either. But I do hope to have one soon. If I'm real lucky I should get one around the 12th or the 13th. No new list is out, but I have a feeling. (I've had "feelings" before though, darn it.)

I did smile at the confusion between spark plugs and pistons, Mother. That's a charmin' ignorance you have and I love it.

I read the sermon Sunday eve. It was fine. Also Sunday eve I went to church in town. At the youth meeting I made an announcement for a lady and it was fun.

We have a formation now so I must quit.

August 4, 1944

Now it's my turn to be three letters behind. After my last note we have had three mail calls netting three letters from you. I hope such good service keeps up.

Marcy's address: Marcine Percy, Fireplace Lodge, Easthampton, Long Island, New York.

We do receive all packages here in the field. And believe me they are welcome. Of course there is a risk of spoil because of delays in our getting mail. But I would appreciate getting some cookies and am looking forward to the salted nuts.

Lucky for me we didn't have to do the push-ups for

our test. They just transferred our records of the push-ups, etc., we did after basic training. Still, I'm sure I could do more than John's 20. It's harder for more heavy fellows. Results of the test haven't been made known yet. Perhaps they'll withhold the badges until Sept. when they can award them with a parade, the usual procedure.

We have learned about ticks. Usually I can feel them before they "dig in." The information about my great grandparents was interesting. I never have been straight on that. Often we talk about what our ancestors were, here in the army.

Last night I piled some pine boughs up, spread my blanket, took off my shirt, and went to sleep. Amazing as it seems, not a single mosquito came around. It was a perfect night. The moon is so beautiful now!! Tonight we won't be sleeping much as we attack a position some fifteen miles from here.

Mark is still in the army, isn't he? I haven't answered his letter yet. So Merrill is still around too. I wonder if you will be getting this letter soon. Your last letter of the 31st didn't take so long. Let me know how the mail is coming through.

There are rumors going about that we may get passes Sunday and that trucks might take us into Leesville, a town nearby. That would be nice.

I'll write again this weekend. It is good to get such newsy letters from home.

August 6, 1944

WESTERN UNION - Leesville, LA. Aug. 6 1944 to W. S. Westerman, 608 2nd Ave., Gallipolis, Ohio

FURLOUGH THE 10TH. WILL PHONE YOU TUESDAY NIGHT JUST GOT THE NEWS YESTERDAY.

PRETTY CERTAIN THIS TIME. WOULD RATHER COME HOME JUST CALL TUESDAY WHOOPEE. SCOTTY

August 6, 1944

Hello, hello, hello. And this will probably be my last letter for a couple weeks. Since you have my night letter by now you know why I am so excited. Yes, Thursday just after I mailed my last letter to you, and just before we started on our long problem, the 1st Sergeant told me I would start on furlough the 10th. Isn't that swell! It will be sooo wonderful to see you again.

With the pleasure comes plans so I guess we better talk those over. No doubt I'll be talking to you on the phone before this reaches you; but just in case air mail gets there fast, I'll say some things now which we can further discuss on the phone.

First and foremost, being home and with you both is what I want most and most of. My tentative outline goes like this: Home the 11th, 12th, 13trh, 14th, 15th, 16th, 17th. Leave for New York Friday the 18th. Spend Saturday and Sunday there. Come home Monday (Sunday night) for another 24 hours. Be back at camp by the 23rd mid-night. I haven't Frank's swell schedule here with me and I don't know exactly when I'll get home or what hours trains leave for New York. Things should run pretty close to the above schedule.

I'd love to see Ellen. In your today letter her letter said she would be home the 24th. I hate to even think of being so selfish as to let her come home early missing that grand last week of camp. I'd rather she didn't disrupt her schedule like that. The only condition I'd permit it (listen to whose shouting orders) is that she accompany me to New York with me paying the ticket. I have been skimping and I would love to spend my pinched pennies this way. ($70 weight me down now.)

I hate to think of people running around just for me. Really all I want is home. Seeing Frank, Joanne, Joey, and Marcy is a too wonderful addition. So don't go beyond that in extras, please.

I'm rattling this off at 90 m.p.h. I got a chance to come into this burg of Leesville tonight. In two hours we go back to our rugged field life. However I get to go into camp Tuesday morning with all the men who are getting furloughs this week.

Don't expect much in me. This field life isn't exactly the way to get into glamorous shape for a furlough. If you'll skip the heat rash, jigger bites, mosquito bites, rough complexion, I'll feel better.

Gosh but it will be wonderful being at home again!!

It would be possible to tear right to New York right off the bat. That way I should arrive at New York Saturday the12th morn sometime. But since I'm lugging more stuff home this time, and since it would be almost impossible for me to go through Hamden without jumping off, I'd rather stop at home first.

I am so thankful for this second chance to see you. For a while I thought I wouldn't be seeing you 'till after the war. ('Course I'm not on the train yet.)

If Ellen stays at camp could I talk one of you into going to New York with me. I honestly will have the money almost to pay another ticket. Think it over. I tried to put a fast phone call thru to you tonight, but it was no go.

Try to cohere that which isn't coherent. Excitement, hurry and weariness make me sort of hazy.

August 7, 1944

After I told you so emphatically that I would phone tomorrow I find I can't. I'm not going to camp until Wednesday, the same night I catch the train. However if I get a chance I shall call first.

The slight delay is caused by the first-aid tests which we take tomorrow. I guess it's a very important test, something to do with overseas.

About an hour ago we killed a four foot black snake. Did I tell you that we also killed two of those deadly coral snakes plus a baby rattler?!

Really it is quite silly for me to write this. But since there is always the possibility of further delay of personal contact I thought I should let you know by mail why I didn't call Tuesday night. Gosh I'm sorry I told you so definitely that I would call. Now you probably will be waiting up for the call. I hope not.

Your letter of the 4th arrived today which is certainly record time for this desolate spot. How interesting that you also, Mother, are reading "Pendennis." My volume is II and I'm on page 289 beginning chapter 25. Are the volumes the same? Our stories seem to coincide.

It's getting dark and bed is calling. I'm skipping daily events in these hurried conversations. We'll have plenty of time for leisure talk in a few days, I hope.

Furlough August 10 through 23

August 23, 1944

Here I am back at camp feeling right at home (?) writing letters in the service club. I haven't been to the company area yet since I wanted to make sure no details would stop me from writing first thing.

The trip was swell. As I expected, I slept most of the

day. And as I had hoped, I met Bob in St. Louis. The finale for the perfect furlough couldn't have been any better. This afternoon we saw a show in Alexandria, "Thousands Cheer." It wasn't bad. We were anxious to find out if our 86th was back from the field so we came out here at 5 o'clock.

It's only 6 o'clock now, and the 86th is back in camp, and has been since the 17th or 18th. This means I didn't miss much of maneuvers and also I'm not going back in the field. Oh goody!! Other news is that we seem to be moving to another camp middle of September. Exact camp I don't know, someplace on the east coast, it's rumored.

Gosh, but the furlough was wonderful. I honestly don't know how it could have been any nicer. I enjoyed every second of it.

This afternoon I had a chance to get you an impractical gift for your birthday, Mother. Just this once, excuse the impracticability. It is nice though, and you'll like it. Have a "Happy Birthday."

It was so swell of Ellen to quit camp early so I could see her. I appreciate it 100%!! Everybody went all out to give me a grand time.

I should go to the company area and start getting settled since I'll have K.P. tomorrow. Did I tell you K.P. is standard equipment the day after furlough? It sort of eases you back into army life, I guess.

Daddy, I'm sorry we didn't get our fishing trip in, in that little pool across from the boat club. Maybe you and Ellen will decide to try it without the West Virgina license. I think that would be a good way to enter a protest to that silly law.

I will write more about what's what around here in a while. First I gotta' find out myself. Till then, thanks again for the swell time.

August 24, 1944

After 24 hours of army life I can say (and you can quote me on this) that it isn't too difficult to get in the swing again after furlough. Yes, the ol' life ain't bad. Today I missed K.P. and got in on a soft training schedule, which the fellows have been having for a week now, so they tell me. The whole day was made up of a five mile hike, movie, class on airplane identification, two hours of basketball (or baseball, your choice), and two hours of cleaning equipment. Pretty soft compared to the field which I expected.

You know I think I made a screwy mistake in my letter yesterday. Did I say I was expecting to go to the east coast? I didn't mean that at all. I meant the west coast. Sometimes I think I'm batty. Especially after incidents like "Grandview, and Crescent Parkway." Gosh!! I am expecting to visit the west coast in a while. You will get a change of address card when I head for there. In fact you'll probably know my new address before I do.

I have K.P. tomorrow. Our company won the bond drive and as a prize we're having a beer party. It really isn't a beer party. It's a chicken dinner with ice cream, etc., plus beer. They brand it a beer party to get the nuts to come too. There will be plenty of cokes, so my thirst won't go unquenched. I'll probably be eating chicken all day.

Jack Sarvis returned from his furlough today. He too had a wonderful time!! He said it was cold enough to wear O.D.s in Wyoming. Can you imagine that?

How are things at home now? I'll miss being in church Sunday. Maybe Jack, Bob and I can work out a trip to church in town. I hope so.

I was disappointed when I learned that my name was omitted when they handed out the Expert Infantryman Badges a week ago. Oh well, I'll try next time and probably get it then. I'm satisfied thinking that I deserve it anyhow.

All the fellows ask about your furlough and really you're quite the center of attention. You'd be surprised what a big happy family we are, interested in each other's welfare, etc. 'Course we're quite heterogeneous (or is that the word?).

This is hurried 'cause even after this easy day I'm yawning something terrific. I guess I got too much sleep at home. But it was a grand furlough. That'll last me the duration and six months if necessary.

August 27, 1944

Sunday has been nice. Jack, Bob and I went into town this morning for church where we met Packy and one of his friends. So really the day has been one of rest, worship and reunions. This evening we enjoyed the youth service again too. The day has been swell! Yesterday was fun too. We had an inspection in the morning, played basketball in the afternoon, and Jack and I shot pool and bowled in the evening.

The Friday beer party wasn't too bad. I skipped out at 7:15. The cooks were busy drinking, so another K.P. and I took off for the show. "Dragon Seed" was playing and it was pretty good. I enjoyed it quite a lot.

The khakis plus the delicious candy came yesterday afternoon. I wish the camp laundry would do such a nice job, Mother. Also, that candy is the best yet! Maybe our new camp will have better laundry service. By the way, we know quite definitely where we are going. I'm almost positive I'll be only about 300 miles from Tommy R., and in the same state. I can't say more as it is best to be safe in writing. It will be hard to get adjusted to limiting yourself in the things one can say in letters when, and if, we get overseas. Probably we will be winning enough to not worry much about censorship when I get over. I hope so, anyhow.

Did your gift arrive safely, Mother? And, how do you like it? Gee, I hope you do like it!! And I hope your birthday is a happy, happy event.

Packy is leaving sooner than the rest of us. And he is destined for a port in the opposite direction, I believe. I think I'll get another chance to see him too. He is a fine fellow and I'll miss having him around.

Since news is scarce I'll wait 'till tomorrow noon before finishing, then maybe a letter with some questions to be answered will be in the mail. 'Till then, "night," for it's time to snooze.

As I had expected, your nice letter came this morning. I'm glad Ellen is feeling fine again. It must be fun having her around home for a whole month.

You might tell Tommy Woodward, Mother, that you couldn't locate the book. Thanks a lot for the trouble. I might have lost it myself. Will you remember to put the cars for Joey in the box you're sending Joanne? You probably did that already.

This morning was more strenuous than usual. We had a lot of drill and, believe it or not, calisthenics. It was nice to stretch your muscles again.

I'm back in the full swing of army life again, and I'm enjoying it more than ever. With the certain end in sight, even though it may be two years before getting home, this life is more enjoyable. It isn't so hot now either. See you again.

August 31, 1944

The swell pictures came Wednesday and the pop corn and knife this afternoon. You would think it was my birthday instead of Mother's. But your lovely "thank you" letter came this evening, Mother, and I am happy that you enjoy the music box. The place where I bought it had many different types and tunes. Although yours wasn't the most expensive, it had the most mellow and full tone. I am glad you like it, Mother.

Today was payday and I was pay-roll guard. Just before I left for guard I told the buddies to help themselves to the popcorn. Well, they certainly took me literally for when I came back there was one left for me. I had two, one before guard and one after, and they were delicious. I was satisfied to have the boys enjoy them too.

I got a nice letter from Joanne too this morning. It certainly is swell to have such wonderful sisters.

This evening between 30 and 40 men from our company alone are leaving on furlough. About the same number is leaving from each company so there is bound to be an awful rush at the station. It's nice that I had mine earlier.

All the men who haven't returned from furlough since July 1st are getting furloughs now. This will make our whole bunch ready for overseas duty. These men leaving tonight will return to our new camp instead of Livingston. Bu the way, it is now all right to tell our destination. We are going to Camp Cook, California. Thrilling new country and interesting new training. I am happy over the prospects. Camp Cook is located in nice territory for weekend passes.

And speaking of weekend passes, I have another one this weekend, my second one since I've been in the army. I'd like to go someplace in Texas, but may just lounge in Alexandria. What with all the men leaving, no one wanted passes, so I took the chance to get one. (By weekend pass I mean a pass which starts Friday night and ends Monday morning. I'll write about what I do.)

I'll be looking for the identification bracelet. That's swell!! Thanks so much!

You may continue writing this address until you get the postcard notice of a change. Then there may be a one or two week's silence, but I hope not.

September 3, 1944

Your air mail letter with the pictures came yesterday. They aren't bad for such a gruesome subject. Do send a couple on to Marcy, Mother. Maybe the one without the hat would be enough. Use your own judgment.

My weekend pass didn't come through as I had hoped. Instead I am on guard. I'm runner for regimental headquarters 'till this afternoon at 4:30 o'clock. The official stamp is just added for color. If any telegrams come in, we stamp the exact time we received them on the telegram. Cute arrangement, eh wot?!

Night before last "Packy" came over to my hut, and we talked together 'till 1 a.m. He left for P.O.E. yesterday, and since it was our last chance to talk together, we made the most of it. He is going to port very near Joanne. If he gets the chance, he will phone her. He is one grand fellow and I hate to see our roads split. At least we'll be getting together at Wesleyan, I know.

This morning I had a most unusual experience. I was told to wake up a major at 6 a. m. So at that hour I went to his hut and shook him and told him to wake up. He said, "Sure, you bet," and then started snoring again. So for ten minutes we ran through that same routine. Finally he woke up enough to tell me to come back in a half hour. So at 6:30 I went back again only to be met with the same problem. It was a question on how rough a private first-class should treat a major. Finally I lost my patience and just shook and shook him. I disregarded all his answers 'till his feet hit the floor. Of course, then he was fully awake and thanked me. I hope I never have to wake him again.

It's a beautiful Sunday and I'm sorry I have to miss church. However, just sitting and writing letters isn't a bad job. By the way, when we move, there will probably be a period of a week or so that you don't hear from me. So, when there's a silence, you'll know we're on the move.

I'm getting more and more excited about seeing California. It will be a nice experience.

Ellen's Y. F. program sounded swell. The token was clever, too. Ellen will make a super minister's wife.

That's about all the news. Ah, and I have an errand. A new fellow just came in and I have to show him his company. Several new men are coming in.

September 5, 1944

Your newsy letter of Saturday came last night. I'm waiting now to hear the results of the planned fishing excursion. That cove looked sooo bassy. Maybe you won't catch a thing, but at least you'll be in a fishy atmosphere

As you see, we're still here at Livingston. And, wow, are we busy!! Yesterday I was a carpenter all day wielding a saw and hammer. It's fun building things, even if the object of your work is only crating for kitchen stuff. I can hardly wait till the day when I'll be carpentering at a summer camp. I even asked the guy I was working with for hints on how to saw, etc. He taught me a lot. It's surprising how much you can learn if you want to.

Has Major Halliday been overseas yet? I haven't heard much about him.

Twenty more men went on furlough Sunday night. That makes a total of some seventy men gone all at once. Our company is really small now. So, whenever a detail comes up, why naturally we all get in on it. I just returned from a range detail. I'm scribbling this now half expecting to be grabbed for another detail. It's all exciting, though. The "move" makes for high morale among us. We are all enjoying everything.

Last night, Wedel, the company goldbrick (bugler), got a large box from home. About six of us swarmed his hut for two hours and went to bed with tummy aches. It was fun. I enjoy your smaller, more frequent boxes more, though, Mother. However, you better not send another one for a couple of weeks.

I am happy you like the music box.

By the way, you asked a couple letters back if I needed money. I don't need any, and probably won't. If I do, I'll let you know. So, don't worry. Thanks for asking.

Could you ask Mrs. Tanner for Mark's new address? I forgot to get it while I was home. I'd like to drop him a line again soon.

How's the weather now at home? It is nice here; still warm all day, but at night we sometimes use blankets.

Write again in a couple of days.

September 6, 1944

Your long letter came this morning. I wish I could tell you where Camp Cooke is, but I'm not sure myself. The only news I've heard - "65 miles north of Hedy Lamaar's house," "Hollywood's only 130 miles," etc. I know I will be located there, or around there, as long as Ellen's chief counselor's husband was. A nearby town that I'm certain of is San Louis Obispo. It will be thrilling, being in a part of the U. S. I've never been in before.

Today I did more carpenter work. I get a big kick out of it. I guess I looked pretty professional for the cook yelled to me, "Carpenter Westerman, come and fix this door." It was an easy job. He asked me if I did carpenter work in civilian life. So, I almost burst with secret pride.

We are still working hard. However, it won't last long. There is no griping and everyone is working hard, whistling and singing. It's such fun. There's no feeling like the feeling that comes when a whole gang of fellows work hard together and like it. The army is a great organization. Too bad it's organized for such gruesome ends. What do you think of the idea of a year of compulsory training for 17 year olds? I think if it were carried out correctly, it wouldn't be bad at all.

I think I'll shower and shave now. I'll finish after dinner sometime.

9:30 p.m.

Jack and I walked over to Dick's (Arentson) regiment to see if he had returned from his furlough. Sure enough, he had, and, of course, he had a wonderful time. He's the boy whose father is the head of a large forest. Dick spent two days completely alone fishing. Also, he got to fight a forest fire, so his perfect furlough was complete. Quite a fellow.

Remember me telling you about waking that Major Sunday morning? Well, I guess I won't ever have to wake him again. He fell off the train while heading for California and was killed. Isn't that startling and sad? Gosh, I was shocked to hear the news. He seemed to be such a fine fellow (after I got him awake). He packed for that trip Sunday after I awakened him. He was going ahead of us early I suppose. That's life. One day waking a man; two days later he's permanently asleep. (I couldn't wake him because he was drunk, a fact I didn't report to my parents.)

Probably you won't be hearing from me again for a week or ten days. So, don't be expecting much more mail from me for awhile.

Your letters are so interesting and welcome. Marcy and you keep me feeling right at home. You're great morale builders.

See you again via mail sometime.

CHAPTER FOUR

CAMP COOKE

CAMP COOKE
   CALIFORNIA
   September 13 - October 2, 1944

September 13, 1944

Well, here we are at Camp Cooke. First impressions are 1.) a cool, foggy place; 2.) nice double barracks; 3.) ocean only six miles away; and 4.) everything is hunky-dory and swell.

Five hour delay for detail.

I just got your two very interesting letters. Wow, the news about Marge Walters (Friend of Ellen residing in Beverly Hills) has caused comment no end. I must hide the letter and her address or she will be deluged with all types of "M" Company men. By the way, I will try for a weekend pass every week until I get a chance to go to Beverly Hills. I would enjoy meeting her again and seeing Hollywood. Thanks for the tip, Ellen.

The trip was absolutely wonderful. Our train was made up of Pullmans and troop sleepers.   We had a

Pullman. Two men slept on bottom, one on top. We were comfortable all the time. Although we left on Saturday at noon, and didn't arrive here till last night at 9 o'clock, there was very little restlessness. The beautiful, changing scenery occupied most of our attention. We had a lay-over of eight hours at Los Angeles. Since we were confined to our cars, I finished Pendennis.

If you would like to trace our journey, here are some of the major towns we hit: Alexandria, Houston, San Antonio, El Paso, Tucson, Phoenix, Los Angeles, Santa Barbara, and camp. These include Louisiana, Texas, New Mexico, Arizona, and California. It took us 32 hours to go across Texas. We are still arguing as to whether or not we went into Mexico. We did see the country, that's for sure. We rode right beside the Rio Grande for quite awhile.

The central part of Texas is the most desolate country I've ever seen. The west of Texas is lovely. Hills and grass begin here. In fact, in 30 minutes we saw 23 deer running wild in this territory. Isn't that terribly amazing and wonderful? New Mexico isn't bad. Arizona has sandy areas, but hills prevail there, too. California is beautiful. All along the trip we saw tumble-weeds, cactus, century plants, and other exciting Western plants. But, in California the top is realized in beauty for unusual plants. Palm trees and everything are really wonderful.

The trip is one I'll never forget. Everything was so well organized. We even had porters who made up our beds. Last night was especially thrilling. We donned our O.D.s (woolens) and in this cool, delightful climate we rode for an hour right next to the Pacific. The stars and everything made it a romantic jaunt. Really, though, no part of the trip was any better than all of it. Every mile was exciting. The mountains were wonderful. They must be the Sierra-Nevadas. Are they? In one spot we rode over a canyon some 200 feet deep, but only a 100 yards or so across.

Our camp location is queer. To the rear of my barracks are big, beautiful hills. But our land is desert and sandy. The ocean is to our front some six miles. We can smell it. Trees are nil close around here. But, in the distance we can see plenty of foliage.

If this letter seems a little incoherent, it's because I'm sticking my two cents worth in about twelve different conversations. These two story barracks are really chummy. They hold seventy men. We fellows who were in the hut together in Livingston are all lined up close together on the second floor. The whole set-up will be OK when we get settled, I'm sure.

So Kenny is giving in to Mommy. (He decided to leave Ohio Wesleyan.) If that's what he wants, I suppose it's all right. But, if he's doing it just for Mommy and for money, phooey on him. He owes me a letter and will probably explain.

Mother, will you send me my other ODs which are in my closet? I do believe I'll need them. I'l appreciate it a lot.

An interesting note on our trip is that we stopped three times for exercise: once in Del Rio Texas, once in Tuscon, and again in Los Angeles. We just marched around town and then had calisthenics.

I'm glad you wrote Marcy, Ellen. Did you send those pictures, Mother? I got two letters from you today and two from Marcy. A nice, quick welcome.

I'll write a more organized letter when we get more organized. This is a lovely territory. I wish so much that you all could enjoy it with me.

September 15, 1944

Having become more oriented to this camp and this

country, I find I like it immensely. Everything is really OK. Last night a buddy and I went to Santa Maria, some 20 miles north of here. It's a lovely town of 12,000 inhabitants. Soldiers are few. And, believe it or not, everybody said, "Welcome, boys. We're glad to have you." One middle-aged lady even shook our hands.

This weekend I may go to Los Angeles. It looks as if this may be my only opportunity. Yes, we're moving again. In just two more weeks you'll be getting notified again of a change of address. The move won't be far, just up the coast fifty miles or so. I figure perhaps I should take advantage of being closer than what we will be to L. A. (What a sentence.)

We aren't working very hard. Details for straightening up take most of our time. However, already we have had some net drill. That is crawling up and down tall landing nets. We had a hike scheduled for today, but it was postponed. Instead we paraded for our Colonel who has been boosted to brigadier-general and is leaving our regiment.

I've been getting mail wonderfully fast. So far I've had four from Marcy, two from you, and one from Tommy Robinson. Marcy's air mail letters take only two days. Yesterday morning I got one she had mailed at 9 a.m. September 12th. Pretty fast! I'm sending all my letters air mail from now on.

I just finished sewing on some stripes on my ODs. Say, Mother, I wonder if you would mind putting a couple on my shirt before you mail it. I'll enclose some. Perhaps it's too late, though.

Ah, mail call and two letters from you. Wes' church sounds interesting. Also, it was good to hear of your enthusiastic freshman group. That's fine! I would like to see Robby again. If it's possible, we'll arrange a meeting. He leaves on furlough the 6th of October. I don't believe I'll be able to see him before then.

The weather is crisp and snappy. It makes you feel all full of pep. I wish you all could be enjoying this country, too.

Thanks for inquiring about Mark's address. Perhaps he is changing camps. That seems to be the popular thing to do in the army now.

There isn't much news. If the day in Los Angeles works out, I'll have a lot to tell you about, no doubt. Probably I won't have a chance to see Ellen's friend, darn it!! I will call her at least, I promise. Trouble is, we won't get there till Saturday eve and will have to return Sunday. Doesn't seem very worthwhile, but I do want to add Los Angeles to my list.

September 19, 1944

I started a letter just 24 hours ago, but laid it aside being too busy. So, I'll start over hoping this time to finish. Most of the group that went on furlough from Livingston have returned. Now we are back on a full training schedule, and I do mean full.

This weekend we didn't get to make our little jaunt to Los Angeles. I was on guard from Saturday morning at 5 a.m. 'till Sunday at the same time. It was an unusual type of guard. I sat in a little 4' by 4' hut only 500 yards from the ocean. It was a desolate spot. My job was to stop all cars to check for passes. One of the fellow an adjoining post got restless and shot a coyote. Coyotes run free and are plentiful all around here. The fellow cleaned his carbine and the one round wasn't missed. He could have got into trouble. Lucky he didn't.

Sunday after guard I went to Santa Maria to the Methodist Church pictured on the card I sent you. It was sort of a disappointment for the congregation was very small.   The preacher didn't have much on the ball.   I thought it was a shame that such a lovely building wasn't being used and appreciated by more. Next Sunday I think I'll try another church. The fellows claim I always talk them into going to my church. A Catholic buddy especially wants me to go once with him. I believe I will.

This morning (It is now noon-time) we had a nice leisurely 9 mile hike.   A couple of the miles were right by the sea-shore. Being next to the ocean is such a thrill. More and more I like California. The sun doesn't shine here. But the days are just about right anyhow.

Your nice letter of the 12th came Sunday.   I wish I could have seen the Kelloggs (an associate minister with Dad in Dayton). I always liked them. I had to laugh at the Brown twins and Phil's episode. I'll bet they grow up to be real fellows. Wow! All the clippings were very interesting. The Lloyd family must be very happy to have both the fellows home, or, that is, in the states.

Well, guess what. Just this second the mail orderly gave me another letter from you. It was mailed the 15th. And such very, very interesting news.   Especially about Ellen and the Red Cross. I think that is absolutely terrific. I don't understand exactly the type of work done, but I know that it is a service organization of wonderful standards and Ellen will be a huge success, as she is in everything.

It sounds as if the choir has real possibilities this year. Isn't it interesting to have new families move into the community. Especially when they have daughters. Hmmm.

Marcy is as fine as her letters, Mother. In fact, she is even finer.   I'm counting on everything working out perfectly in time. In the meantime, I have something to be my very best for.

I hope John Lupton does visit you.   I've been wondering exactly what he has been doing. Give him a big "hello" for me.

When do you leave for school, Ellen? I was talking to a Northwestern fellow and he really loves the place. I know you'll have a grand time. And If you go to the Red Cross, I think that will be wonderful. If any fellow has better sisters than I, my name isn't Westerman.

Sunday afternon several of us played basketball at our sports arena. We had a grand time. Jack and I were on opposite teams this time. Although Jack is 6'4", I had fun stealing the ball from him on rebounds. He doesn't jump as high as he should. We want to practice more often. Since the weather is so so delightful, we hardly even work up a sweat. The arena is only two blocks from our barracks. The set-up is ideal. Too bad we won't be here longer.

Tomorrow we are going to fire our weapons again. We are having refreshing schools now. I'm an assistant instructor. It's fun helping fellows name all the parts and explain the mechanical function of the machine-gun.

Has G. A. H. S. played any games yet? Keep me posted on the scores.

See you again soon via mail.

September 25, 1944

What with three of your letters to answer, three boxes to thank you for, and three exciting days to tell you about, I don't know where to start. First of all, thank you so very much for the fine chain (identification bracelet). I've been wearing it ever since it came, and I don't know how it could be any better.

It's exactly what I wanted. It arrived Thursday eve. And this morning, the O. D.s and the candy came. The stripes are on just right and the clothes are pressed beautifully. The candy has disappeared already in the customary fashion. It was delicious. The puzzle will fill a free hour soon. And, oh yes, thank you for the ten dollars. I got that this morning, too. I borrowed ten from a pal Friday, so I got the advantage of really using your ten this past weekend.

I did receive my two-day pass. Here is a play-by-play account of how I used it. Friday eve we (four of us) caught the 6:30 bus from Lompoc which got us into Hollywood at 1 a.m. We found a nice hotel and slept late in the morning. Then we got up and went to the Hollywood Guild where we reserved beds for that night. The Guild is sponsored by several stars and everything is free. It is the nicest spot I have seen yet for servicemen. We left there after breakfast and went to the Hollywood U.S.O. From there I called Ellen's friend, Marjorie. She was very nice to me. However, she had plans and couldn't show us around. I wasn't expecting her to, and it was nice talking with her.

At the U.S.O. we got free tickets to the Shipstad and Johnston Ice Follies. They were positively gorgeous. We saw them in the Pan-Pacific Auditorium. I have never seen anything quite like it. The whole show was 100 times more wonderful than I ever expected. At first we were sitting in the rear; but an usher gathered us G.I.s and took us right down on the front row, straight across from Guy Kibbie and Gail Patrick, the movie stars. What a seat! The girl skaters threw flowers at us once. Wow! If ever you get a chance to see it, I recommend it completely.

We chose the Ice Follies over the football game because it was so very hot. I'm glad we made that decision anyhow.

In the evening we visited the Hollywood Canteen and the Palladium. Also, we windowshopped at the N.B.C. Studios, Brown Derby, and other places. We had both our meals Saturday at Melody Lane, a lovely restaurant with reasonable prices.

Sunday we went into Los Angeles proper, and there I

went to church. It was a pleasure to hear Tippett again. His sermon was swell. "Workmen Unashamed" was his title. I wish I could have spoken to him afterwards. The whole service was very worthwhile and inspiring. Sunday noon we splurged and ate at the Biltmore Hotel. After that I broke over the Sunday Show Rule to see "Going My Way." It was fine, and I hope you see it, too. Still, I think it had rough spots.

All in all the two days were great, and I wouldn't have missed them for anything.

Now to answer some of your questions. Feel free to lend my things any time to anybody. "Share and share alike" has become my motto since being in the army, especially. And about Marcy's Christmas gift, the earring set sounds very interesting. Perhaps they would be ideal. I was wondering about a jeweled Delt pin to match her lovely Gamma Phi jeweled pin. However, that might be better later when I can be around personally. Quiz Ellen on the perfect gift will you please? I would appreciate it.

Ellen is going to have a real experience at school. And she will be such a success. Speaking of bright people in the family, Joey seems to be going to town on his talking. Wow! Maybe I wasn't imagining "Unky Scot." Hmmm. It must have been sort of terrifying for Joanne and Frank, and all New Yorkers, to be without electricity. I hope no one suffered for it.

So Billy Betz is safe! Hurrah! And how interesting the news is about the other fellows.. Did Lupton get over to visit? Say, we must have a good football team. Greenfield is usually plenty tough. 20 to 13 isn't bad at all. I hope we beat Point Pleasant, the old rivals.!!

I got a welcome surprise from "Packy." Ninety percent of his group went overseas. But, he has been reassigned to an infantry outfit in South Carolina. I'm glad to hear that he's still around. Gosh, but the army is queer in some of its doings.

I'll wager that we will be enjoying California for quite awhile. Timne will tell!!

The Upper Room bulletin arrived this morning. Thank you, and I'm going to try to be more regular than I have been.

Queer as it may sound, I have the day off today. Why? Because I have to sign a certificate stating that I'm free from injury. (Do I hear you saying, "What is he talking about?") It all started last night on the way back from Los Angeles. Miles and I got separated from our two other buddies, so we caught the bus after theirs. All of the buses were specials and were sort of ancient Greyhounds.

We were riding along peacefully (but quickly) when I saw the lights go out and heard the driver yell, "Look out boys, here it comes." I hit the floor. Next thing I knew, we were rolling down a cliff. Picture 46 men in an old bus rolling down a cliff at midnight and you have our plight. After what seemed an eternity, it came to a rest. I felt as if I had just stopped a 200 pound fullback; but, aside from being jolted, I was sure I was O.K. I yelled for Miles, and he said he was all right, too.

That was the sensation of a lifetime. There I was wondering which way was up, and also wondering if we were ever going to get out. My biggest worry was that some fool would strike a match. Finally we got a chain going and we all filed out a broken window. Some went out the rear, too, where the top had broken open. The whole business was very orderly and organized.

To make a long story short, the total casualty list was three or four broken arms and several bad gashes and bruises. Miles gashed his face and hurt his shoulder. Four men were pinned in, but we soon got them out. God was being especially careful of the soldiers last night. And. believe me, I thanked him, and am still thanking him, and will always be thanking him for it. The driver was injured the most. But, I believe he, too, will live.

The pay-off, which sounds almost unbelievable, was what happened to the second bus we boarded. We had ridden only five or six miles when a terrible grinding noise brought the bus to a halt. The oil pan had fallen off. Wow! So on the third bus we finally arrived here at camp at 2 a.m. Ho-hum.

Quite an adventure, eh wot? I believe I will sneak a couple of hours of sleep while I have the chance. Thanks again for everything.

P. S. Don't think that I got hurt. I haven't even a sore muscle. Not a scratch. And, I am indeed thankful.

September 27, 1944

The account of the football game was certainly thrilling. Gallia Academy must have something this year. I was surprised to hear that they held Greenfield to 20 - 13. It's such a bigger school. Tieing Point Pleasant was no mean feat either. The Blue Devils must have their pitch forks (or whatever it is devils are supposed to carry) sharpened.

The agreement made between the schools and the church is terrific. It's going to be a must in my school. Who got the idea? I really think it's grand! In fact, I believe it is almost as perfect as it could be. Even more will depend on how the administrators handle it.

This evening I got an excellent "Chapter Mu Newsletter." However, it brought a piece of terribly sad and surprising news. Norm Scrimshaw has been killed in France. He died August the 18th. And, I wasn't even aware of the fact that he was overseas. You remember me talking about Scrim, don't you? He's the one I met at Fort Benning on Christmas eve. Probably he was one of the most efficient of Delt presidents. I am so very sorry to receive this news. I know you will be, too.

The "Newsletter" explained why I haven't been hearing from Bob, too. He is overseas now. It all makes me anxious to get in the fight. A step nearer that end will be our next move. This weekend we are moving to San Louis Obispo. There we will begin our amphibious training in earnest. By the way, did I tell you that all men, now, who returned from furlough before August 1st are on furlough again? This means that if they give furloughs again after we finish this training, I'll be one of the first on that list. Maybe I'll be home for Christmas. It's exciting to wonder about these things.

I got a letter from Marcy (a daily occurrence lately) today with desires expressed for being in the WAVES or Red Cross. I tried to squelch them. And, I don't think she really will want to go into either one. If she were finished with school, it would be different. I read an article written by a woman the other day. Its title was "Why I don't want to be a WAC." Actually, it seems the services aren't using the women as they might. At any rate, it doesn't seem wise for a woman to enlist.

We have been hiking a lot. Tomorrow we have another fifteen miler. Last week I was issued my 5th pair of GI shoes. Quite a record for only eleven months. Absolute proof that the infantry walks!! 'Course now I have two good pairs.

Joanne wrote a swell long letter. She enclosed three small snapshots of our New York visit. Joey is darling.

Talk about poor structure! I'll blame it on a race with the lights. It's almost time for taps.

CHAPTER FIVE

CAMP SAN LUIS OBISPO - PART 1

CAMP SAN LUIS OBISPO
CALIFORNIA
OCTOBER 2 - NOVEMBER 26,1944

October 2, 1944

I just returned from 80 miles farther north. I was on a detail sent to one of our battalions with food rations. They are on a problem 80 miles from here. It's really late to be just getting off detail. It's almost tomorrow. I did want to say at least "hello" today.

We moved here to this camp Sunday. This camp is terrific. We have those cozy little five men huts again. The whole camp is cradled in mountains. I can look out our door and see that we are entirely surrounded by hills. It's very beautiful. Especially with that beautiful moon tonight, is it lovely.

Gosh, but Gallipolis is going all out on the home front. That's just grand. And, the church people are backing the church 100%, aren't they. That's excellent news too.

What with the move yesterday and this 18 hour detail today, my eyelids are really having the "dropsies." I can't keep them open.

The ride today was nice. Almost the entire way was on four lane highways. California is going to always be one of my favorite states. Enormous diesel trucks are prevalent. They have whistles like trains and are beauts.

I was disturbed to hear that you hadn't received any mail for a week. I'll make sure that won't happen again, even if my letters have to be poor ones like this.

Thanks again for the boxes. All four were swell. I'll write again very soon.

October 3, 1944

At last I have time to write you in a leisurely manner. That hurried note I whipped off last night was a poor excuse for a letter. Also, now I have air-mail stamps again. Perhaps I can get back in my more regular letter writing routine again.

It occurs to me that it was silly to have even mentioned the bus accident to you. Although I haven't received your comments on it as yet, no doubt you worried. Really, it was nothing for me. It's hard for me to believe it even occurred. Now, this afternoon, I was told by the division adjutant that I may be reimbursed for my troubles. I told him I didn't even get a scratch. Still, he claimed I might get money. Miles, the man riding next to me, will probably receive at least $200. A bruised shoulder and six-stitch cut were his injuries. If I do get any money, I'm sending it home to be used in the church gymnasium. Or, maybe you could buy a lot of football tickets for the poor little boys who have to slip under the fence. Anyhow, I want you to spend it for me in some charitable way. Actually, I shouldn't get money. Being unharmed is more than enough.

No one, except the driver, was seriously hurt. The fact that the bus was reserved for soldiers and the equipment was faulty, is worrying the bus company. For that reason, they're handing out money.

Ohio Wesleyan defeated DePauw 35 to 0 Saturday. Isn't that swell! Marcy was present for the game. I wish I could have seen it with her. One sore score was that Michigan 0- Indiana 20. What do you think of that? I'm disappointed. I always count for the best from Michigan. From all rumors and scores so far, it looks as if Ohio State is going to be the big threat this year. Football will always be interesting, no matter what the personnel of the teams. It's a great game.

I'd like you to meet my new hut-mates. They are one swell group. We balance and counter-balance just about perfectly. 1.) Corporal Gleason- whom you have met before. Still a jolly fellow and a good squad leader. 2.) Atone Aziglio- 2nd gunner. Aziglio is tops. He is Italian, but doesn't look it. Rather, he is more the Brooklynite. Formerly of the Air Corp and Tank Destroyers, he has over two years of army service. Going on 22, very intelligent, and, I repeat, a grand, clean-cut fellow. 3.) Isaac Villar. Villar comes from Louisiana where his wife and three children are waiting for him. He's 34, but still rarin' to go. Aside from "lovin'" his beer, he's a fine chap. His duties are 3rd gunner. 4) Minges. (I can never remember his first name.) Minges is also from the Air Corp. His father owns five Pepsi-Cola plants. And, Minges owns a beautiful '42 Lincoln sedan. He has his car here, too. He has never been bothered with money troubles. Still, he is a good guy. Always sharing his car and money, he has lots of friends. It's unfair to speak of him only in terms of money, for he's a fine fellow all-around.

Now you've met my buddies. We are already having a grand time together. 'Course we have known each other for four months, but just now we are really getting to be an intimate team. Our squad is bound to be one of the best.

This is such a lovely camp. I wish you could see it. We are exactly in the center between Los Angeles and San Francisco, 205 miles to each city. The countryside is beautiful and the weather is even nice. The nights get darned cold. But, the days are just right. We have oil-burning stoves in each hut, so the cold nights don't bother us much.

When we will come in contact with boats, I don't know. This Thursday we go 80 miles farther north for a three day firing problem. We go to the same spot where I took rations yesterday. It means that we will miss our weekend, but the problem won't be too difficult. By the way, I probably won't be able to write during that period.

Ellen seems to have such an ideal set-up. She wrote me all about it. Her Tutorial Fellowship will give her valuable experience. I had to laugh how she told me about her Wednesday nights. It seems that's the only evening she and Wes will have free together. No question about how they'll fill that evening.

I got a nice long letter from Joanne. (Or did I tell you!) Gosh, but I held my breath when I read about Joey chewing on glass. She sent some swell snaps of the three of us, and of Joey alone, too. I sent one on to Marcy. Have you got any yet? Joey is the best looking baby I have ever seen. Have you got that picture of Joanne and Joey sitting by their cabin in New Hampshire? That's one of the most adorable pictures I have ever seen. Almost makes you want to cry.

I still have time, but I find I'm running out of news. Seems as if if it's not one it's the other. I should get a letter from you tomorrow. I'll try to answer it before we go out for our three days.

P.S. I have seen "Dragon Seed." It's excellent. Have you had a chance to see "Since You Went Away?"

October 5, 1944

This is another "minute note." In just 45 minutes we start on our three day problem. I won't be able to write again unitil Sunday or Monday. Your swell letter written the 28th came yesterday. I'm certainly lucky having such a good letter writer for a mother. (Wonderful mother, too, naturally.) Your letters are like conversations. I do enjoy them.

Since I am so positive that I'll be around for awhile, I suggest you forget about the Christmas gift business 'till the holiday. Who knows, I may even be home on furlough then. I'm glad you are so enthusiastic about the jeweled pin for Marcy. It is quite expensive. In fact, it will probably come to around 35 or 40 dollars. It's an investment I would love to make. I believe I'll be able to pay that much easily. I think she would like it a lot. If Ellen would enjoy taking care of it, I'd very much like to have her do it. I'll write her next week.

After all these years of fixing electrical appliances, a fuse finally blew. That's not a bad average, Mother. Really good! Betty Faulkner and Charlotte must have had an exciting time. Nursing is a great opportunity for a lot of girls. You mentioned a new English teacher. Who is she replacing?

Since I broke into this letter to run to the PX for some candy for the problem, I'm almost out of time. We will load up very soon now. We're going 80 miles north to the same spot where I delivered rations Monday. It will be a nice long ride.

So long for now. See you again soon.

P. S. I can't get over the wonderful year you are expecting in the church. If this is your last one, Daddy, in Gallipolis, I'll bet it will be your best, and that's saying a lot.

October 9, 1944

I go out on a three day excursion and come back four letters behind you. Not bad at all! If you don't mind my being behind, I must confess I like it. Letters from home are so welcome. Your most recent letter sent the 7th arrived this noon. Considering that it was an answer to my letter of the 3rd, that is record time. Only six days to exchange thoughts at 3000 miles. It's a wonderful world we're living in.

I think I'll sort of take your letters one at a time. The one written the 30th came in the field. I especially enjoyed and was interested in your viewpoint about Marcy and the WAVES. It was an approach I hadn't thought of. If I don't get a chance to see Marcy on furlough before New Years, I think I'll drop her a word of encouragement. It's becoming more obvious that I will be in the services longer than I first expected. One of the big objectives of my post-war plans is to have a chance to be with Marcy more.

The Forster's (Dayton, Ohio friends)visit sounded swell. The row of antique shop visit all must have been fun. A visit by them has always meant good times. I'm so glad they could come once more. He must be busy with all those phone bills, etc. The debate about race equality interested me. Have you read the article in the Digest about the raw deal the South got during the Reconstruction Period? I had known some of it, but it brings out very well the reasons for present day disputes. We Yankees and rebels here in the hut have come to a better understanding on the situation because of that article.

So Merrill and his brother got together in France. That is swell. So many memorable and happy experiences come out of war. They will never counterbalance the bad ones for the fellows overseas. But if a guy stayed on this side all the time, the army could be considered strictly a nice time. Too bad Tommy had that disappointment. Say "Hello" to him for me. Also, Billy Betz, if you see him. I always thought John Lloyd was a good guy. I'm glad he has such a pleasing wife. Where and how did he meet her?

The boxes sounded like a lot of work. But you can count 100% on their being appreciated. All the fellows will love them. The news of the change Mr. Higgins plans for is wonderful. Goodness, but that is grand. If I get any money,

I want every cent of it to go for the stadium. Gallipolis will be even better than Athens or any of the Southeastern schools now, or rather when plans are completed.

Louise's husband sounds nice. (Even if you said he reminded you somewhat of me.) The wedding must have been lovely. It's the type I would prefer someday. Quite in contrast to Eloise's. I hope both marriages are great successes.

Hip, Hip, Hooray!! So finally vacation plans are coming through. That's wonderful. You should have a swell time in Michigan again., I'll bet even the car will love the trip. What will be your address? Grandmother's?? I hope Michigan doesn't disappoint you too much. What game will you get to see? That's really swell!!

I got a long letter from Tommy. He must be in Gallipolis by now. Say "Hello" for me again. I think there is a good chance of our getting together when he returns. Rumors say our next move may be near San Diego.

Our three days in the field were fun. I acted as squad leader in the absence of some sergeants. We ran through four different types of problems and did well on all of them. Even though our camping area was 80 miles north of here, it was warmer. Perhaps it was because we went further inland. The jaunt wasn't difficult and really lots of fun. I enjoyed leading a squad. In fact, I wouldn't mind being a squad leader permanently. Chances are no good though. We have our quota.

This doesn't make up for your four swell letters. I'll write again soon.

October 11, 1944

Your letter of the 9th arrived this morning. I can't get over the excellent mail service. It is really super! No doubt the box will arrive very shortly. And, I am looking forward to it.

You don't need to worry about my writing too often. I write when I feel like it, and I never sacrifice recreation to write. In fact, it's recreation to write. I scribble my letters to you hurriedly. I could write less often and longer, but I like writing more but shorter notes. Today I wrote Ellen asking her to investigate the pin. I hope it won't inconvenience her. Maybe she'll enjoy it.

Last night I was on guard duty. I enjoy guard for it gives you a chance for serious thought. Nothing makes a fellow think like a beautiful night when you have nothing to do but walk by yourself.

Perhaps you are right about Ellen and Wes. I'm positive everything will work out fine, though. Both are smart enough to realize a mistake if there is one.

Proving my point about short notes, I'll sign off already. Guard makes a guy a little sleepy the next night. You are still making plans for the vacation, aren't you? I hope so.

P. S. Have you ever received a box of fruit from me? You should be getting one soon. Also, an 86th Division magazine is coming your way.

October 16, 1944

Here it is Monday morning, and a nice weekend finished. I have a few minutes before morning drill call, so I'll dash off this note, hoping it will reach you before you shove off for Michigan Thursday.

Your letter of the 12th arrived yesterday, and I am happy that the vacation is really coming through. Goodness, but the church is in fine order. Certainly there won't be business worries while you're on this ten day jaunt. I'll bet Frank (church custodian) is thrilled with the stoker.

And, I know you are too, Daddy. It is wonderful the transformation that has come about in Grace M. E. since you arrived, Daddy.

Michigan came through with flying colors against Northwestern. Hurrah! Also, Ohio State did well. The real tussle will be the Michigan-Ohio State game. Wow! We listened to the State-Wisconsin game Saturday.

The weekend consisted of two shows, church, a couple of big meals and rest. The shows were "Arsenic and Old Lace" and "Barbary Coast Gent." I think you would enjoy both. The first one is a scream!! We went to the Presbyterian church and the service was really lovely. I can't get over the high caliber of California people. Even the cab drivers seem to be well educated. Poverty is at a minimum. I'm enclosing the bulletin, plus a picture of the church.

Eddie's little message does sound preposterous. It would be nice if it came true.

Since it's almost time for the whistle, I'll sign off. Be sure to have a grand trip. Have one great time.

P. S. I know that I will be around for a longer period than you think. So, don't think that I'll be sailing before you get back.

October 19, 1944

How's the north-land? How did the car run, and how are Grandmother and Grandfather? In fact, how is everybody and everything in Ann Arbor??? This must be a beautiful period to take a trip. Are the leaves almost all off the trees now? I figure they should be at their loveliest right now. I miss the colors. We have the hills here, but they are minus the colorful trees.

I have been on KP today. And, it was a nice day to have that detail. I missed a fifteen mile hike, and now, this evening, a four hour night problem. However, in a short while I'm going back to the kitchen to help make donuts for the fellows when they return. So, I will have put in equal hours, but softer work. KP is fun ever so often. Now that our company is up to full strength, we go on KP only once every two weeks, which isn't often.

Chances for meeting Tommy are pretty good. After we train here for two or three weeks, we will move to Camp Callen near San Diego for a short period. Perhaps then we can get together. Speaking of pals, I got an interesting letter from Kenny. He is really enjoying his work at Athens. Already he is singing in the church choir. And, as you know, he has transferred his letter. He says that he has had opportunities to begin the actual embalming, and he "loves" it. Perhaps he has found his real place in life. As a sideline, he is trying to help the boss's 15 year old high living son to be a better boy. He seems very much satisfied.

Billy Betz has had an experience. I only hope that he will be able to forget the bad parts, and, perhaps, the good ones. Maybe it will be all right to talk over the army days for one or two years after the war. But, I don't like the idea of children listening and getting glory complexes, or sumpin'. In other words, our deeds shouldn't sound heroic, because they aren't, when you come down to brass tacks.

No boxes have arrived yet, but I'm expecting them soon. Hot dog! Your last letter of the 15th didn't come till today because it was miss-sent to the 342 infantry. That's the reason I'm slow answering it. Don't worry about writing on schedule. And, for heaven's sake, don't think I dread getting a lot of mail from you. On the contrary, I love it. Write when you have time, whether it be once a week or four times.

Daddy, a fellow just told me about a spot where soldiers can go deep sea fishing for only two or three dollars. Believe me, if I get a chance, I will too. The Navy takes men out in their boats every weekend. Not bad! I hope you get a chance to throw out a line. I'd love to be going with you. Catch one for me, if you get the opportunity.

One of the cooks just stuck his head in the door, so I better go. Do say "hello" to everyone for me. And, have a real vacation. Don't bother to write while you're there. Write a big one when you get back.

P. S. Am enclosing that sweet shot of Joanne and Joey for you all to enjoy. Please send it back after a while.

October 20, 1944

I'm so glad the fruit arrived before you left for Michigan. Although it was probably in your way a little, it was better that way than to have it spoiled when you returned. It was nice that you could share some of it with the Lovett children. No doubt they enjoyed it. How many avocadoes were there? I was told that there would be four. I just couldn't resist sending the box. You send me so many, and it was fun to do a turn about for once.

Last night, or rather Wednesday night, at the movie, I saw a major whom I swore was a Haskins. I pointed him out to a buddy and told him I was sure I knew him. However, I was under the impression that Major Haskins was in the Medics, and this man wore an engineer's insignia. Today, when I read in the gossip column about the Haskins, I decided that must have been he. Do you suppose it was? Too bad I didn't speak with him. Is Jim Gillingham around here? There are several "sailors" about.

By now you are probably in Ann Arbor! Is it cold? The weather here is perfect. The cool nights are fine for sound sleeping. Today we were having a class in the sunlight when all of a sudden big rain drops began coming down. Not a cloud in the sky, not a sign of rain; but,, it did come down for a few minutes. Quite a freakish weather incident, eh wot?

Today we had another routine physical. I'm in good shape. Height - 71", weight - 156 pounds, eyes - 20/20, pulse - 74, blood pressure - 112, etc. The army food and exercise agree with us all. I was hoping to weigh more, but that isn't bad stripped. My only defect was my feet. They are getting just a lttle flat, which proves I'm an infantryman. Ha Ha. Also, I have one tooth that needs filling, and that will be taken care of soon.

Did I tell you of the picture, "American Romance?" It's excellent and would be a good show to take in during the vacation. See it if you can. One other evening this week, I went to the camp library and read about "Education" in the encyclopedia. It was interesting reading, and makes me believe that the field is still in the pioneering stage and is open for worthwhile work and excitement. I plan to do more reading of that type. Only three or four times have I visited the library during the army career.

Next week we run a seven or eight day problem in the field. Probably we will both be returning back to our respective dwelling places about the same time. I hope you continue to have a swell time. I'll be thinking of you and everybody. I'll write again after this weekend. We may fish, play basketball, or climb a mountain tomorrow and Sunday. How's that for interesting choices?! I hope you get to take in a game there.

October 22, 1944

I received your letter from Ann Arbor today. Air mail does the service up super. Less than two days to hear from you, even from Ann Arbor. I'm glad to know that the trip was nice. Also, the early plans for fishing sound great. Twelve hours isn't long considering today's speed limit.

Pretty soon the odometer will be ticking up 50,000 miles. We never thought we would be putting that many miles on that car, did we? I bet it will carry us 50,000 more safely, if we want it to.

Just the few sentences about sitting in front of the fire, and Grandmother making mince pie, really hit the spot. It must be nice to be there again. I'm so glad you are finally getting the vacation you deserve.

This weekend has been another pleasant one. It included a football game between San Luis Obispo and Santa Maria, the picture "The Merry Monahans," a couple of hours of "touch" football, a lovely church service, two big chicken dinners, and rest. The church service this morning was especially inspiring. The preacher was quite young, but very good. Enclosed is the bulletin.

We had a big time cheering at the high school football game. San Luis is the same size town as Gallipolis, but I'm positive we had much better teams. (Aren't all past high school players??) Eight of us went together. We swore one end didn't hit the ground the whole game. S.L.O. won the game 28 to 0.

I got a letter today from Bill Eells, president of Chapter Mu at Wesleyan. He said Bard and his father had been present at a recent initiation. Well, blow me down! I'm certainly happy to finally get some word about Bard. Other good news was that Manning has been made social chairman.

Does your information about Ellen mean that she is going ahead with the Red Cross deal? Has she decided to not wait for a semester to pass by?

General Benjamin Lehr (sp.?) is going to inspect our division this week, so our jaunt in the woods has been called off. (This may be a rumor, but I believe it's true.) This makes the 3rd or 4th time generals have been nosing around. I'd like to know exactly how they conduct their personal inspections?! At least, they keep us on the ball, which is good enough reason for them inspecting, I suppose.

I'm having the two rolls of film I brought back with me from furlough developed. There should be some fair snaps among the shots. I'll send them on pronto.

Keep enjoying yourselves. And, don't forget to give my greetings to everyone.

P. S. Did Michigan play anyone this Saturday? I couldn't find her scores.

October 25, 1944

The Christmas box and the box of popcorn balls and fudge arrived last night. I opened the popcorn immediately, and about ten of us had a big gab fest between gulps. All asked me, "Who made them?" I answered that you did, Mother. 'Course, they said to tell you they were really luscious. Thanks ever so much. I planned on saving the box marked "Christmas," but I must admit I saved it only three hours. Last night my hut-mates persuaded me that I should open it, too. Then I remembered about the pecans, so I rationalized my way into opening the box. The pecans are delicious!! And, all the gifts are swell. Azeglio is reading from one of the little books now. I'm keeping the assortment in one box, and will "reserve" my use of them till Christmas and after. Thanks ever so much, again. The box is fine for Christmas. Is it the type the church sent to all the servicemen? If so, I think you hit the nail right on the head.

Your letter written Sunday came today. How do you like trout fishing, Daddy? Is it as fun as reeling in a bass? Did you catch anything on your excursion to Devils Lake? I'm still hoping to get a crack at deep-sea fishing the Navy offers on weekends.

Today we ran an all-day problem right next to the

ocean. The breeze kept blowing the smell of the salt water to us. "Problems" are twice as much fun near the ocean. We fired some two thousand rounds. A brigadier-general observed us for awhile. General Lear, commander of the ground forces, is supposed to be around soon. So far, we haven't seen him. Our squad is getting to be very efficient. We claim we're the best heavy machine gun squad in the regiment. Just ask us. We'll tell you how good we are. Hmmm.

I have trouble recalling exactly what Jean and Miriam look like. It was fun reading about Bob and Hansi. And, now I'm wondering how Fritzi is? That hour-and-a-half of supervised sports everyday for Bob sounds pretty rugged. No doubt he's enjoying it. Uncle Bob must be working 24 hours a day, what with two more factories. I'm glad Ted is going to buy that footage. I think I know the land. Probably that one on the left as you go down the road into camp. That's swell.

It's great to hear that everything is swell on your vacation. Isn't it a coincidence that I sent the picture on almost the same day you thought to ask for it. That is the one you wanted, isn't it?

We're firing the same problem tomorrow, so I'll get plenty of sleep tonight. We have to run quite a bit on the sand. Thanks again for the boxes. And, have a good trip home.

October 28, 1944

Your swell long letter written right on Devils Lake came yesterday. I did enjoy it. All the news about the relatives was so interesting. You answered many questions I have been wondering about. You put me right in the mood when you described the "gentle breeze, and the rhythmic breaking of the small waves." Your vacation has been like a visit for me, too. All the descriptions and news were so very interesting.

I have always been sort of secretly proud of my ancestors and relatives. Both sides of the family have such good records physically, mentally, and morally. Too bad about Uncle Harold's daughters. Rather they are victims of circumstance. The Westermans and Wuerfels are two great families. I certainly can't blame heritage for any mistakes or failures I make in life.

Finally I'm sending you pictures, via Joanne. Since I'm writing her this evening, too, I'll enclose the snaps in her letter. For fun, we'll reverse the "sending on" methods. Besides, she is two or three letters ahead, and I do want to write her. The shots turned out much better than I expected. In fact, 15 out of 16 came out perfectly. Developing is easily and cheaply done here in camp. You'll enjoy them, I believe.

General Lear arrived yesterday and left today. We certainly were on the ball during those 24 hours. We had a big review for him. In fact, we stood at rigid attention for over 30 minutes. I saw three men keel over, and , of course, my field of vision was limited, since eyes were straight ahead. He walked all through our ranks. There were four brigadier generals with him, plus our Division Major General. I have never seen so much "brass." This morning we ran through our attack problem, and, sure enough, he was there to watch part of it. He looked us over pretty thoroughly. I was under the impression that he wouldn't leave his car, but he certainly did.

Even though we have been restricted to our area all week because of this big inspection, I'm staying in tonight too. It's fun to relax and write letters and read for a change. The new "Digest" came today and it looks good. I want to read if through in awhile. I'll go to town tomorrow for church. A lot of us decided to do our relaxing in camp this weekend. Financial reasons are many of my pals' troubles. However, I have money.

I got a nice letter from Ellen today. And, I realize now her birthday has gone by without so much as a card from me. Why didn't you remind me? I'll send her something a month late. Sometimes it's more fun that way anyhow. She is busy now, isn't she. Grad school isn't the leisurely business I supposed it to be, especially with all the extra work she is doing. She mentioned the fact that working with Wes threw a different light on the subject. I'm positive Ellen will know what's right or wrong. Since I don't know Wes, I don't voice any opinions. (Not that they would have any affect on them, anyhow.)

Gosh, but it's nice of Grandmother and Grandfather to ask about the car. Perhaps, after the war I may want to offer them cash for it. It would be to trade it in on a safer Ford, though. It's a 1933 model, isn't it? Should be in good shape, too. I do want some kind of car after the war. Probably I will be able to afford one, I hope.

I'm enjoying my hut-mates more and more. By devious ways I have been carrying on a sly reform movement. Villar is too much of a drinker. Menges hits the bottle ever so often, too. I got hold of a couple of anti-alcohol books and left them lying around. They read them, and soon we started talking it over. Always they say it's different being in the army, but I think they realize they shouldn't waste money on the stuff. Actually, they are both grand fellows. At present, Villar is home on an emergency furlough. His youngest child (18 months) has a type of meningitis. He was so worried and sad. I hope so much that it will recover. Villar loves his wife and children fiercely. Menges is now in the hospital with skin rash. He should be out very soon.

Sgt. Gleason just returned from confession. He is a good buddy. Aziglio went to town for the show. Usually,

"Zig" and I stick together, but this eve I let him go alone. He's the tops of the outfit. The family "attitude" of our company is amazing. No longer is there any distinction between non-coms and privates. Actually, we are one big happy group.

One thing sometimes bothers me. That is the fact that I am only a PFC. Do you mind having me only be a PFC? Actually, if any openings for squad leader should come about in our platoon, I probably would get it. However, I will probably be discharged a PFC. And, I hope you realize that it's not really a lack of ability, but rather a case of being where needed. If you don't mind, I'm happy. I'll always be satisfied being only a PFC. It's a rut I know I won't carry into civilian life. If I thought it affected my post-war desires for success, I would worry. But I know it doesn't. As long as you understand, everything is swell. Margaret's husband in France, (Bill Dewey) no doubt, has the same viewpoint, as do a million other good privates.

I'm stringing out on subjects not necessary, so I'll close. I hope your return trip was swell. I'll bet Gallipolis was glad to have you back.

P. S. I'm sending money orders home first of the week. Put it away till I tell you how to use it, please. Thanks!!

Did you catch any fish on Ken's Lake?

October 28, 1944
To Joanne, Frank, and Joey

Mother is probably sending on letters of mine ever so often, since they are meant to include the whole family. However, I want to thank you personally for the swell enlargements. They are nice, and I'm happy to have them to add to my group of pictures. I have almost two dozen different snaps of members of our family now. It's fun to share them with my pals, and they do act as excellent "subs" for seeing the real McCoys.

When I was at home last August, I brought back with me two rolls of film and Ellen's Baby Brownie. Since then, I have taken pictures off and on. Finally, I used up all 16 shots, and they have been developed. Maybe you'll enjoy looking them over. Some were taken at Camp Livingston, a couple at Camp Cooke, and the remainder here at San Luis Obispo. I wrote "helps" on the backs of the pictures so you might understand them a little better. Send them on to Mother and Daddy when you're finished. They aren't much in the way of photography, but some of them are interesting.

I appreciate your queries about when and where to direct "Santy." I believe we fellows will be hanging up our stockings right here in California. I hope you haven't gone to any trouble in the way of gifts, etc. Gosh knows, the swell time I had visiting you is enough of a gift for all year 'round. The snaps ever so often of Joey are adorable, welcome presents, too. Don't do anything extra, please. The recording of Joey's voice would be keen. But, then again, I don't know where I could play it, and it would probably end up smashed. Better send mine to Ellen or the Folks. Thanks a lot, though.

This week we prepared for an inspection by Lieut. General Lear. Yesterday and today he examined us. He gave us a thorough and critical inspection. So far, I have heard no bad complaints, and I think the division came out with flying colors. This morning, our section of machine guns ran an attack problem for the General. He was actually there to see it, too. Quite a thrill acting for the commander of the ground forces of the U. S. This evening he moved on to inspect another nearby division.

You asked if Marcy was an art major. She is majoring in history and sociology. However, she has had courses in art, and she is good. She illustrates a lot of her letters. All around gal. Yep!!!

The fellow I thought might call you back in September, is still in the states. Instead of going across, he was re-assigned to an outfit in South Carolina. I was happy to hear that he was still around. "Packy" is an unusually fine fellow. He has written twice from S.C.

I do enjoy descriptions of Joey. Your Sept. 21 letter was so interesting. (I should have written you long ago.) Also, your more recent letter was good. So he is really developing a vocabulary!! (Note: the remainder of this letter is missing.)

October 30, 1944

Your very interesting letter came yesterday. My, but you are having a good time! I was a little mixed up on the dates you would be there, so probably you will be reading two letters from me at once. I'm glad you can be there till the 1st. That's a fine vacation.

If nothing comes up, I will actually go fishing Saturday. We investigated and we find that for only one dollar we can fish all day. Of course, our catches go to the boat owner. A big barge will be our boat, with rods and bait furnished. Hot dogs! This last Sunday we spent quietly, church again in the morning and reading in the afternoon. In the evening, we saw a show put on by the 342nd. It was pretty good.

Remember Faria? He returned tonight! He was put out of the paratroopers because of a sore leg muscle. At present, he is assigned to a rifle company. We're hoping he will come to our company again. He was so happy to see all of us again. And, we were glad to greet him. He's a good fellow.

Tomorrow evening the USO is holding a grandioso Halloween party. Soldiers are furnished masks, and a good time is promised all. It will be fun dunking for apples, etc., again.

I'm returning the one picture before I forget. Did you receive my group of pictures yet? Probably Joanne hasn't had time to send them on.

Because of recent announcements, I'm almost positive we'll be hanging our stockings this year in this state. Singing "Auld Lang Syne," too, no doubt.

P. S. You were even more beautiful 15 years ago, Mother. You must have always been a queen, and will always be. Keerect, isn't it, Daddy?!!! The picture goes into my billfold.

November 4, 1944

What exciting letters! Dad, yours was a masterpiece. The fishing trip, the Michigan-Purdue game, the church service, the visit at Willow Run, all were terribly interesting. Goodness, but you did have a wonderful vacation. Your visits with Pryors and Bob and Becky and everybody sounded so very worthwhile. In fact, everything about your entire two weeks seemed to me to have been tops. The good weather, good fishin', my, but that's swell. Your letter written the 1st arrived today, and it sounds as if the trip home will be nice too. I'm so happy the vacation worked out so well.

We had a surprise two-day wilderness jaunt Wednesday and Thursday. That's the reason for the longer than usual silence from this end. Weather was perfect for the 40 hours we were in the field. The full moon, the surf, plus the coyotes howling, put me in a romantic mood. Our "problem" was held in mountainous terrain. It was some job lugging our weapons up and down the hills.

Today is dismal and rainy. If it is clear in the morning, we still hope to get in our fishing. If it isn't clear, we will have other chances, though. One fellow was telling me that the guys fish while on the ten-day boat ride from San Diego. It seems only one practice landing is made every day, and there is plenty of leisure. Sounds good. By the way, we expect to move to Camp Callen the end of this month. However, my address will remain the same, I believe.

I remember the snap. What a picture. I think I may send it on to Marcy just for fun. Speaking of Marcy, I'm wondering how, exactly, to go about getting the pin. It has to be done through the chapter at Wesleyan. In other words, one of the active brothers has to buy it for me. I wonder if Manning would be willing to do it on the sly for me? And I wonder if he is still coming home often enough for you to contact him and make arrangements? I could write him, but it might be easier if he is still making those weekend trips. What do you think?

Halloween eve a bunch of us went to a dance at the USO in town. Apples, cider, and all the good things that go with the season were there. We even wore masks. It was a lot of fun. I met a USO hostess who was formerly a Delta Queen. She's a Tri-Delt, and her husband is in the Philippines. We had a nice friendly chat.

Last night I played basketball, as I have been doing this afternoon, also. The sports arena in camp is one of the best equipped I have ever seen. We had several good games.

I'm sending twenty dollars in money order tomorrow or Monday. I wanted to send more, but Villar has ten dollars of mine. He borrowed it from me when he went on his emergency furlough. I'll have to leave the money for the stadium till later, darn it. (I was afraid I'd have to do it.) When Villar returns, I'll send more. Put it aside for Marcy's gift.

Have you received the snaps yet? I got another nice

letter from Joanne today. She didn't mention the pictures, though.

The hut is rather noisy, so I'll sign off for now. We plan to see the show, or sumpin', this eve in town. I hope the trip back was nice.

P. S. Hurrah for Michigan again this week. Ohio State ended up on top, too. Wow!

November 7, 1944

Your very interesting letter of the 3rd came today. I can't get over what exciting descriptions you've been sending me about your vacation. Bob and Becky's home is certainly thrilling. Your visit with Jewell and Alf and Tom and Alice sounded so nice, too. Also, the experience at the airport must have been something. It all has been so very wonderful.

I have been telling some of the former Air Corp boys about Bob (Lowrey). And, about your experience in the link trainer, Daddy. My, but I would like to visit Lockbourne while he is there to show you around. Such class having the guard expecting you. That's swell!

Yesterday an unexpected box came from you. The "open" sign was very prominent, so, of course, I followed directions. It was another fine, welcome bunch of gifts. The cookies were delicious as usual, too. And now today a box arrived from Joanne. Gosh, but I'll be spoiled if all this attention keeps up. You've given me more than I would ordinarily expect for Christmas already. Thanks so very much.

The weather kept us from our fishing trip as I was afraid it might. However, we attended church and had a nice quiet Sunday. Saturday eve I met an old Wesleyan pal and we talked and talked. Also, we saw "None But the Lonely Heart," a pretty fair show.

I have gotten tired of attempting to get money orders. So, I'm sneaking 15 dollars in this letter. The decrease from the planned 20 is a safeguard. I don't want to run out of money before Villar returns to pay me. I'll be sending more.

This morning we fired the flame thrower. What a weapon that is! It's good to have knowledge of all weapons. Combat conditions often switch you completely to a different job. And we are prepared to handle almost any job now.

Joanne sent a couple pocket books which are cute. One is "How to Tell Your Friends From the Apes." It's a wow! I'd like to send it on to you. If you see it around, buy it.

News is scarce and it's late, so I'll sign off. It's nice to have you home again, and I did enjoy all the vacation news.

November 9, 1944

Wow, just a year ago tonight, I was bidding you so-long and heading for Columbus! Remember? The year certainly hasn't been one of displeasure. In fact, it has been very interesting. And I am thankful for the 12 months of opportunity to see different parts of the U. S. And now I'll predict at least two more years of army life. Although they aren't likely to be as quiet years as this one has been, I'm sure the time will teach me much.

This morning I was called to the dental clinic. They looked over my teeth very carefully, and I go back tomorrow for some fillings. I don't know how much work has to be done. Probably just two or three fillings, and that won't be bad for over a year of just personal care of the teeth. By the way, for this year of service I get that little red and white "Good Conduct" ribbon. It seems silly to wear it considering the small amount of effort put forth for it, compared to the battle ribbons.

I'm so glad you like those little snaps. I, too, was surprised that they came out as well as they did. The films were old, the camera is old, and the picture-taker inexperienced. I want to take some more, if I can find film somewhere.

Goodness, but I'm being smothered with boxes. And, I "gotta" confess, I love it. Yesterday a box came from Grandmother made up of popcorn balls and cookies. It was good! I noticed your handwriting, Mother; perhaps you mailed it for Grandmother. Do thank her for me! Another package is coming my way. Marcy is sending me a bigger shelf size photo of her. And, I'll really go for that. Marcy is so very wonderful! Her letters hit the spot so completely! More and more she seems to be the ideal of all ideas I've had about the perfect woman. And, when I get back, I'm betting I'll find that she's enough like my mother and sisters, so that I'll want to marry her. I'm not getting anxious, though. Just rolling out thoughts spurred on by the romantic patter of the rain on the roof.

We are still waiting to begin our actual amphibious training. Any day we should start. This waiting is rather nice. Training films and non-strenuous work are taking up our time. In fact, this evening I felt like more exercise, so we went to the arena and played two hours of basketball.

I was sorry to hear about Don Slagle(Gallipolis friend). Sometimes, however, a combat wound is nothing more than a bad floor burn or a cut. That's why it doesn't pay a bit to worry. A pal of mine was reading a letter to me today about a friend of his who was "wounded." His wound was so slight that he was ashamed of all the heroic questions and sympathies asked him by the people at home.

Ha, your predictions were correct. The "Presivelt" is back in office. Perhaps it is for the good. Time will certainly tell whether or not he is highly capable. The big worry is the fact that Truman might be called upon sometime to take over. Heaven forbid.

Last furlough I wasn't aware that there were any misunderstandings in the church. I am happy to hear that they are ironed out, though. That must have given you a wonderful feeling of triumph, Daddy. I'll bet ol' Frank is really happy to be relieved of some of his furnace duties. That is wonderful. Also, the work on the house sounds as if it will be definitely all right.

Yesterday we had a company picture taken. It is similar to the one we had taken at Benning. Already the proof is furnished, and it isn't a bad group picture. I seem to have a tendency to squint one eye in pictures. I look like a crook or sompin'. But, I'm sending you one soon.

I've been reading more heavily recently. I finished the "Digest," plus the "Coronet" (a magazine surprisingly excellent most months). And, we in the hut have been using the little books off and on as brain teasers. They are fun. No good shows have been here this week, so our leisure has been spent reading instead.

Have you had a chance to see Manning yet? Did the money arrive OK? No doubt a letter will be coming soon answering these questions.

I better get rest for the jaunt to the Dental Clinic. Drilllllll!! So, good night. It's nice having you back in Gallipolis.

November 12, 1944

Today is another lovely Sunday, and we have been spending it in town per usual. This morning I attended a Catholic mass in a mission here which was built in 1772. They held communion. Their ceremony didn't impress me as much as ours does. I grew tired of all the rapid Latin. And my opinion of the Catholic church, though a primitive one, is still that I believe the ceremony and ritual part is overdone. Also, I miss the congregational singing.

One of the boys met me awhile ago, and he said a package and a letter from home were at camp. That's great! That must be the anniversary present. It was kind of you to remember the 12 months in that way. I, too, am so thankful for this entire year of training. And we are thoroughly trained. I am as confident as I will ever be that we're ready for action.

Speaking of training, Saturday afternoon we began our "amphibious antics." We were taught how to ascend and descend the big nets. Now tomorrow we go to Morrow Bay (10 miles away) to use boats actually on the ocean. Wednesday we'll finish this preliminary amphibious training. When we finish all the training, we'll be prepared to make landings almost anyplace. All we lack then is ski troop instruction.

Thank you so much for wanting to get in touch with Manning for me. It makes it much easier for me. I was speaking to a jeweler's son, and he said the pin shouldn't exceed $35 in cost. Perhaps it won't be too expensive.

Friday and Saturday I made a couple of trips to the Dental Clinic. As a result I have four new fillings now. But, what's amazing is that I need four more. I have to return sometime next week. It has been quite a while since I've visited the dentist.

By the way, I got a glimpse again of Dr. Haskins (Major). He is down here. I don't know why "Kitty," or is it "Ami," sounded so sure that he was leaving for overseas soon. If he is attached to the 86th (and I think he is), he will still be around for awhile.

Joanne's note about Joey's begging sounded so darling. I can just see him now in poppa's shirt. He must have been a scream! I still insist I have the best nephew ever.

I used Grandmother's two dollars today. A chicken

dinner and a steak supper were my investments. And, they were good. A restaurant cooks its steaks on a big barbecue pit. It's picturesque and good. Reasonable, too. This noon we passed a "Hot Tamale" sign. So, we knocked on the door and each bought a tamale. They were good, too. And, they were hot.

The weekend football scores interest me again. I still believe that the Ohio State-Michigan game will be a humdinger, in spite of OSU's terrible strength. We'll see.

I believe I'll wait till camp to finish this. Then I may thank you for the box and answer your other letter correctly.

With a cookie in my left hand and a pen in my right, I thank you very much for the delicious variety of cookies. "Zig" and "Wedel" thank you, too. The three of us have put an awful dent in the big box in these past fifteen minutes. Thanks, also, for the clippings. GAHS must have a pretty good team! All the news was interesting to read.

The warm bed looks very inviting, so I'll climb in right away. Isn't it interesting that I should be getting my teeth repaired the same period you think I should be doing things like that?!

November 16, 1944

In a few days you will reccive another change of address card. In spite of the address, I will be at Camp Callen in San Diego for ten days or so. However, our mail will be received at Camp Cooke, as the card will read. I imagine it will be forwarded on to us, but, in case it isn't, and in case we don't get to write from San Diego, don't think that we are shoving off as yet. After we finish the advanced amphibious training at Camp Callen, we will be stationed at Camp Cooke for an indefinite period, which may be quite awhile.

I am looking forward to our coming experience at San Diego. A ride on a real ship for nine days is the big attraction. From the ship, we will make landings on islands, etc., ever so often. Now I'll get a chance to find out how much I can stand without getting sick. I wonder?? Also, being in San Diego will give me a chance to see Tommy, which will be great!! He has written me his phone number, so getting together shouldn't be difficult.

The past few days of preliminary amphibious training have been fun. In fact, I sort of think the Navy would have been a nice dish. We made four practice landings from landing craft in the bay. Everything works with clock-like precision. You would thrill to see the exactness of it all. We had good boat drivers, and only on two of the landings did we have to wade through water. The Navy knows its stuff! The Army does, too! Together they make an unbeatable team. No wonder our beach landings have been such successes.

I plan to phone Marcy sometime soon for the fun of it. I would also like to give you a ring. I'll pre-arrange the evening so we can be sure to get together.

The prospect of going over is exciting, even though it's still indefinite. But when I think I may be over for a pretty long time, I wonder if, perhaps, it won't get boring, especially with Marcy on this side. (Maybe I can stow her away. Hmmmm) Sometimes I wish she could come to California for a short visit with you, Mother. But, on second thought, I realize it's too inconvenient for all concerned. Besides, even if another furlough doesn't work out, I have the wonderful memories of the last one. And, I know I can count on Marcy being around so that we can pick up where we left off after the war.

The night before last we played basketball again. Results? 76 to 74, our favor! What a game that was! I was ready to drop when we finished. We have the possibilities of an excellent team here in M Company, several high scorers, and a couple of tall men. I'm gradually improving, too, I think. Tonight we play another company. Maybe we won't be so lucky this time.

Last night a bunch of us saw the movie "Doughgirls." Although it was nothing wonderful, we were in a slapstick mood, and we laughed very long and loudly. Wow!

I'm happy to hear that Ellen believes she and Wes will actually be married someday. For awhile I thought, perhaps, she was beginning to think differently. I sent her a box of chocolates about ten days ago - a birthday present a month late!! Will I ever learn to remember birthday dates?

This afternoon I returned to the dentist to be fixed up the rest of the way. Three more fillings to go, I guess. Sometimes I go to the office, only to be told to return at a later date. I have been excused from several hours of drill because of their blunderings. Not that I mind, though.

So, Don Gothard is finally leaving? And Charlotte went to see him off, Hmmm. I'm not in favor of the last minute goodby visits. I list those visits under your "futility" classification. There doesn't seem much sense in it. Better they stay at home and be useful.

Say "hello" to the Melungs for me. And. tell Mrs. Slagle I hope Don gets along fine, and I bet he will. I'll write again two or three times from this camp.

November 18, 1944

Just before I mailed my last letter to you, your splendid note of the 13th arrived. Now I have just loads to talk to you about. And,

also, lots of time; so, pull up a chair for three or four sides of this sloppy writing.

First of all, thank you a million for the wonderful

Christmas gift. Wow! Fifty whole dollars! That's a lot of money. And I had to smile how you suggested doubling that already huge amount so that I would be sure to accept the "small gift." It will be more than enough for all my pre-sailing needs. I do appreciate it so very much. Please keep it there and use it for Marcy's gift and any others I may want to ask you to shop for later. With a big wonderful reserve like that, I can spend my pay freely. That is truly the perfect gift presented at the ideal time. Thanks again and again!

It makes me happy to know that work toward buying the pin has already been started. I hope it can be gotten by Christmas. Chances are it might be a little late. Marcy will love it, I'm sure! I'll feel swell knowing she's wearing it. I want to give Manning something for his trouble. Perhaps a belt, tie, or something similar would be appropriate.

Your suggestion that Marcy might visit home after my excursion sounds terrific. In fact, that prospect is almost as thrilling as a furlough would be. I know she would enjoy visiting again, and I know you would find her most enjoyable. With me not around to steal her away for myself, you'll find out more what a girl she is. Do plan on it!

Guess what?! Yesterday I finished at the dentists. The experience was most enjoyable. The captain had some nova cain, so he said he might as well use it on me. So, I had an hour of painless drilling. I have one tooth that may need to be pulled out sometime. However, chances are it will last three or four years more, so he left it in.

What I really started out to say was this. I saw Major Haskins again. This time I decided to speak to him in spite of rank differences, etc. I talked with him for some fifteen minutes. We had a good short visit. It was so much fun that I forgot the "sirs" and salutes. He has only been with the division for two-and-a half months. That's why I haven't seen him before. He's a very nice man.

I want to tell you about our thrilling beach landing we

made yesterday morning. We got up at 3:30 a.m. By the time we had driven ⓓ Morro Bay, it was 7 o'clock. We boarded our crafts and went out of the bay into the ocean. The swells were fun. By 8:30, we started in for our landing. The surf was rugged. We got pretty wet, and had to wade waist deep in the warm water into the beach. Sometimes the boats get right on the beach, but we didn't quite make it because of a sand bar. It was really fun! I didn't think the surf had been too rough, but the officer in charge said it was as high as it had been since running problems. I don't blame you for loving the ocean

so much, Daddy. It gets in your bones, all right.

The wonderful Thanksgiving box arrived this evening. It is tops! I opened it only to check on the condition of the food. It's the kind that keeps, so I'll not indulge till this coming week. The pigs feet and everything look so inviting. Black Jack gum, all my favorite items! It's a wonderful box again. Always you send exactly the right, most welcome things.

Next weekend I may already be visiting Tommy. I'm sure we'll get together in San Diego. That will be fun.

It occurs to me that your box only took four days this time. That's really fast! I thought you would like to know that. "Special Delivery" was stamped all over the box. That must have sped it up In spite of all the rumors and factors pointing to an overseas movement of this outfit, don't count on it too much. Really, I may be around quite a while. To be completely frank with you, it hasn't yet reached the point where people are whispering "weeks." It's still in the "months" stage. However, no one but the chosen few really know, I'm sure. Furlough outlook is poor! If we're still around the end of January, I'll get one. The only furlough requirement is that all men must have had one in the last six months before going overseas. It will be a relief in several ways to be overseas. No more will we be "rear-guard commandoes," and, finally, we'll be doing our real duty. The education factors are worth looking forward to, too. Foreign countries, new customs, everything will be exciting. And, the sooner we put in service, the sooner we'll be home after the armistice.

Villar has returned (or did I tell you already). His baby is getting along much better. He repaid part of my money, and will repay the rest pay day. Borrowing and loaning money in this company is always easy. Everyone remembers their debts. Villar is a good, honest man, anyhow. He has money in civilian life, so I don't feel a charity need there.

Today I was on KP! The cooks were cleaning chickens for tomorrow. They were throwing away the gizzards. Another fellow and I grabbed the "pocket books" and cleaned 'em and fried 'em. I had a "pocket book" sandwich that was good. I wish Joanne could have shared it with me.

Tomorrow morning a gang of us are going in town to church again. It's a regular occurrence and at least six of us make the trip weekly. Since we're a mixture of faiths, we've been volleying between Presbyterian, Methodist, and Catholic. I believe it's Methodist's turn this week. I wish I could attend church in Gallipolis again. That service tops them all. Can you spare me one of your sermons sometime again, Daddy?

Football scores today were a little sad. I had hoped Michigan would wallop Wisconsin. And, now, Michigan and Ohio State??!!

Than you for all you're doing. Gosh, you are spoiling me at 3000 miles, and I love it. Good night, once more.

November 22, 1944

At this moment I am a little perturbed. All this week I have been wanting to write you and catch up on correspondence in general. But, we have been too busy. Now tonight, more of our free hours are chained down by a swimming class. I wouldn't mind except I went to the same class last week. Maybe I won't have to go yet. The class is interesting, though. In it we are taught how to remain afloat by blowing up our shirts. Another trick is removing our pants, tying the legs, and blowing them up as water wings. The methods are pretty ingenious.

Monday, from 10:00 a.m. till 3 o'clock, we ran an attack. It was a thrilling problem, using actual air support and field artillery. These beautiful hills are real challenges to one's stamina. Now this morning, we arose at the early hour of 4 a.m. and made another beach landing.

Hot dogs!!! They just announced no swimming for those who had gone before, and that's great. Now I can write you in a decent manner.

Your wonderful letter written the 16th came yesterday, and today your epistle of the 19th arrived. So I have six swell pages of conversation to talk with you about. It's appropriate that your letters should be typed in red letters, for each day I receive mail from home is a "red letter" day in its own way.

I was sorry ot hear about David Beard. I remember him well. It's good to know that Dan Eachus is having a chance at college life. He'll enjoy it, no doubt. The further news of J.T. and Merrill was interesting. Also, it's about time that Mark should get a furlough. The Air Corp is slow in handing out "vacations." Where exactly is he now? Too bad Mr. Brumfield is so ill. I hope he recovers. By the way, where is Luther now?

The evening at St. Johns sounded good. Mr. Higgins and Mr. Brown are fine men, and I'm happy to have their boosting words. Education seems to be my future. If it still interests me after being away from the book "larnin'" angle for awhile, that should be a good sign of permanent interest, shouldn't it? Marcy has promised to send on some of her more interesting literature and theories.

This noon I got five letters. Wow! One from each of the wonderful sisters, one from you, one from Packy McFarland, and one from Marcy. Packy is in England someplace now. The fog, rain, and cool weather are discomforting to him. However, he says the sincere kindness of the English people is great. Already he has been invited to dinner and has made friends. Packy is swell!

I have written you before about the visit with Major Haskins. It is nice to have another Gallipolitan in the "Blackhawks."

I opened and started demolishing that wonderful Thanksgiving box Monday morning. The sardines went on the problem with me. This afternoon, two candy bars and the nuts accompanied me on a close combat course. We (the hut) "wrecked" the box of deeelicious candy last night. And now today, we unwrapped the smaller box of cookies. The few that are left lie before me now. And, between paragraphs, they are rapidly disappearing. Mmmm. Soon only the chewing gum will be left. Thanks again! It was, and is, swell. Forgive the jumping the gun a little.

How unusual! A woman colored preacher!! I'd like to hear her sometime. As long as she gains people's respect and reverence, she should do the usual man's job well. The preacher I usually hear here gives an interesting child's sermon. However, it seems to hold no lesson or point. It's funny to see the children nod enthusiastically when the preacher asks, "Do you have a dog?," or something similar. I would love to hear another one of your sermons, Daddy. Will you send me one? The Thanksgiving one sounds swell! Dr. Shaw sent one titled "Are You Listening." Spiritual inspiration is sometimes a little difficult in the army.

Sunday morning church excursions are apt to turn into more of an excursion than a trip for worship. You would enoy seeing our whole row of fellows in church.

The letters from Joanne and Ellen were nice. Ellen must have had a close call cutting her finger in the lab. I do want to write Tommy Pryor encouraging him to attend Wesleyan. As soon as any member of the family has his address, I'd like to have it. Ellen asked about the ring on my finger in one of my pictures. That's the Delta Tau Delts ring Marcy gave me for my birthday.

For heaven's sake, don't ever hesitate to lend any of my things, Mother. Joanne asked if it were OK to borrow the sleeping bag for Frank. I'd love to have them use it. Don't even bother to ask my OK before passing my stuff out. It's fun to know different people are enjoying them

Tomorrow being Thanksgiving, I realize so much that I have an awful lot to be thankful for. This year of invaluable training in a time of necessity is on my list. My wonderful, wonderful Mother and Father, and sisters, are always on my list. So many, many things come to mind!! If possible, I want to make a chapel service during the day. Even if I don't, I want to spend more time than usual thanking God.

YourThanksgiving schedule sound fine. I know you'll enjoy Mrs. Plymale's hospitality. The river ride sounds fun, too! We don't start south until Friday, so we, too, will be having a fine meal and celebration.

CHAPTER SIX

CAMP CALLEN

Camp Callan
  San Diego, California
  November 26 - December 12, 1944

November 26, 1944

Your letter written the 21st arrived Thursday. This evening is the first chance I've had to answer. Thursday we had a delicious dinner; but eating time was our only leisure. The rest of the day was spent packing and preparing for our move down here. Friday morning at 4 a.m. we rolled out of bed to board our trucks, Half the company made the trip by vehicles and the other half by train. I drew a jeep. The ride was very enjoyable. We wore overcoats and were comfortable. Friday eve at 5:30 we stopped in a large field just beyond Los Angeles and pitched tents. Yesterday we came on arriving here at 10 o'clock. Although the entire trip was only 350 miles, at maximum speeds of 25, we rode along quite slowly.

Camp Callan is positively terrific. It's a pre-war camp having all the luxuries a really good camp provides. The natural surroundings are fine, too. Our double- decker barracks is only 500 yards from the ocean. Right now a beautiful sunset fills the skies. I wish you could enjoy the scenery and the countryside. We were ordered to keep awake in our jeeps. It was no job at all what with such views.

Arriving early as we did I thought surely we would have free time today. However, we have been busy continually. A training schedule filled today. And, for the first time in my army career, we had reveille and retreat on Sunday. They did allow us to attend church. I believe we may expect a busy time of it here. A twenty-five mile hike tomorrow sort of proves that. Hmmmm.

Wonderful, wonderful, about the pin!! That is inexpensive. But, if you say it looks beautiful in the catalogue, and it's the best, that's great! Thank you so very much. You are a super secretary. I'm calling Marcy this next Saturday. As I understand it, we won't be able to receive or send mail for eight or nine days (from the 3rd to the 12th). If phone connections are easy, I want to call you, too. Then I can call again when Ellen is there. However, don't count on it too much. We may not even be free.

I am perfectly satisfied with my lot in the army for the duration. I would never trade the army for the navy if it meant not meeting Marcy. And, that's another instance proving that most things work out for the best.

I just phoned the number Tommy gave me. He wasn't on duty, but I can reach him tomorrow evening. So, chances are that tomorrow night at this time I'll be talking to good ol' "Rob" again. That will be fine! San Diego is only 12 miles from here.

Goodness, but Chet Sealy must have seen a lot of action. Give him my regards! Also, say "hello" to Don for me. I am glad he came through with not such bad injuries.

The chapel service this morning was lovely. We had

communion, too. I got more from the service than I have from many of the civilian church services I have attended recently. There is a feeling of real power when worshiping with a full house of fellows. The singing and the responsive readings reminded me of the conference service I attended with you, Daddy, in Columbus. Everything was done with gusto and real feeling.

We board our boat next Sunday, and are supposed to be off the boat and back at Camp Cooke the 12th. It will be unusual not receiving mail for such a long period, if we don't. Probably it's a good conditioner for the real Mc Coy when it comes. If you are interested in our whereabouts in the Pacific during this period, we will be around the Coronado Islands. They are on most maps, just south of San Diego in the bay. It's fun telling you "info" now, 'cause someday it will be limited.

Wow, how do you like the O-M score?? That must have been a thriller. As I understand it, Michigan was leading in the last quarter 14 to 12. Then Ohio State came through with one more to win 18 to 14. Some game!

Will write again soon. Don't forget to address my mail to Cooke instead of here. I hope your Thanksgiving was as nice as you had planned. Ours was quite nice.

November 29, 1944

Busy with a capital "Bee" is again the report from this end. However, we're having fun, and that's what counts. Monday we took a twenty-five mile hike. Only two men fell out from "M" Company, and we're proud of that record. We started at 8 o'clock and finished at 4. In the evening we busied our free time by going into San Diego. What an amazing town that is! All marines and sailors! I wouldn't have believed that soldiers could be so definitely in the minority in any town. During our evening there we saw only a dozen or so G.I.s.

The purpose of the San Diego visit was to see Tommy. I talked to him on the phone, and because he was on duty, we decided to attempt to get together later. I think I may have a chance to see him this evening. Even though that evening's objective was not attained, we had a good time just walking about looking over the city. A fine Y.M.C.A. helped occupy a lot of our time. The city is nice, large, and interesting. It seemed to us that all of the sailors and marines were wearing ribbons. We felt very definitely like rookies. Several crutch cases were on the streets, and many purple hearts.

Yesterday we were given another ground forces test. It's the old business of push-ups, dashes, etc. I surprised myself on the 300 yard dash. Another fellow and I tied for the company record with a 42 second run. The terrain was a little rugged, and, also, we were suffering from the effects of the day before hike. Perhaps we could have done better.

Last night we got more shots: typhoid and small pox. Before I went to the dispensary, I put in a call to Marcy. I had returned from the dispensary only 20 minutes when the call came through. One hour and thirty minutes to cover 3000 miles is pretty fast. We had a fine talk! I mentioned your desire to have her visit. Her vacation is short, but I know she'd like to visit, probably after the holidays, though. The call cost more than I had expected, so I think you're right in suggesting I wait till Ellen's home before I call you. I'll call home after the 16th when you'll be sure to be there.

Today has been rather restful. This morning we had more or less routine classes. Now this afternoon our squad is on a detail. We just sit at our guns while patrols go by us and record our position. Pretty soft! And, it's swell to have this chance to answer your last letter.

Your letter written the 22nd, with Manning's and Ellen's letters enclosed, arrived last night. The mail takes longer being forwarded, I guess. Thanks again for the wonderful job you're doing in buying the pin. That is swell and I appreciate it. I do want to write Tommy Pryor, and I will this week before we go on the boat, if it's possible. I like him alot. He had a certain aloofness and pride which I admired. He would enjoy Wesleyan, I'm positive.

So that you may speculate with me, I'll pass on a recent rumor. People say we might have a ten week training schedule after we reach Camp Cooke. What reasoning such a rumor is based on is beyond me. But, if it came true, it would mean maybe another furlough. Probably all poppycock like 90% of rumors. Am passing it on just so you may expect anything. Might be here for Valentine's Day. Might be gone by New Year's. Who knows?

I continue to enjoy California. We passed some wonderful high schools on our ride down here. Maybe the state even has vocational opportunities. I still love Ohio and Michigan, though. They're first on my list.

I have changed around my allotment plan for overseas. Since you are such a super secretary, Mother, I'd like to have you do some banking for me. Every month, beside my bond, you'll receive 30 dollars in your name. That will make $48.75 I'll be salting away every four weeks spent overseas. I'll have a dozen dollars for myself which will be more than enough. If I'm gone two years, I should have over $1500 dollars waiting for me. Not bad at all. That, plus the free college, should start me off right, and how!

I still don't know whether we'll be able to write next week. I hope so. At any rate, you'll hear again by the 14th or 15th. No doubt, much sooner.

What is Tommy Pryor interested in? What are his life plans and service plans? I'd like to know. Maybe we can begin a correspondence. Manning is a good fellow, and I'm glad Wesleyan is agreeing with him. HIs letter was well written.

I'll save the rest of this page in case a letter comes this evening.

Hello again,

No mail this eve. Tomorrow morning we get up at 3 a.m. I called Tommy, and we'll meet tomorrow night instead of this evening. Rest is essential tonight. I'm going to write T. Pryor right this minute. I hope I can help convince him about O.W.U.

No more news. I hope it isn't too chilly up North. And, I hope everything is running smoothly. I'll write again before the jaunt.

December 2, 1994

Although the mail man hasn't been favoring me with lots of letters from you, this evening he came forth with a wonderful box, which is really swell. The assortment of sweets is definitely welcome. Thank you so much again! I wasn't expecting it, and it was a nice surprise. No one is getting much mail here. No doubt when we return from our jaunt we'll be swamped. The last letter I received from you was the one with Manning's and Ellen's letters enclosed.

Maybe tomorrow, before we go on the boat, we'll have one more large mail call.

It has been longer between letters than I had meant it to be. The extra busy training schedule is again the 'scuse. However, last night an evening of frivolity with Tommy was the reason for not writing. We had planned a meeting for Thursday, but being paid (pay day) kept us apart. But, we did have a grand reunion last night. Rob is thinner than I had expected. I met him at 8 o'clock just after he had finished playing a basketball game. Incidentally, he scored 18 points. Still good! We spent most of the evening talking. It had been some 14 months since we have been together, A show and bowling, plus a good dinner, added variety to the get together. We finally split up at 1 a.m. And, by the time "Zig" and I returned to camp, it was after 2. Ho-hum. (So, I'm going to bed early.) Tommy has a fine set-up in San Diego. He thinks he may go out on a hospital ship soon, though.

Our small boat trip of last Thursday was interesting. We were introduced to the vessel that is to be our "home" for this next week. It's a regular troop transport. Bunks are five high and look rather precarious. There is just enough room for everybody, and that's all. The same ship also carries the boats which take us to the beach, so you can guess its size. Landings are getting to be like every day matters. The Thursday one ran smoothly and was a cinch.

Tomorrow we start on our jaunt. During our seven days (approximately), we will make only three landings. At our last landing, Gen. Lear will be present to watch operations. I told you already about no mail, didn't I? I'll surely write a long one after the week or nine day silence. Expect to hear from me by the 15th, probably.

And speaking of the "finis" of this practice jaunt, we are returning to San Luis Obispo instead of Cooke, a recent change. You will be notified when the mailing address is to be changed. Obispo is the nicer of the two camps, so the news is nice.

A lot of the fellows have gone into Diego tonight. I'm enjoying a nice, quiet service club. A talented soldier is playing classical numbers a few feet away from me. He is good! And, it's so very nice to hear him. I do love good music. Ah, there goes the "Brook" a number Ellen used to play often. Or, is it the "Brook?" Anyhow, it's lovely, and I'm enjoying it.

It occurs to me often that to be acquainted with and to enjoy a number of good things is to set up a barrier to the bad things. If music, books, sports, etc., thrill a person, he isn't going to look for cheaper and more shallow thrills. And, I am so thankful that you raised me to have a natural barrier against the bad. So many of the fellows didn't have the good rais'n' I did. No one can blame a man for something his parents didn't give him. And, along with the parents come the schools. That's why school work seems to be the vocation I want.

Tommy said he thought Don Slagle may be in the hospital there in San Diego. He's going to see if he is. Has "Chet" returned home yet?

I'm enclosing a list of the names of the fellows in the company picture I sent you. Those starred are the closer buddies of mine. Keep the list along with the picture.

I'll want you to do a little Christmas shopping for me in awhile. Any suggestions for gifts will be welcome. How much exactly did the pin cost? How soon will it arrive?

Remember me mentioning the possibility of getting in some fishing on this deep sea excursion? I have heard no pros and cons on the subject. Also, we haven't had time to look for tackle. I believe I'll spend my free time on boat reading. I have the new Digest which I haven't perused yet, also, a Newsweek and other magazines. Maybe during the time we're on one of our landings we'll get to throw over a line and sinker. We'll soon see.

It's going to be queer not hearing from you regularly. Our mental telepathy sets will be keeping us in touch, I'm sure. And, before we know it, the short week or so will be gone.

I can't recall anything more I wanted to say this time. I believe I shall write on the boat so that as soon as we land I'll be able to mail a letter to you pronto. Take good care of yourselves. I'll be writing and hearing from you in about 10 days. So long for awhile.

December 5, 1993

If you could only see the perfectly beautiful cove our convoy is resting in now. It's such a peaceful picture that it's almost impossible to believe the ships are warships. About a dozen sailors have fishing lines out. This adds to the peacefulness of the scene. The evening is lovely!

I'm beginning the promised diary of events a little late. But, since sleeping and reading occupy most of our time, daily epistles might not be interesting. I'll sum up what we've done so far day by day.

Sunday we boarded ship as we were scheduled to do. However, the day was spent moored in the harbor. We got used to our limited quarters and just generally loafed around.

Monday was a more exciting day. At two o'clock we felt the ship beginning to move. At six o'clock we were unable to see any land. The immensity of our convoy was a surprise. Twenty or more ships made up our group. And, by ships, I do mean ships. A battleship, destroyers, transports, etc. The sight of such a complete assemblage started rumors spreading. After an hour of riding the waves, some of the more prolific rumor spreaders had us heading for the Philippines. Three or four blimps or zeppelins added to the realness of the move.

The swells of the open seas failed to affect very many of us. I know of only two men who ran for the bucket. The ship is large enough to ride smoothly. We traveled continually Monday and Monday night. The gentle rocking during the night was sort of a nice cradling feeling. I slept like a baby.

This morning about 7 o'clock, the boat (I mean ship) anchored. A glimpse outside showed me an island some two or three miles away. That was to be the object of our landing. We loaded into our boats (boats are craft carried on ships) at 9:30 a.m. At 11 o'clock, after an hour and a half of waiting, we hit the beach. The preparation before any boats landed on the beach was astounding. Naval guns blasted away and planes strafed. It all looked like the real McCoy.

We were in the third wave of the third attack battalion. In actual combat, that would mean a fairly safe position. However, the positions in the attack are changed about. The surf was very slight, and we went from the boat to beach getting only wet soles on our shoes. That's wonderful compared with some of our former waist deep wadings. We returned to our ships after an hour or so on the beach. Our landing craft took us back, too, naturally.

It's certainly miraculous the complete, expensive training the army is giving men now. We'll be sent into battle with thorough training! Wc have another landing Thursday and a last one on California's shore Saturday.

The sunsets, the smell of the sea, everything is so romantic and restful. This is just like an ocean cruise. The cramped quarters aren't real inviting. I think I would choose the occasional rain and mud in the infantry, plus the wide open spaces, rather than the close quarters of the easy living navy man.

Everything is run with clock-like precision. Meals are

tops. And, gosh, but we are getting plenty of rest. All I do is read. Ask me anything about this month's Digest, last week's Newsweek or Colliers. Also, I've been reading the Bible and some literature passed around by the ship's chaplain. Much of this life and I would get fat.

A seal is playing around the ship tonight. Did you read the article on sea lions in the Digest? After watching this one tonight, I believe they are clever. He, or she, kept coming up right under sea gulls, scaring the day lights out of them.

Tomorrow I'll have to trade literature with some of the men. There really isn't room on the ship for classes or instruction of any kind. Staying in our bunks is the only way to be comfortable.

As soon as more news collects, I'll add to this. Till then.

December 8, 1994

Three days since I last wrote, but still there isn't much exciting news. The problem yesterday was a diller, however. We took the entire island. Over hill and dale, for a long time. I thought that this lazy life might make us soft. But we were able to go the terrain in fine shape. It makes me think that rest is as good for you as exercise. Actually, of course, it's a combination of the two that's best.

I finally learned the name and location of this island, which has been the object of our two landings. It is San Clemente. It's located midway between San Diego and Long Beach, about 100 miles from the coast. There is no vegetation on it. Cactus, rocks, and dirt make up the whole place. The cactus brought about some humorous scenes. I got one on my shoe. I sat down to remove it only to gain another in a more painful and conspicuous place. Ouch! It was funny, though.

Last night we had a movie in the mess compartment. It was "The Tuttles of Tahiti." Do you remember it? We laughed at it and enjoyed it.

For the last two days we have been out of reading material, that is, all except the literature the chaplain passed out. Now everybody is reading intently "The Upper Room," "Secret Place." "New Testament," "Stop, Look and Listen," and other pamphlets of a religious or moral nature. Now I'll bet the fellows would rather read them than other magazines. Everyone is interested, and it's good for all of us. Reading and thinking in those lines brings one close to God, and that brings a wonderful feeling.

Tomorrow we land on the beach near Camp Pendleton, a Marine base. We'll probably stay overnight there, and then return to Obispo by rail and convoys. This week has been enjoyable and restful. Also, the training has been worthwhile. I'll always remember this week.

I just left you for a minute. I threw away some trash. Just as I dumped the box, I noticed a dollar bill. How's that for easy money. Nobody has claimed it, at least not seriously.

I mentioned "The Secret Place." I believe the Baptist church prints it. It's very similar to "The Upper Room." I enjoy reading numerous persons' ideas and convictions.

Mother, will you send me the amount of money I have left of the fifty, that is, just the information, not the cash. I'm making a mental list of what I'd like to have you purchase for me. As soon as we return to Obispo, I'll send details.

I have missed the regular letters from you and Marcy. It will be nice reading the accumulation. Then I'll have a lot to write in answer to your letters. Now news is scarce.

I won't be able to mail this till Monday or Tuesday. By then I will have written you again, no doubt.

CHAPTER SEVEN

CAMP SAN LUIS OBISPO - PART 2

**CAMP SAN LUIS OBISPO - PART 2
DECEMBER 12, 1944 - FEBRUARY 12, 1945**

December 12, 1944

It's nice to be back in a home camp again. We arrived here this noon. Although we landed on California's shores Saturday the 9th, we camped there until last night. While we were there, we merely cleaned weapons and did other routine work. Last night, those of us who rode down on jeeps got to board a train for the ride back. So, we choo-chood merrily all night. It was fun to be on a train again. While we were bivouacked, I got one of your letters, which was most welcome after the long silence.

This afternoon we had a big mail call. It took two whole hours to give out all the packages and letters. And I got five more from you. Goodness, but that's a lot of mail. Besides that, I received one from Manning and three from Marcy. Incidentally, at the other mail call I got a letter from Joanne in which she enclosed a letter from Doug. I am sending it on to you. It's a thrilling letter!

To begin with your letter of the 25th: I am happy that

Tommy Pryor has decided on Wesleyan. I did write him a rather lengthy letter. (It wasn't a very good one, though.) You were busy that Thanksgiving weekend what with the funerals and all. All the news about E. Holzer, Farley's husband, and Helen Wheeler was so interesting. I would like to meet the recent secretary. She sounds like a good addition.

I'm looking forward to the fruit cake. I like all fruit cakes now. Yours will be most welcome!

We fellows had a laugh over your comparison of jeep and car, Mother, dear. There isn't much in common between the two. However, they aren't bad riding. We never use tops, though, and that makes it a bit windy.

Mr. Brumfield's case must be serious. I hope he recovers. I hadn't realized he was so seriously ill. I feel sorry for the boys. And, Luther's fights must be because he's still in civies.

Daddy, I received your sermon in the field. I read it that night by the fire and again Sunday. I enjoyed it thoroughly. It's a fine one, as always. We do always have so terribly much to be thankful for.

The news of a real snowfall is wonderful. Gosh, but it must be thrilling. I'd love to see more snow. Your fine descriptions are good substitutes for the real McCoy. I can picture easily the beautifulness of it all.

I am happy to learn that John Cunningham has graduated as a navigator. That's super. He must have worked hard. John always had the "go get" necessary to be something. He showed it in his football. Though small and handicapped, he was a threat always to the opposing team.

Ten dollars or so will be plenty for overseas pay. Money just rots where we expect to go. Some of the men are planning on only five or six dollars. Chester could tell you the same, no doubt.

As silly as it seems, for our maneuvers on an

uninhabited island, we're entitled to wear the American Theatre ribbon. Wow, that makes two I could wear if I wished. Ha!

I will surely thank Mrs. Brown or anybody sending cards or gifts. I plan on sending several Christmas cards as I did last season.

Have you noticed a tension or peculiarity in this note? It's justified. A fellow just informed me emphatically that I would get another furlough. So I may be wiring you for money one of these days. I do so hesitate to say this, but the rumor is loud enough to bear listening to. Wouldn't it be wonderful to have another visit. Gosh, but I've had my share already! I would love to see you again. Seeing Marcy would be grand, too. (She sent a picture plus an identification bracelet today.) I'll keep you posted very soon. Probably sooner than you think.

December 18 1944

This letter should reach you about the same time I do. But in case I'm delayed a little, I'll explain now how I'm coming home. The boy in our squad who owns the '42 Lincoln is also going on furlough. He needs someone to help him drive. Since he can drop me off in Knoxville, Tenn., I'm grabbing this chance. Three of us are riding with him. We plan on driving 20 of the 24 hours. Averaging 40 we can make an easy 800 miles a day. It's 2500 miles to Knoxville from here. Since we're going by private conveyance, we get to leave tonight at midnight instead of tomorrow at 9:30 p.m. This should put us in Knoxville Friday morning sometime. And that means I'll be home a day earlier, or sometime Friday night.

We follow two roads all the way, 66 and 64. They are excellent highways. It's all a southern route so we don't have to worry about snow, etc. The car is the safest on the road. It's a 1942 Lincoln Zephyr sedan. Harold (Minges) has taken fine care of it. Just four months ago he wangled four brand new white side-wall tires for it. We won't be driving too fast. Three thousand miles of continual hard fast driving would be too strenuous even for a Lincoln.

Picture me sailing along the country enjoying the beautiful scenery. It will be a fine trip. With only four of us in the big sedan there is room for two to be sleeping stretched all the way out in the back seat. The car has red leather upholstery and is comfy. Harold and I will do most of the driving. However, the other two buddies are drivers, too. Incidentally, the fellows are nice guys. I went to church with one of them yesterday.

You would never guess what we are doing today. It's a long story. Do you recall the three or four Sundays we were busy? It seems our new regimental commander submitted a schedule to the division commander. This schedule called for ten seven-day weeks. When the division commander saw it he was mad. And he was more disgusted when he realized that we had been working for the last four Sundays. So- we have today, Monday, free. I am simply amazed , and, also, the report that we will work on Sunday no more unless absolutely necessary. I guess Maj. Gen. Melasky is a fine division commander. It's swell having today off. Now I can get ready for the homeward trip.

About the cost of the trip home, Harold is charging each of us only 15 dollars. Of course we'll have to buy our train tickets back here. However, we may buy round trips at furlough rates of $65. Then I can cash in and receive almost $30 back. That will be a saving of $15, not including dining car meals, etc. Not bad!

Your letter written the 14th just arrived. As you can tell by my recent letters, I, too, am writing incoherently and excitedly. It is so very wonderful!!

Although I have known about riding in the car for a

couple of days, I thought I wouldn't tell you 'till now. Such a long ride in a car might worry you. There is no reason for worry. I thought it over carefully before deciding. The long train ride seems to me to be more dangerous. Recent reported accidents don't sound so good. Harold's car is absolutely the best there is. Three thousand dolars might buy it here in California, but I doubt it. And, Harold is a fine driver. He's been driving a car as long as I have. So far he's had one accident. A flat tire or engine trouble could slow us up. If that occurs you'll understand that the delay is nothing.

I am so very happy over this coming furlough. I don't know what could be more wonderful. I am so thankful!! Christmas at home! What could possibly be more perfect!

I'm going into town to do some last minute shopping. Be seeing you - actually.

December 21, 1944,
12:39 p.m., Telegram from Knoxville

Will arrive Huntington by train, 2:05 a.m., 22nd.

December 21, 1944,
4:22 p.m., Telegram from Knoxville

Train three hours late. Can take bus if you are busy.

January 5, 1945
(On the Train)

After a fourteen hour snooze, I realize that it's time I say "hello" again via the mail method. It's hard to believe that it was over two days ago that we were talking together. So let's check up and see what has made the time fly by so quickly.

The train ride from Gallipolis to Columbus was fine. Don and I had fun talking together 'till Athens. From there on in I read about some operas. At Columbus (the train was one hour late) I investigated weather conditions and learned that no buses were running. So I phoned Marcy pronto. We had a wonderful time talking together again. I got the thrill of a lifetime when she announced that if having a career meant being alone, she didn't want one. We had talked over that subject and I was pleased with the outcome. But that was her first emphatic statement which led to an answer to the question as to whether she might become Mrs. W someday.

The train was again late arriving in Chicago. From there I wired Marcy an orchid. Also I phoned Ellen. She didn't have time to come to the station since my train was late. But we talked quite a while. The night before Ellen had been riding an "EL" when she spotted a guy who looked like Miles. A Black Hawk patch on his shoulder prompted her to ask him if he might be Miles. He answered yes, and I can just picture his surprise. Ellen said he just stood around with his mouth open. I'm so happy Ellen spoke with him. I can hardly wait to get his reaction.

At first when we left Chicago the train was jammed. Luckily I got a seat after only a half hour of standing. And except for a couple of short periods, I have had this same seat all the way. It's really ok. Most of my time has been occupied by sleeping and reading and talking. Also, I wrote Marcy a couple of letters yesterday. The time is passing quickly, and I'm enjoying the whole trip.

Last night I had this seat all to myself. I went to sleep at around 8:30 p.m. When I woke up to check my watch again, once more it was 8:30. I had slept twelve full hours. I snoozed two more hours and then had a late breakfast. It's now about noon. Pretty smooth!

Gosh, but this furlough was perfect. I can't possibly

imagine how it could have been nicer. From beginning to end, I enjoyed every second of it. I knew I would have a swell time, but it was even more super perfect than I had expected. It's wonderful to be a member of such a wonderful family. Mother, Daddy, Ellen, Joanne, and Joey, gosh, how could you be any better. Add the Feelys, Brashares, and maybe the Percys, and we certainly complete a perfect family double circle. I am thankful for this. And just wait 'till more grandchildren start arriving, what a super gang we'll have then.

Joey is such a great guy. I certainly felt like sneaking him along with me. Thank you so much for coming over, Joanne. And, you are the lovely mother. Gosh, I just burst with pride when I inspect our present family and its future. Wow!

I'm ashamed to say that I don't know where we are. I remember vaguely somebody saying Salt Lake City. We probably are still in Utah. We haven't stopped for a long time. This train is running on time, so we'll be in Los Angeles in just about 20 more hours. Most of the fellows on this train are already late. I'll make it in plenty of time, though.

Will you sort of smooth over the visits I failed to make? As I look back now, I realize I didn't see Mrs. Robinson or Mabel McClung. Also, I didn't say "so long" to a lot of people. I should have been more carful with my time.

As soon as we stop I'll mail this. There is still snow all around. And, it is cold on the platform. Maybe it will be cold in California, too. It will be interesting to see how things are at camp.

I'll sign off in preparation for mailing this. If we don't stop for awhile I'll add more later. Again, I want to thank you for the wonderful furlough. It was superb.

January 7, 1945

Back at camp! And it isn't bad at all. The temperature is surprising. It must be 70 degrees at least. In fact, it's almost uncomfortable. Various rumors are still flying about, but none of them are founded on anything at all. Most reliable of all seems to point to maneuvers at the end of this month. Probably they will be held right here in California, too.

The train got me in Los Angeles at 7:30 a.m. as planned. In the station I met an M Company pal and we went to a show downtown. The picture was "Meet Me in St. Louis." It was fine. I caught the 6:00 o'clock train for San Luis and I arrived at camp at 11:15 p.m., forty-five minutes early. On the train during this last lap was a cute little girl just about Joey's age. Although Joey's age, she was inferior to him in vocabulary and action. From comparison I could see that Joey is actually really very brilliant. And that's not a prejudiced uncle's opinion either.

Last night just as I was going to sleep, the whole hut returned from town. They did give me a royal welcome. We talked until 3:00 a.m. They are such a swell bunch of guys. I'm fortunate to be with them. This morning Minges returned, late, but not late enough to make trouble. He drove back in his car again. He didn't telegram because he was visiting with a brother in Birmingham and wasn't sure of his plans.

I'm sending back my ration sheet. You may need some more points while Joanne and Joey are there. The sheet is good for two more weeks. Also, I'm returning the train ticket for you to cash in. All you have to do is take it to the ticket man in Gallipolis and he will refund you immediately. If I send it in from this end it might take two months. Also, show him the enclosed statement so he'll know you didn't just find the ticket. If for any reason he should fail to give you the money, return the ticket to me and I'll go through the available red tape from this end. Don't forget it for it should amount to 30 dollars or more.

By the way, I found a ten dollar bill in my pants watch pocket. I don't recall how it got there. It boosts my cash on hand to over 30 dollars, so keep the ticket money, of course.

The only thing seemingly missing is my brown pen. It may turn up yet. Or, have you seen it at home? This black one isn't running smoothly as yet.

Every time I think of the wonderful furlough, I almost swoon. It was so nice. Today I opened the accumulation of mail. It included a box from you, the hickory nut cake. We ate it immediately. Also, Ellen's swell Christmas box!!

I'll write again real soon.

January 8, 1945

Today has been a lazy day. "Showdown Inspection" was our schedule for the entire day. Everything we had over the allotted amount of clothing, etc., was confiscated. Anything we were short of we were supplied. Now this evening we learn that tomorrow we will go through the same routine. So breaking into camp routine is being gradual and enjoyable.

Tonight rumors are flying thick and fast. But still no one knows anything definite. Lt. Cox just dropped in the hut to ask us if we knew anything new. Minges popped up with a rumor that skiis had been ordered for the entire division. And that's how ridiculous some of the stories are that are going about. The amount of uncertainty and talk points toward something definite developing in the near future. So probably in another week we'll know for sure our future for the next couple of months.

A short while ago I drew my squad leader equipment.

It includes rifle, bayonet, compass, clinometer, flashlight, wire cutters, bolo klnife, whistle, and many other things. A new list of things just came out for squad leaders, and I'm getting the benefit of it. You should see the bolo knife. It's almost two feet long and wicked. I'll use it as an axe to clear bushes away from the gun. Being squad leader is proving fun. I hope it continues.

I can just picture Joey helping (?) pull down the Christmas tree. That must have been a riot. I hope the river doesn't rise high enough to be harmful. If it's lowering already though there should be no serious flood scare. The clippings were interesting. I'm betting that Jo Wells and Kenny Iron will want to get married. Too bad about Eugene Plymale.

No more men have gone on furloughs. I do hope more men will get some soon. Gosh, there's nothing like a furlough! Especially a wonderful one such as I had. This evening I wrote Mrs. Percy a thank you note. Pen and paper still balk my thoughts. A few more letters and I should be back in the writing groove. But, perhaps, some letters are difficult most of the time anyhow.

Everything about this last furlough was so fine. It will honestly last me a long time if necessary. Christmas at home was wonderful. All my gifts were grand! I thank you for everything every night.

After always saving all of my letters, I have finally decided to stop the practice. Since we're being asked to get rid of all excess things, I think I'll have to include most letters. I will save them 'till I've answered them anyhow.

I hope everything is buzzing at home as happily as ever. And I hope the weather is nicer. I loved it, but it's better for only short periods. See you again soon.

January 10, 1945

How is the weather now in Gallipolis? Is it still so very cold? It's getting cooler here now. In fact, this evening makes me believe perhaps California will never have winter. But I guess really it won't be cold. It's just cool enough to wear field jackets.

Your letter today was interesting. I'm happy to hear that another good Gallipolis man is joining the 86th. I'll be watching for him. All the clippings were interesting. Too bad GAHS got defeated. Maybe they'll be better for it. They acted a little over confident and cocky.

The last two days and for the next two I'm working with the personnel section. It's an interesting job. I pop questions all day and in the evening. Three of us are helping out. The hours are pretty long but the work is soft. It's quite fun. Cpl. Dipompeo and Cy Troyan are working with me. We aren't on a regular training schedule at all yet. This week is sort of a cleanup period. Odd jobs which need being done are being cleaned up. We worked until 9 o'clock tonight.

Miles is still excited about seeing Ellen. 'Course he says she's beautiful. I knew he would be taken by her loveliness.

Although there is nothing in particular which makes me mention this, I want you to remember if at anytime you don't hear from me for a longer period than usual, probably we were unable to write for some reason similar such as the last one. So don't forget.

It's late and I'm pretty sleepy even though I'm not working hard. So I'll make this only a short note. I keep thinking about the wonderful furlough. It was certainly perfect!

Good night. Give Joey and Joanne an extra kiss for me.

P.S. Today I got a card announcing a year's subscription to the Digest, a gift of the Feelys. That is grand of them. I'll try to write a thank you note.

January 11, 1945

Am I right in saying Joanne and Joey left today? Gee, I'll bet the house seems quiet now! Isn't it restful, sort of? I can readily see how Frank would miss them. Just being an uncle and brother, I miss them enough. I still hope and pray that my children will be just three-fourths as sweet as Joey.

Today I got a set of pictures we took at Percys. I'm sending them on right away. And, will you send them back after you've enjoyed them. The one of Marcy and me under the tree is too bright and isn't so good. The rest are fine, though. Marcy mentioned that her mother was writing you or something. I hope she does. Mr. Percy usually wears glasses. Perhaps you'll notice them missing in the pictures.

We're working nights at personnel and I have to return there now.

10:00 p.m.

Back from the office! By tomorrow eve we will have questioned almost 5000 men, or the entire regiment. Then I'll be back to my squad leading job. It's pretty late now, so I'm going to sign off.

I'm sending another bunch of stuff home. It's all stuff I don't need and It's just in the way here. I'll let you know when I mail it.

The main purpose of this note was to enclose the pictures.

I hope it isn't too quiet in the house now. We're always there in spirit anyhow.

January 14, 1945

This coming Tuesday evening all of us Wesleyan men

are gathering together at the service club for dinner. Last night I met a former Phi Psi and we decided we should take action to see that a meeting could be accomplished. We mailed post cards right away. There are seven of us still here. I hope we'll be able to make it. Just so night problems and details stay away from all of us!!

Last night I went to the camp studio and got my picture taken. (Didn't break the camera either!) Tomorrow I get to look at the proofs. Since the arrangement calls for payment before pictures, you'll be receiving a "pic" good or bad. I may send you all three of them and ask you to mail one to Marcy and the other one to the persons you wish to. It would save me the trouble, and the studio, too.

Speaking of pictures, the number I have gathered here has grown large. I'm sending some back for you to keep for me. I want to be free from any excess equipment. It's so much neater and easier in case maneuvers actually come about.

I was sorry to hear about Baxter. Probably he is a prisoner in Germany. They captured an amazing number. War news seems to be excellent now, though. I'm sure 1947 will see me back at studies, etc.

I am constantly aware of the excellent company I am in. I am lucky. The men are tops. The six men I have in my squad are tops. The roster now includes "Zig," Villar, Minges, Roberts, Tickvica, and Woeltjen. "Tick" is a former driver recently transferred to my squad. Woeltjen is our driver. New York, Louisiana, North Carolina, Michigan, California, Illinois and Ohio are represented.

Last night Bill Herndon, Cy Troyan and I talked for three whole hours. Bill was governor of Texas at the Texas Boys' State. The honor included living at the governor's mansion for five whole days. Cy was captain of his wrestling team. Neither of the fellows smoke, swear or drink. They are fine! This morning Bill and I went to chapel here at camp. The service was pretty nice.

"Keys of the Kingdom" is showing at the theater tonight and tomorrow. I do want to see it. Have you seen "Meet Me in St. Louis?" It's good, and you would enjoy it.

"Zig" and I are going to walk over to the 342 area. I want to make sure the Wesleyan men there know about our meeting. The get together should be most interesting.

I'm glad Marcy and the Percys dropped you notes. By the way, would you mind mailing that other company picture I have in my room to Marcy?

There isn't much news so I'll stop writing for now. I hope the new quietness isn't annoying. I'll write again soon.

January 15, 1945

Last night I finished reading "Papa Was a Preacher" written by Alyene Porter. It tells the story of a Texas minister and his wife, plus eight children. Naturally, it was an especially interesting story to me. Read it if you get a chance. One of the fellows in the company gave it to me after he had finished it.

Also in the line of intellectual enjoyment is the "Keys of the Kingdom." It wasn't as powerful a picture as I had imagined it would be; but still it is worthwhile!

I examined the two proofs of my pictures. They look too much like me. One of the three is being tinted. You should receive them in the mail by the 30th or so. If you like the tinted one better, keep it and send one of the others to Marcy for me, please. Really, they aren't very good, So don't expect much.

The boys in the hut laughed with me over your first typed paragraph written on the 12th, Mother. You must be psychic! It is about time something like that occurred. What will be the outcome has us baffled. We honestly have no idea about anything??!! Even though you have guessed correctly,   I suggest you don't make it a subject of conversation, just for super safety reasons.

The pens arrived yesterday with the socks. Thanks a lot. I am now writing with the brown pen. It writes more smoothly than any pen I have ever owned. Both are very good. There is another brown one about someplace. If you find it, throw it away or something. Thanks again.

Please don't send any of the ticket money. I have more than I need. Also, I have fifteen dollars loaned out, and that will be another source of income next pay day. I have even thought of sending some cash home. I get paid the 10th, you see. Also, this coming pay day I'll be getting additional ration pay. Did I ever tell you the army pays a soldier for the meals he ate on furlough?

Being squad leader is hurting my conscience. Take this morning for instance. We aren't having regular drill. Instead, all the men are working on various details. Squad leaders don't have to do detail work, so I'm sitting here in the hut all alone writing while others do odd jobs. Naturally it involves other things which sort of counter balance the niceties. For instance, if something comes up to be done in the squad at a time like now, I would have to do each man's job for him since he isn't around. I do like the job since it is a change. Probably by March I should be a sergeant if everything goes well in the squad. The extra money would certainly be welcome to store away for post-war use.

Time out for work

Just now a job came up to be done. At least now I don't feel as if I weren't doing anything.

Tonight is the planned meeting for our Wesleyan get together. I'm keeping my fingers crossed. A lot of details are keeping the men busy through the evening. I'm afraid I may not even be able to get there. I certainly hope so, though! We're just hoping for an informal meal at the service club together.

The few days working with personnel we're certainly interesting. I must have questioned at least fifteen hundred men. Five thousand (approximately) came past our desk, but three of us were working the desk. I spoke to each man for only a minute. However, I began guessing at their intelligence rating, amount of school, and home state after glancing at them. It was surprising how nearly one could guess. I couldn't help but notice the intelligence ratings of the men in "M" Company. Our first sergeant, who is a college graduate, has a score of 140. That's the highest in the company. There are six of us, all college men, who have over 130 or 135. A couple of non-coms have 75! Hmmm. On the whole, we're a pretty intelligent outfit. Scores of 110 and 115 were required for the air corps and ASTP, so may of us are above that. My squad's average is 123, and that isn't bad for seven men from seven different states. Working with people will be a joy. Each one is such a surprise package. I can hardly wait to begin studying toward that goal.

You would be pleased to see the reform movement which is in full swing here in M Company. When I returned from furlough, several fellows told me that had given up smoking. I thought to myself, "Bet you don't." But three men haven't even had one for over two weeks now. And, they're happy about it too! Others are still trying to stop, but having trouble. It seems every smoking or drinking man realizes he is doing wrong. I'm happy to see them self-disciplining themselves.

The weather here is still lovely. Not even one drop of rain as yet. Some days are almost too warm. Sunday it was uncomfortable to walk to chapel with a blouse on. I hope winter doesn't stay with you in such force for very much longer.

My correspondence is very apt to be limited to you

and Marcy only. I would like to write to many more, but it's difficult now. Do give my regards to people for me as often as proper.

Marcy is so wonderful! She is exactly what you would like!! I wish I could have spoken to you more about her family. Although her parents haven't had college educations, they have certainly made the most of their high school educations and what they have learned since then on their own. They are so kind and sincere. Unless some unforeseen event steps in, one of my first post-war plans is a ring for Marcy. And, if the war lasts longer than 1947, it will not be a post-war project. There are no doubts in my mind about her. All my thoughts about the future include her. It's essential for her to be with me. And, it makes me so happy to know she has agreed to be included in my future plans for happiness. Time will pass quickly 'till I can be with her again with that thought in mind. And, with time and distance acting as testers, we will know surely then that things are right.

I didn't mean to get "mushy." Still, I wanted to tell you a little more about Marcy.

Enough for now. It was so nice having your letter written in the station. Don't work too hard straightening things up.

Are you getting to see many basketball games? How does the team look to you?

January 19, 1945

We have been rather busy for the past few days. I haven't been writing as much as I'd like to. This morning, however, we had an interesting break in our steady work routine. The whole regiment gathered in our lovely amphitheater here for an assembly. There we met every officer in the regiment, and also had a nice talk by our regimental commander, the colonel. We originally thought the colonel was no good. From observing him today, he must have a lot of fine qualities. His speech won me over considerably.

We got a big thrill when our battalion commander introduced our Captain Brydon as the commander of the best heavy weapons company in the division.

Since there are nine companies like ours in the division, we felt really proud to know we were thought of as the best.

I have a confession to make. Night before last I let the barber give me the works. Call me baldy now. It's the closest shave I've ever had. If you remember some of my former haircuts, you'll realize how short this one is.

Phil Campbell's loud praying made me smile. What a boy he must be. As for Joey, I repeat, he is a darling and a heartbreaker. I'm afraid I'll be judging my children as to how they stack up in comparison to Joey. By the way, I've finally decided to be sensible and agree on only seven or eight kids. And, if boys predominate, I won't be sorry. But I do want at least three girls. (Pipe dreaming.)

This evening, even though it is late, we are working. My job calls for work for about five minutes out of every hour. So, I'm lucky in being able to talk with you tonight.

Did I tell you about the outcome of our planned Wesleyan get-together? We were working that evening also, so I wasn't able to attend. And, since then I haven't met any of the fellows. Perhaps we'll be able to meet yet.

Your trip to come in March sounds swell, Mother. It will be a nice affair! Isn't it wonderful that Grandfather and Grandmother are still so well and happy!

This weekend I hope to get a chance to write you a real honest-to-goodness full length letter. I can't recall even one good letter I've written since that wonderful furlough. I hope everything is still going well at home. Everything is really OK here.

P. S. Some fellows say I may not get to phone Joanne. I myself strongly disbelieve this. Maybe in a couple or three weeks we'll know. (I'm considering distance when I say that.)

January 23, 1945

Your letter of the 20th arrived this noon. Sometimes air-mail takes four days, and once in awhile I receive one in one or two days flat. Most of the time three days bring the good word from you to me. Are mine still coming through on time and all right? I hope so.

Last night a group of us played some more basketball. I'm enjoying that game more than ever before. Finally I'm learning not to get disgusted at missing shots. It's much more fun that way. How did GAHS come out against Athens? Ohio Wesleyan seems to have a good team, as does Ohio State. It's nice being from Ohio. It's such a well known state, and we do well in sports and everything, it seems.

This morning we went on a hike. It was my first "walk" since furlough. The weather was so lovely, we couldn't help but enjoy it. We saw a group of red-wing blackbirds. I didn't realize California was another home of theirs. Also, a meadow lark or thrush of some kind added its presence to the beauty of the morning. I repeat, California is a beautiful state.

I hope Merrill came through the German's push all right. The rate of casualties doesn't seem to be very bad. If J.T is in Headquarters Company, that means he may still be playing in the band. Or, perhaps he is with a wire laying outfit. Headquarters is the home of the miscellaneous, but important, groups.

I'm glad Kenny Iron had a nice visit with you. Kenny

is a fine fellow. Did he mention anything about getting married? I was under the impression he was planning on it. So Don Gothard is home! I thought he had gone overseas. I'll bet Charlotte is happy.

All the snow and cold at home there must be exciting and discomforting at times. Marcy writes that some profs now have one-horse sleighs.

Perhaps Mrs. Cardwell would do better with a horse drawn vehicle. A sleet storm would certainly leave a slippery road.

When you wrote about finding a tire for Frank's bicycle, I wondered if it would be the proper size. That's fine that it is satisfactory. I'll bet he does appreciate it.

Baxter was probably taken prisoner during the big German push. When a man is "missing" in the ground forces, I'm inclined to have lots of hope for him. I sincerely hope good news comes very soon.

Will you send me Ellen's address. I have forgotten it, darn it. Marcy wants it too since she owes Ellen a letter. And, I have never thanked her for her swell Christmas gift. Northwestern is another school with one of the better basketball teams this year. Maybe she's getting to see some of the games.

What is the matter with Fred? Goodness, but he sounds as if, perhaps, he is off the beam a little. I was surprised to hear that the Foldens had sold their store. What are they planning to do now?

These days aren't too busy. We put just enough work in to eat well and sleep soundly. In fact, it's quite the life. I'm appreciating the laziness. A few men even get 24 hour passes. I may take one Thursday or Friday just to look in town. I haven't been to town since furlough. There really isn't much there.

Gosh, I wish you could be sharing this lovely weather with me. It's exactly like spring would be at home. At this moment some of the fellows are passing a football outside my door. I think I'll answer their calls and join them. Everybody is in a happy spring-like spirit.

I hope the convention goes well. I know the music will! So long for now.

January 30, 1945

Pretty soon you'll think that we aren't doing a thing. And that's what life here amounts to. Witness another 24 hour pass Zig and I just finished enjoying. These last few days have been so much like vacation days. It's really a lazy, lazy life. Our pass was fun again. Last night we thumbed thirty miles to Paso Robles where we bowled a little. After a big meal we thumbed back to Obispo. Or at least we attempted thumbing back. We got marooned in Atascadero, so we took a greyhound the last few miles.

Last night we again slept 12 full swell hours at the same place. I honestly believe I might get fat if this life continued. I tipped three different scales around 174. That's just about my lifetime high.

Lewis Stevers is taking a lot for granted. Don't be surprised if things don't turn out so favorably. Also, they haven't any business throwing rumors around like that. I'm surprised that they have said so much.

What a wonderful long letter I got from you yesterday, Daddy. Goodness, but it was swell! Thanks for the advice on singing I hope everything went splendidly at the State Pastors' Convention. All your news was so very interesting. I ran into something which might interest you at chapel Sunday. It was a pocket size edition of the "Upper Room." It's an identical copy, only one-half, or maybe one-third, as small. Have you seen it? I like it a lot for handiness and convenience. It might be better to send to service men.

Easter is coming near! How I love the Easter anthems. "Ice is gone from all the rivers" will always be one of my favorites.

Do you suppose Mrs. Feely sent that box Railway Express? A card came to the company from Railway Express for Walch S. Welchner, or someone?? I stopped in the office today, and if the box is from the Feelys, they'll forward it here from Camp Cooke.

Your last letter mailed the 27th, arrived today. I never thought about flying weather affecting air mail service. Surely it does. Merrill's promotion and safety is great news. I remember Vic Hager well. Goodness, will it never stop snowing there? You must be tiring of white landscape there. Certainly the cold weather is bothersome.

Tonight we're going to play more basketball. We do have fun playing. Too bad Gallipolis lost so badly to Athens. But we must have a pretty good team.

Retreat is sounding, so I'll have to run. See you later.

Hello- it's after basketball now. We had a swell game. And, tonight I got a swell surprise. Yep, the "sarge" rating came through. An hour ago I was notified of the raise to sergeant. So, I have to start sewing on those bothersome three stripes. But, I'm glad! Whoopee! Overseas I'll be getting

$103.60 monthly, including the expert infantry pay. That's a good sum. Wow! The army system of ratings is most unfair. Any man in the company could do the job I'll be doing. But I'm happy over the advancement, anyhow.

I have to start sewing, I guess. So, I'll leave you for awhile again.

February 2, 1945

Busy with a capital "B" is just what we are now.

Things are buzzing once more full speed. I am "charge of quarters" today. It's a 24 hour job starting last night and ending tonight at 6. I'm glad work is coming my way cause it makes me feel more worthy of my new rating. And, golly, I have been busy! A constant rain hasn't helped our efforts for efficiency lately. This noon for the first time in three days the sun came out for a moment.

Charge of quarters (C. Q.) consist of being errand boy for the company commander and the 1st Sergeant. I got the company up this morning, and have been chasing men and details the captain wants all day. Every hour I walk to battalion headquarters to check for new news or info. A constant rain hasn't helped our efforts for efficiency lately. This noon for the first time in three days the sun came out for a moment. The job brings in a lot of walking.

Before I forget, Mother, do send Marcy the nicest corsage for Valentine's Day. I'll appreciate your help, and she'll enjoy the flowers as always. Make it real special and nice. I haven't anything else for her. Just put "Love you always" on the card. Thanks a million.

I'm so glad the new Youth Fellowship set-up is going so well. That must have been a job handling the whole evening alone, Mother. Marcy sent the same clipping and picture of you, Daddy, as Mother did. I hope everything went well at the convention. Two thousand singing preachers must have been a thrill!

Lewis Stevers immediately impressed me as being a fine fellow and swell guy. I am glad he's staying with the 86th. Mrs. Haush's nephew was starting rumors he shouldn't have been talking about. However, since everything is just speculation, I don't suppose any harm was done. There are some things I can tell you. For instance, this is apt to be my last letter that will go direct from me to you. After this, a company officer will be checking the content to make sure I don't allow any important info slip into my letters. Your messages to me won't be censored, as far as I know. You will receive more letters from me while I'm still around. I don't believe I'll be able to phone you anymore, though. If I'm extremely lucky, maybe I'll be able to see Joanne. But, that chance is one in a thousand. Distance and opportunity will probably both be against that.

Your regular wonderful letters have been so nice. Daddy, yours was so swell to receive. The classes on doctrines, the cards, everything was so interesting. The advice on my voice was welcome, too. It's hard to believe that in less than two weeks we have Valentine's Day, soon followed by wonderful Easter. Time is whizzing! This will probably be my first Easter really away from home, but I'll be home in spirit always regardless of surroundings. I'm betting on this being a more peaceful world this Easter than last.

Of the six men in my squad, five are now Pfcs. Only Minges is still a Pvt. Surely he'll get the raise soon. There were several ups in ranks along with my boost. It's hard answering to the call of sergeant. I suppose I'll get used to it. I'm happy to have the position, and I do want to do well at the job. Still, I'm disgusted with the army system of making non-coms. Circumstances get the men the jobs. Worthiness hasn't much to do with it.

Now is a good time to tell you about my overseas saving plan. You will be receiving $30 monthly to deposit for me, Mother. Also, The $18.75 bond will continue to come. And, then along with that, I will be saving $30 a month in the soldiers' deposit plan. That leaves me $13.45 spending money, which is more than enough. The army recommends that you have only $10.00 to spend. My total pay will be $97.60. Subtract $78.75 savings and $6.40 insurance and that leaves the $13.45 clear. Isn't it swell that I'll be able to save so much!!

Don't be alarmed if you don't hear from me for the next week or ten days. It won't be longer than that before I'll be able to resume writing. Later will come the other delay in letters. 'Course I'm speculating again, and there may be variations in that schedule. And, I may be able to write one more letter before the first silence. I'm pretty sure we will be getting much more desirable duty than we first expected. I am glad that you aren't the worrying kind, 'cause there will never be any sense in worrying. 99% of the time I'll no doubt be safer than most civilians.

I wish you could have seen the rollicking "SNAFU Handicap Race" we had yesterday morning in the sport arena. (SNAFU means "situation normal, all fouled up.") It was a howl. The entire regiment attended, and the division concert band "made music." The

"race" consisted of a pie eating contest, a tug o' war battle, a pack rolling race, and some clever skits. It was really clever and fun. Everyone was in a fun mood, too.

I have written much more than I thought time would allow. But, I started over five hours ago. It's almost time to go off C. Q. I'll write again tomorrow, if possible.

February 3, 1945

This is just a brief note to say everything is going just fine. Although you won't be hearing from me for the next 10 days or so, you'll know everything is OK. My next letter will probably be real long as it will be a composite of several days' writing. So, expect a note again the 14th or so.

I'm really caught with my hands tied this Valentine's Day. I did so want to send things to you and Ellen and Joanne. But, I guess I'll be unable to. You know how very proud I am of my family. Naturally, you all have my best love. It seems funny to even mention it, it's such a constant feeling. I am so thankful for the most wonderful parents in the world, plus the most wonderful sisters.

By necessity this has to be brief. And, so already I'll say so long. Be seeing you again via mail pretty soon.

P. S. Thanks again for finding a corsage for Marcy. I haven't been able to get her a single thing. Maybe an additional dozen roses would be nice, too.

February 8, 1945

These recent new regulations on letter writing sort of cramp my style. We'll have to get used to omitting several topics from our conversations from here on in. However, the things we can't talk about really aren't important in the long run. You, Gallipolis, friends, news, beauty, the future, are subjects that are lasting and real. And we can talk all we want about them.

In the last three days I have read five books. Four were murder mysteries and one was a compilation of essays on the home, family

life, sex, etc. by Havelock Ellis. Reading so much has been fun. All four of the murder stories were thrillers. Two were of Nero Wolfe brand. One was an S. S. Van Dine creation, and the other a Captain North best seller. I have never read many mysteries before. Choice of reading matter isn't very large here. The mysteries are swell reading, though.

We've been having interesting geography lessons. A bunch of us from different states get together and tell what our individual state produces most and what the terrain of the country is. Usually we end up saying our home state has anything and everything. We're too prejudiced to present educational point of views. Take Ohio, for instance. Hmmmm!! Tell me, is the weather still so rugged? I'll bet you still are having snow.

Gosh, but the war news is swell! The freeing of the prisoners at Manila was something! Is Mrs. Miller's husband in that group? I hope so. The suspense between the news of their freedom and the publication of the actual list must have been terrific. News from all fronts is heartening! I'm counting on my prediction for 1947 coming true. Isn't it interesting how Mrs. Stivers' forecast came approximately true!

Did the pictures arrive? You should get them very soon. I hope they aren't a disappointment. What do you plan to do with the third one?

In just a couple of days I should be getting more mail from you. I believe I'll wait till them before I write much more. You probably will have some questions I can answer. So I'll sign off for a little while anyhow.

February 12, 1945
(In the eastern part of the U. S.)

Our mail will go out this evening finally. So this is a good time to write. And now I have two swell letters from you to answer. It is nice to be receiving mail again. Also, I got a nice long letter from Ellen. Did I mention the letter Joanne wrote ten days ago? News from the family is the sort I love. It is good to hear from you.

Now I know more about the big snows you have been describing. It's swell plodding along once again in real deep snow. The cold weather is invigorating. But, it's easy to see how a whole winter of snow would get rather bothersome. Surely ol' man winter will get snowed out soon.

Your news items were very interesting. Too bad about the fire. Mrs. McCormick is nice. I have always liked her. I hadn't realized she was 76. How did the fire begin? Major Haskins will want to know about it. Too bad Frank didn't get his Baton Rouge assignment while Joanne was home. I wonder how he'll like Louisiana. Colonel Bush's interest shows he must be a fine democratic officer. Too bad I won't be able to meet him. Your most recent news about Tom Roe is coincidental.

I am happy to learn that Ellen is returning to camp and with a substantial raise. Or is it definite as yet? Marcy's camp plans are pending, too. Incidentally, Marcy mentioned receiving a lovely letter from you, Mother. Also, she's writing Ellen very soon. Ellen's future plans sound swell. Her present is by no means dull either. Goodness, but she is piling in the work. As I re-read her letter, I see she wants to visit Joanne this summer, maybe. Can't say I blame her. I wish I could again see her. Those things are for post-war, though. I'm looking forward to a new "pic" of Ellen. If It's large though, the other beautiful small one I have will do fine. So Wes is in the Golden Gloves! I'd love to see him go far. But I can see it would be difficult to keep in top shape while working hard at studies.

I have to laugh every time I think of some of Joey's sayings which Joanne wrote about in her letter of the 28th. The "Daddy candy, Daddy Coke, please.", is a scream. It's hard top believe Joey is almost ready for Sunday school. Only a month more and he begins. But he is growing up. That fact amazed me last furlough. I must admit I had to smile when Joanne wrote of seeing a Marine who resembled Earl Fox; and, then, upon asking him, found out definitely not. So often you see someone who might be an old acquaintance. I'm still amazed over Ellen's lucky recognition of Miles.

Whee, another mail call. And a swell letter from you, Daddy. Also, a cute valentine from Ellen, and three more notes from Marcy. I love all these letters!!!

Daddy, you must have had a grand time in Columbus. What a thrill it must have been leading over a thousand people, including the governor, in singing. I want to sit in on more pastors' conventions. I can't imagine a more exciting group for singing and whole hearted group participation. Thanks so much for writing about it. Too bad about the game with Jackson. I'm afraid Charlie Swanson is no coach. The lack of training rules may well be the reason for the one point and two point losses. Those games are heartbreakers. Thanks for the address. I would like to use it. If I get a chance, you know I will.

Remember Bob Rahn? Of course you do! He just gave Janet Stansell a diamond. I wrote him last night sending heartiest congratulations. They'll make a wonderful pair. Bob is in action now. The engagement was via mail.

I hope good news comes through soon about Tommy Fife. Has anyone received anything on Baxter? I'm confident that they will return safely. It's good to know Mr. Brumfield is recovering. Also, Tom Lewis' recovery is good news.

The next silence in letters may be longer than this last one. Don't worry a bit, though. You should know that really I am as safe as any civilian.

Maybe I'll get a chance to send valentines yet. I hope so, 'cause I do have the gandest parents and sisters in the whole world. That's a fact that I'm always aware of and constantly appreciate.

I'll write again first chance.

CHAPTER EIGHT

CAMP MYLES STANDISH

CAMP MYLES STANDISH
BOSTON, MASSACHUSETTS
FEBRUARY 13 - 18, 1945

February 13, 1945.
TELEGRAM

ARRIVED SAFELY IN EASTERN US   ALL IS FINE

February 15, 1945

It almost seems queer writing you tonight. Our two phone conversations were so real and fun that it does seem as if you were right next door. In fact, I don't know exactly what to talk about tonight. We did have such swell actual talks. The telephone is definitely a wonderful invention! And, the set up they have here adds to its effectiveness. Yep, it's really OK hearing your voices so clear and natural again.

Checking on my accumulation of unanswered letters, I see you are three up on me. I have yours of the 6th, 8th, and 9th. As always, it's wonderful to hear from you. You always write exactly what I want to hear. And, between you and Marcy's regular supply, I can count on at least one letter every mail call. I love the way you are spoiling me.

What a waste Johnnie Phillip's root beer accident was! HMMM. Today in our mess hall a fellow dropped his whole tray of food. Another fellow rising from the table caused the accident. It was such a coordinated movement it looked as if it were planned. We all laughed, as did the victims.

Thanks for being such a super secretary, Mother. I appreciate it a lot, as does Marcy. She really likes hearing from you. She loved the flowers. I guess Valentines Day expressed my thoughts better than I expected. I did want to send something to Joanne and Ellen. Maybe I will even yet.

In talking to you this evening about the ring, I didn't say much definite. The reason I didn't was because the time for giving her the ring isn't really important. We know we want to get married someday. And we know there will never be anyone else for either of us. That is positively definite. A ring would mean announcing that to everyone, which isn't so necessary. That's why I originally planned to wait till I could look around for the perfect ring in the U. S. But since Marcy plans to finish school in one more semester (after this one), I thought maybe it would be swell if she could have it before leaving Ohio Wesleyan. But, darn it, I would love to buy it and give it to her personally. I'll decide before next Christmas anyhow. Marcy is everything to me, and knowing her this much has made me realize life won't be complete unless she shares it with me, but definitely!!

Today's mail brought another letter from Ellen. This time it was a V-mail, my first one. It's thawing out in Chicago, too. I'm glad to hear spring is finally shoving winter out. Gosh, but you have had a long, rugged winter. Have you really been without colds or sickness? There are a few sniffles in the outfit. I feel fine, though, and really we are all in top spirits.

I'm glad the pictures arrived. Thanks for sending one on to Marcy. I think she got it on Valentines Day. Did you send the third one to Ellen? I didn't phone the other call tonight, but think I will in an evening or so.

It was so very good hearing you both again. Maybe we can work out even another call. We'll see. You sounded fine and healthy as ever. Mother, you're still planning on your March visit to Ann Arbor, aren't you?

Before I forget, Marcy's birthday is April 18th, I think. Gosh, I don't know what exactly to get. If perchance I should be unable to tell you what it should be, please get something nice. Maybe costume jewelry, or something similar?

I think Zig and I are going to get passes for tomorrow evening. So, I'll write again probably by Saturday at least

P. S. A gang of us have given up candy for Lent. Easter is slipping up on us.

February 17, 1945

Last night Zig and I went on pass. We had lots of fun taking it easy. The city had several fine facilities for servicemen, so the evening wasn't a dull one. I had a funny surprise. We decided to look in on a dance, and finally we danced a couple. The girl who was my partner was average, as are all girls compared to Marcy. She asked my name and was surprised to hear it was Scotty. Her boss's name was also mine. The pay-off came when she said her name was Marcine. That really floored me. Too bad the only similarity was in names! We walked around the town a lot, Zig and I. Its antiqueness is queer and homey. Cooking was OK there, too. We ate two fine meals during our eight hour pass. Window shopping was a big phase of the evening.

Your letter of the 12th arrived yesterday. How really wonderful that spring is finally coming. I can't imagine seeing a robin already. Your church service sounded fine. "Be Prepared" was an appropriate sermon subject for scouts. Lewis Green is a nice fellow! Wasn't it kind of him to remember his mother and friends in that way. I am sorry to hear that Col. Miller wasn't on that release list. Surely he is all right. But it's too bad to be disappointed after having high hopes.

You mentioned your discussion on the colored situation. Gosh, I don't believe two days go by without a friendly (?) little argument here. This morning we argued about the Red Cross. It seems some of the fellows are acquainted with one or two unfavorable "deals" the Red Cross had a hand in. I'm sure it's a fine organization, though.

How interesting about "There's Moonlight on the Lake." I'll bet it is a lovely number. Life is so full of interesting unexpected surprises. I'm still chuckling over last night's coincidence. I hadn't danced since I was last with Marcy, and I really didn't want to. But then when I did, finally, and got that surprise, that floored me. I danced only a couple with her, and then Zig and I went on our way.

I had planned to call again, but I don't believe I will. We did have two fine conversations, anyhow. I didn't phone Joanne either. All my memories from the recent furlough are so vivid, a phone call isn't a "must" for happiness. Recently the booths have been really crowded. Other fellows, no doubt, have more essential calls.

Probably you are prepared for another silence from this end. 'Course we won't be able to tell you when not to expect mail. But I'm reminding you again just in case this resumption of this letters may have made you forget.

Marcy is getting a well-earned vacation the end of this

semester. Rumor has it that maybe they'll get from the 22nd to the 6th. That would be super! She has been working so very, very hard. I'm afraid part of her vacation may be used working on the Bijou. I hope not! Have you ever written again about her visit? Since Manning left Wesleyan, the opportunity and convenience isn't so good. I hope you can work out some kind of get-together sometime soon, though. Next semester her work may not be so strenuous. Maybe then you can work it out.

News is scarce. We're just getting fat. I'll keep you posted every chance I get.

CHAPTER NINE

ABOARD THE SHIP S S LEJEUNE

ABOARD THE SHIP S S LEJEUNE
ON THE ATLANTIC OCEAN
FEBRUARY 19 - MARCH 4, 1945

Date not Reported
At Sea V-Mail

It seems a little queer being on the sending end of V-mail. No doubt it's a service we're going to appreciate from now on. I am told regular mail may be as fast as this. We'll experiment to find out. I'll alternate the two to make sure we are sharing thoughts these first few weeks. In order to save space I'll omit the system of paragraphing, You can guess the change in thoughts, which is probably something you've been doing for quite awhile in some of my hurried notes. The trip continues to be lots of fun. We are wallowing in leisure. Reading, talking, and sleeping are our three main time killers. And the time is whizzing by. I'm wondering lots of things about home. Will Ellen get a vacation between semesters? Are you still planning on your trip to Ann Arbor, Mother? Has Frank returned from Baton Rouge? I have the neatest little picture carrier. It's the ideal auxilliary to my billfold collection. Joey has a prominent place, looking as cute and lifelike as ever. When is his birthday? I've forgotten the exact day. You would enjoy the experiences I'm enjoying. After the war we'll have to spend at least two weeks talking them over. I'll be writing again soon.

Date not reported
At Sea

This is truly a wonderful experience. I don't blame you a bit, Daddy, for loving the sea so much. And, I am happy to state that apparently I have inherited an immunity to sea-sickness. For two days we had waves big enough to cause plenty of trouble, as far as stomachs are concerned. Once or twice my head reeled a little, but my stomach was stable, and I didn't miss a meal. So, now I'm patting myself on the back, and maybe tomorrow will find me in the victim group. So far so good, anyhow.

We're allowed to be on deck quite a bit. It's fun watching the waves and the various cloud formations. I have been reading the book Weather Around the World. It's interesting material and doubly so when you can experience it first hand. Someday after this world gets straightened out I'd like to take another cruise. Next time, though, I want nice deck chairs, lemonade, Marcy, etc. Hmmm. We have plenty of comforts here now. You would honestly be pleased to see how we're enjoying ourselves. Just now I returned from the deck after winning (and luckily) an hour and a half game of chess.

As usual during periods like this, we have lots of time for reading. I have read Clarence Day's Life with Father and Fosdick's On Being a Real Person. Day's style is simple and interesting. I enjoyed him a lot. I had read Fosdick's condensation in the Digest. The book in its entirety is good, too. We have a good library on board from which to choose reading material. Yep, the set-up here is fine.

Church services are held daily. They are conducted in their usual impressive manner, so our spiritual life isn't being neglected either. Everything is so well taken care of that it seems that really we are on land, especially now when the sea is gentle. However, when the going gets rougher, it's pretty obvious our feet aren't on terra firma.

A couple of hours have whizzed by since the last paragraph. Also, a good chicken dinner has vanished in that period. Food is OK. We eat only twice a day, but the meals are almost equal to the regular three. I've been listening to some records. Phonographs, like the one in my room, are available for compartments. Classical and popular records are plentiful. We chose some Kostelanetz selections.

Tomorrow we're going to have some boxing on deck. One of the officers asked me if I would participate. Since the bouts are really meant to be exhibitions, I don't believe I qualify. I wish I were a good boxer. Knowing enough to defend oneself if necessary is good enough, I believe, though. I'll be much happier watching. I hope we haven't shelved basketball for the duration. Certainly we'll have opportunity for football and baseball.

We're getting so much sleep! Maybe we're lacking in exercise?! Too much of this life would certainly make even me fat. We're getting everything prescribed for good health except exercise. Can you see me with two chins?

Everything is going fine in the squad. I couldn't ask for a more cooperative spirit. I'm really fortunate having such swell fellows. In fact, I do have a million things to be thankful for. This page wouldn't begin to hold the list. I'm learning that miles offer no block to the feeling of togetherness one has in thinking of loved ones. Certainly

God is the main liaison in these thoughts, too.

News is rather scarce at present. Although I have more writing time, I have less interesting material. Probably the future will offer less writing time. Don't forget not to worry. It's the most useless practice I can imagine. It pays no dividends whatsoever.

By the way, I may be asking you to do that ring shopping for me. I'm talking it over now with Marcy via mail. If you could send pictures of settings and stones, it would really make it as much my choice as yours. We'll have more on that later.

How is the Easter music coming? Several of us have given up candy for the forty days of Lent. So far we're all doing fine, too. I hope everything is coming along just swell at home, as it is here.

P. S. I would enjoy another one of your delicious boxes, Mother. As soon as you get my next change of address, please send one. Yum, yum!! I'll keep you posted if we need anything else.

Date not reported
At Sea (V...-Mail)

It won't be very long now before I'll get to be reading more of your swell letters. Also, then we'll be able to put dates on our letters. And, probably we will tell you what part of the world we're in. The entire voyage has been and is continuing to be really great. And, now we are all getting excited at the prospect of seeing a foreign country. We have small language books to help us get along with the new tongue. I wonder if I'll ever be able to learn any complete sentences. Too bad they don't speak Latin. (What a joke that is. As if I could understand even that.) Aside from the two days of rough weather, everything has been smooth and nice with the entire gang. This has been a trip none of us will ever forget. 'Course we're all looking forward to this same trip going the other way. Hmmm. Say "hello" to everyone for me. I finally wrote Kenny the letter I have long owed him. Hoping to hear from you soon.

Date not reported
Viewing France from the Ship

Here we are! Not exactly on terra firma, but near enough to see it and view closely some of the conditions war has brought about. Our first sight of the ruined buildings was something I'll never forget. Everyone stood on deck just staring in silence. It was as if we were viewing some terrible accident. You could read the thoughts in the fellows' minds. We were all thinking how lucky we of the United States were. Piles of ruins stood everywhere. One large crane was on its side almost covered with powdered cement and bits of wood, steel, and rail. Not a single nearby building was intact. Some farther away seemed better off. But the whole scene was one of destruction and war. Goodness, but it is exciting and rather awful. There will be so much building to do after the war. I realized bombing was effective. However, this first-hand sight of its results makes one realize it is devastating. One building especially stands out in my mind. It was formerly a large structure about four or five stories high. A bomb must have struck directly in the center for only the four walls were standing.

No doubt we'll soon get very used to scenes of this sort. This first one made us aware, once again, that the U.S. has been so fortunate. Although I can't say this as pure fact, it seems each of our allies have suffered a thousand Pearl Harbors to our one. We can be thankful that home is so safe.

I'm having the most fun trying to learn French. The

small books made up for the army are swell. I'd like to write some things in French to prove my progress, but if we write in a foreign language our letters are censored at some special base, and that would only be wasted time. Having these letters censored doesn't seem to be so bad after all. They are pretty lenient. We may describe incidents and scenes. Sometimes it is best and obvious to omit dates and names. We are kept posted on changes in censor policy. That's why recently I've been omitting the date, but later on I'll be able to add that plus more interesting details.

Symbolic as it may seem and fantastic as it may sound, the following is true: Above all the ruins and crumbled buildings points a church steeple intact! It's an amazing sight. A few boards are missing, but it has suffered almost no damage. Isn't that wonderfully peculiar!? Do you suppose expert bombers could have skirted it purposely?

Did I mention that we are having daily church services on ship? They are so fine, too. Lots and lots of fellows attend. In the mess hall acoustics are such that the group sounds mighty while singing. We sing a lot and all enjoy it. I'm in favor of a daily group devotional service. the regular chapel service at Wesleyan is a fine plan.

Since my last letter I read America by Stephen Vincent Benet and The Lost Weekend. In America it tells of the early pilgrims' voyage of 64 days. Gosh, but that took courage! The book is fine. I liked the beginning better than the later half. The Lost Weekend is swell. You can feel the characters emotions, the writer feels them so well. I had read the condensation, and the book is all just as interesting. Best sellers are reprinted in pocket-book, pulp-paper style for us serving overseas. It's a great idea.

As I have told you all along not to worry, I again re-emphasize it. It's absolutely useless and uncalled for. So put it on the shelf, as I have, for the duration, at least. Ten to one we over here are getting more care and materials than you are. The army and the wonderful U. S. look after us as if we were babies. I'm having a positively wonderful time. There may be some distasteful experiences, but there are so many interesting and enjoyable ones!

Mother, I would love to expect a box a week from you. So, I think I'll ask for one that often. Although we are well cared for, it's a cinch delicacies such as your wonderful cookies, pickles, etc., are rare here. Food will be most welcome always. Right now (just before chow) I'm thinking of pickled pigs feet. Yum yum!!

A pal tells me plain air mail is much faster than V-Mail. Actually, we should use some of both to help save space in air mails. But, let's use the air mail most of the time. If they advise us that the planes are getting crowded, naturally we'll adhere.

The absence of mail from this end means very little. In fact, I fear that I'll be writing less, even though I'd like to write more to make sure you are hearing from me. Being a squad leader involves more responsibilities now that we are getting readjusted, etc. I want to write at least twice a week. I'll always find time for at least one, I'm sure. Of course, many times our mail may be delayed, so you can't expect to receive them on any regular schedule.

I keep thinking of the title of Bob Hope's book I Never Left Home. I don't know exactly the meaning he wishes it to have (I haven't read the book. Have you?), but that's the way I feel. With all the swell buddies still together, and with all the grand memories so vivid in my mind, it seems really as if I were still in the U. S. (except for the ruins, of course). And, when your letters start coming again, I'll really feel at home.

Enough for now. Next time I write we'll be more

settled and there will be more news. Just in case this is the only one to reach you before Easter, Happy Easter! I can just hear the lovely anthems.

CHAPTER TEN

CAMP OLD GOLD

CAMP OLD GOLD
  NEAR YVETOT, FRANCE
  MARCH 4 - 24, 1945

March 7, 1945
Somewhere in France

At last we have our feet on solid ground. And, it is beautiful ground! You should see the perfectly lovely countryside that makes up France. Honestly, it is nice. Our ride from the port (Le Havre) to camp was filled with picturesque sights. Evidences of war are few when you leave the cities. Everything is so neat and permanent. Wood is very scarce, and because of that, things are built with more design and more substantially. Even fence post are iron most of the time. (Rather, most fence posts are iron. Such English I ain't got! Hmmm.)

Our camp is nice, too. We live in commodious tents. Food and everythig is well taken care of. I do wish you could see us. Then certainly you wouldn't have a worry in your mind. The weather is still rather cool. However, warmer days shouldn't be far away. The fields are plowed and several signs of spring are around us.

Best of all the new reports I have to make is that we are again getting mail, and plenty of it. I have your letters of the 10th, 14th, 16th, 17th, and 19th. One came from Joanne written the 20th. And, I have four from Marcy. Yep, it is swell getting them again. Your five dollars arrived safely. But, I'm sending it and another one back your way. It's quite evident that we will be having too much money on our hands. Since we are changing all of our American money to French dough, I believe I'll get rid of these ten bucks pronto. So, here they are enclosed.

The French people are anxious to be friendly. They are terribly short on candy, cigarettes, soap, etc. However, we aren't allowed to do business with them. Some have been known to exchange articles worth ten dollars or more for one measly pack of cigarettes. As we rode through towns, people smiled and waved the V...- sign. Their friendship is by no means just for pecuniary matters. I hope before too long I'll get to learn much more about their language and themselves.

We are really so well cared for. Don't let the word "overseas" worry you. Actually it is a wonderful experience, much more natural than you would expect. 'Course we haven't experienced every phase of war-time overseas, but I assure you this step of it is truly delightful. I'm telling you this now 'cause I don't want the postman to know it when I ask you for some essential (?) things on the next page. What I ask for isn't an absolute necessity. Don't feel you must send it. I'm just asking for boxes for the same reason I like 'em in the U. S. That isn't being too dishonest, is it?? Hmmm.

Please send some small candles. Some "Aunt Jemima Ready Mix" could be used very conveniently! We have neat stoves on which we might practice some pan-cake flipping some cool evening. Any food that would keep during the trip from you to me will be most welcome. Do you suppose cheese might mold? Hard-tack or anything we could chew on between meals would be perfect. Our meals here are fine, but we miss the handy PX. We used to sort of gorge ourselves there, I believe. That's about all I can think of. Candles about six or eight inches long would be perfect.

So the fender has been repaired! Swell! I was disgusted when that fellow bumped me. I'm surprised to hear that all the farm boys are being inducted. Did they volunteer, or is it compulsory now? You spoke of the scouts. This is rather like scouting or camping. My enthusiasm for camping and tent life has never waned. I do love it. I am glad, Daddy, that you asked the ten colored scouts. Racial prejudice is an awful evil we must get rid of. We all smiled, Mother, at your mistake of using the serial number on Mrs. Feely's address. That's a howl!

You answered so well all the questions I have been wondering about. Everything you have been writing about is so very interesting and exciting.

Joy, joy! Another mail call and your letter of the 23rd and three more from Marcy. Time out while I read 'em.

Such a lovely, long letter! Each one is just like a real visit. I can never be homesick since I feel so near to you all the time. All the preparations for Easter sound super! It won't be long until that glorious Sunday is right on us again. Mother, I would appreciate it if you would send Marcy some beautiful corsage. I believe I mentioned that in one of my earlier notes. By the way, her letters were also super! She mentioned seeing "Keys to the Kingdom." It seemed to her, Daddy, that the missionary priest resembled you a little. She said she especially noticed the way he leaned forward in his chair attentively listening to conversation. She has a good memory!

You mentioned about reports on poor food over here. As far as we're concerned, it's excellent! Ours is still up to standard! The usual PX ice cream, etc., is all we're missing. That's why I ask for food, etc.

The "Crusade for Christ" is so worthwhile. Surely those funds will be used on the most worthwhile project there is. I'm glad it is going so well.

We have trouble finding time to write. During the day we're busy doing odd jobs. And, as soon as the sun goes down, we crawl into our comfy bunks. As yet our lighting facilities are scarce. Right now I'm racing with the sun. This way we certainly get enough sleep, at least ten hours every night.

I have decided to send a money order later. It is safer that way. And, since the first page was written, we turned in our American cash. I had fifteen dollars and I get in return 750 francs. Francs are worth two cents a piece. So, expect a money order in a week or so.

Light is dimming quickly so I'll close. I do hope you will have Marcy at home soon. We will probably decide on postponing the ring till later, but it is only a matter of time 'cause Marcy will always be the one.

It is wonderful to be getting your swell mail. I do hope mine is reaching you regularly.

P. S. This is the first letter I've been able to date. You should receive some five or six before this, or maybe four. I'm not sure of the exact number. From now on we'll know what day it is anyhow.

March 11, 1945
Somewhere in France

Today is Sunday, and you may be sure we remember it here as we always have. We had a lovely service in the open just an hour ago. Originally it was to be held in one of the large tents. So many came that it would have taken at least two tents to hold the crowd. The hymn singing will always be my favorite part of the service. It's so easy to picture you singing the exact words. This morning's hymns were "Holy, Holy, Holy," "Stand Up, Stand Up for Jesus," and "America." Usually we sing four or five hymns. All our regular hymnals weren't available, so we sang just the three familiar ones. Did I ever tell you about the fine little portable organ provided? It's very neat. The tone is good and loud enough to be heard in the open. Yes, church is always a lovely, inspirational service here.

Every little village around here has a large stone church. Yesterday we took a hike of some ten miles. In that short distance we saw at least four churches. They are built solidly. Large stones and cement are the main materials used. They must be very old. We saw one building with 1821 inscribed on the cement.

Very appropriately your letter written exactly two weeks ago arrived today. Everything seems to be going splendidly at church. The idea of cooperating church and school in records of attendance is absolutely swell. The more those two wonderful institutions get together the better everybody will be. The Youth Fellowship is going great, too! Gosh, every phase at church is going tops! And, it will continue to be that way as long as you, Daddy and Mother, are heading things. That's plenty obvious.

I want to mention again the handiness of the small "Upper Room" pamphlets. They fit easily into any pocket and don't get frayed or torn. Since I got mine, I haven't missed a day or a page. I hope you'll get some to send to servicemen. I know they would appreciate it.

The larger one isn't as convenient. It is a fine book, and several of us have the habit, as do, certainly, thousands of others.

Daily we get the newspaper "Stars and Stripes." It's printed in Paris making the news "hot off the press." The last three issues have told of the flood of the Ohio, which you predicted, Mother. Did it necessitate a postponement of your trip to Michigan? I do hope it didn't. I'm hoping you'll be there, Mother, 'cause tomorrow I'm sending a cablegram to Ann Arbor. It may be that you haven't yet heard from me. My letters will arrive at least by the 12th, so I'm sending a word to Ann Arbor just to let you know all is swell. The occasion should be a gala one. Grandfather is so vigorous and well for so many active years.

Thanks so much, Mother, for being such a wonderful secretary! I had forgotten the exact date of Joey's birthday. I appreciate your aid in getting gifts, etc., But, I do want to write a letter at least to supplement your help. Please send me a list of everybody's birthday.

Two V-mails have come from Ellen. I wrote her last night, and then this noon another swell note arrived from her. Did I mention the grand, long letter I received from Joanne? The family is certainly keeping me well supplied with the news I love. Today marks one week spent here, and I have received a total of 14 to 18 letters from you all and Marcy. Mighty nice!!! Frank's job is an important one! Villar, who lives in Baton Rouge, knows about that big refinery there. I do enjoy such super letters! Recently the "Stars and Stripes" announced that only V-mail would be assured air transportation from the states to here. The regular air mail is nicer to write and read, but I do believe it's good to make at least half our letters the V-mail style. Then we'll both be sure the word is going through pretty regularly.

We just had a sumptuous meal! We are getting wonderful food now. It may be that our appetites are just enlarging, but we do enjoy the chow. How does chicken, mashed potatoes, peas, gravy, two slices of buttered bread, coffee, and pudding sound? This noon we had beef, carrots, apricots, etc; but, yesterday we had the other menu. Each meal is fine! Naturally, army chow will never equal yours,

Mother. Your candied sweet potatoes, mashed potatoes in the shell, eggnogs, and the other delicious dishes you prepare make my mouth water any time. It is amazing how well the army feeds given the supply problem and the other worries field life offers.

Today our schedule is made up of mass athletics. Before church we had a grand touch football game. We have plenty of sports equipment and a swell field to use it in. Now we have candles in our tents, too. It won't be so difficult finding time and light to write. We are really getting settled in fine style. While we were playing ball, a group of French children gathered to watch. Villar talked with them in his fluent Louisiana French. They are nice kids, just like ours at home. All of them had just returned from mass. They told Villar they liked Americans fine! The Germans stole from them and weren't half as nice. One little boy wanted to trade a loaf of bread for two packs of cigarettes for his dad.

I'm enclosing a ten franc note and a 2 franc note. One franc equals two of our American pennies. It's funny looking money, isn't it.

I do hope these letters are reaching you quickly. Mrs. Stivers, Mrs.Haskins and you should do pretty well on news of us if you keep pooling your resources. I haven't seen Lewis or "Doc" for quite awhile. No doubt I'll meet them again one of these days. Everything is swell here. The squad is getting along great! I'm feeling tops! My hair is long again, which means I'd better get another clipping. Say "hello" to everyone for me, including the children preparing for church membership.

March 12, 1945
Somewhere in France. V-Mail

Your letter of the 27th arrived today. I'm glad you saw

"Music for Millions." It was good, wasn't it. Last night we had a movie. "Sunday Dinner for a Soldier" was its title. I had seen it before, but I enjoyed parts of it again. This morning we all got wonderful hot showers. Washing facilities here are good! Ever so often we will prepare enough hot water for leisurely showers, which is swell. Tonight P.X. rations arrived for us. They include candy bars, chewing gum, soap, etc. Each day seems to bring more comforts. Pretty soon we'll be living like kings. We are well cared for! We had another chicken dinner this noon. Chicken is one of the more plentiful foods here. Needless to say, we aren't very sad about that. You should be on your way to Ann Arbor now, Mother. You'll have a grand time. The paper says the flood waters have subsided, so probably that didn't stop your trip. Isn't it queer how people differ in their ideas of giving. I don't blame you for smiling at that two dollar donation. Maybe they'll realize their mistake. It is nice receiving your letters so regularly! I hope mine are reaching you the same way. I'll be writing again very soon.

March 15, 1945
Somewhere in France

Spring is here!! The last three days have been superbly beautiful. I feel like getting out the spade and digging the whole garden and back yard. Just 100 yards from our tent a farmer is lazily plowing the field. The fresh overturned earth reminds me of your garden. I'm really developing a case of spring fever.

The army seemed to sense the coming of the nice weather and spring fever cases. Two days ago we made a swell ball diamond. Now a company baseball league is going full sway. So, actually we are doing what our fever dictates, a nice softball game with the warm sun tanning our faces. It's a great life. Naturally we have duties to attend to; but we're getting lots and lots of wonderful recreation. Our first platoon has a fine team. Knihtela, the pitcher, is tops. We won our first game and are hoping to win all of them. (Overconfidence, hmm.) Seven teams have been organized within the company. This afternoon we did some more work on the diamond. We have a pretty good back-stop, good bases, and an excellent level field. It's a smooth athletic set-up.

Tuesday afternoon a Red Cross mobile unit visited us. Two nice American girls served us coffee and donuts. It was a nice sort of party. I wrote Ellen a letter mentioning about the R. C. girls. I hope she decides against any service of that kind. Being a minister's wife is the most serviceable position a women could hold anyhow. That same evening the movie "Jamie" was given for us. It was fair. You might enjoy it quite a bit.

I can hardly wait to get an answer to one of my letters written from here. I hope you'll ask me all kinds of questions about the country. I'll be able to answer most of them, I'm sure. Best news we've got lately is the possibility of passes. We won't be able to visit any cities of note, but we will be able to see French life in towns, stores, churches, etc. I'm looking forward to such an excursion with excitement. It'll be fun writing you about it.

Today several men were given Pfc ratings. Minges (the fellow I drove home with) also made it. Now every man in the squad is a Pvt 1st class. I'm glad, too, because each deserves it completely. In fact, it's too bad they aren't all getting the same wages I am. They are so cooperative and swell.

This lovely weather makes me have that wonderful, groggy, lazy feeling. I just feel like sitting and chewing the end of my pen daydreaming. It's really a nice mood for a change. I hope you're having this glorious weather, too. I've slipped a little on my correspondence because of all the ball games and recreation. Probably letters will be so far apart you won't notice if I don't write for a day or two. But I do like to write at least every other day or so normally, inspite of spring fever. We'll have another mail call tonight, and I'll bet it'll bring more letters from you and Marcy. I haven't got any for a couple of days, so no doubt several are on the way. I can always count on lots of mail from you all, and I do love it.

My French is improving a little. It still is sad, though. Maybe by the time I see you again, I'll be sounding real professional like. I can count to twenty. (No doubt the first number I'll want will be 30.)

New news is rather scarce. As always. I'll write again very soon. I hope everything is still coming along wonderfully at home.

March 18, 1945
France

Today I have so many things I want to say and tell you about that I honestly don't know where to start. First of all, your nice long V-mail written the 5th arrived last night. We've been having a sort of contest in the tent to see who could receive the longest legible V-mail. Your typewritten one with 45 written lines tops the list easily., That seems to be the solution to overseas writing problems. Typing a V-mail allows you to say all you want to, and it assures prompt, safe delivery. I suggest you continue writing that way. It's easy to read. Regular air-mails from the states don't receive the priority a V-mail does. Since I can't write all my thoughts in the crowded space V-mail allows, I'll continue to send regular air-mails ever so often. Ours aren't as apt to get side-tracked as yours might be.

Did I acknowledge your other V-mail written the 3rd? I believe I did. I am getting a good supply of mail from you all.

And today is another beautiful Sunday. Every Sunday here has been lovely. Church this morning was again impressive. The coming of Easter makes the service even more meaningful. I got a sturdy new Bible, King James version, for the tent. We have an ink stand on one of the poles. The Bible sits snugly and prominently there. It's very apt to be used. The men in the tent are regular churchgoers. Eight of us are Protestants, three Catholics, and one Hebrew.

Friday afternoon a service unit stopped in camp and put on a good show for us. We all enjoyed it very much. It lasted an hour and was performed by eight or nine servicemen. The master of ceremonies used to be James Cagney's double. After the show a couple hundred books were thrown out over the crowd. The books were the type I've written you about before, small pocket-sized versions of today's best sellers. I grabbed several times for one, but missed. Finally I got hold of a fat one. I looked at the title and guess what it was??? Yep, The Apostle. It was pretty amazing considering that you had just written about reading it, and Marcy had just quoted some phrases for me from it. So now I'm joining the reading ranks again. I've read only the first 50 pages, but, maybe I'll finish it someday. So far, I like it. Lent seems a good period to read it.

How interesting about the milkweed. I hadn't heard of using it for life preservers before. Maybe the type we have in the garden would be even better. Certainly It's worth investigating. Today's many different needs have brought about many new uses for many things, certainly. Isn't spring beautiful? With you at home, we here are all enjoying new blossoms and new life, too. On a hike Friday we saw pussy-willows and lots of daffodils. Judging from your similar observations, we must have the same stages of development. It's fun picturing you enjoying the same weather.

On the same hike, I dreamt up some ideas. No doubt they were the result of that spring fever sickness. Still, I'd like to get some info from you. I think it would be fun having bees as a hobby. I realize it involves quite a bit of work. During college I'll definitely want something to do that will keep me outside and might possibly bring some cash. Bees and their product appeal to me. ('Course it's mostly the product.) I even thought of possibly living on the suburbs of a college town and combining a small poultry and bee business while attending college. These are all strictly pipe dreams, but while the smoke is still in my eyes, how about informing me on the subject. How much cash and time would a small poultry and bee set-up involve? They call for only a small plot of land. When I get real analytical, I realize such a pipe dream is fantastic. But since my plans for college and the future are still very transient, I'd like to learn things about some of the possibilities which might work out. So tell me a little about this, please. You've had experience and do have access to more information than I. 'Course it's not important, but I'd like to know more about the subject.

Time out for lunch

Beef, potatoes, gravy, peas, coleslaw, pineapple, bread and butter, and coffee. A delicious meal!!! Now I feel like a siesta. If my writing is weaker than usual, blame it on a full stomach.

Now I'll tell you about the highlight of all experiences yet had in France. Last night a group of us got our first pass. I'll relate the story step by step.

At four o'clock about 25 of us started for a town some five miles away. Transportation is scarce. We used our two trusty feet and arrived within the city limits at 5:15. Four of us left the large group to do some shopping.

We were looking for something for our wives, mothers, or sweethearts. The shops were similar to our American stores. There is no bartering or bargaining. Prices were moderate, but in some cases too high, just as is often the case in shopping tours in the U. S. The first stopping place was a building advertising perfume as one of their articles for sale. We looked over the stock and finally bought several bottles. I bought two of different odors (?). Also I picked up a couple pins made in France. These four articles cost me a total of $4.80, or 960 Francs.

We wanted some jewelry or scarfs. After looking in five or six more shops, we gave up. The only scarfs worth looking at were $12.00. The jewelry wasn't presentable. It was fun talking with the different shopkeepers. None of them knew any English. But, we managed to understand each other quite well. Finally, I purchased two cute Easter cards, finishing my purchasing for the evening. I'm enclosing one in this letter. Incidentally, I am also mailing the perfume and the pins to you. I'd like to have you mail part of it on to Marcy if you think it's worthwhile. A gift from France might add to the meaningfulness of her bigger birthday present, which you have offered to buy.

The town itself was very picturesque. Buildings were close together. Street were very narrow and of brick surface. Something very unusual, which I learned is all over France, is the street latrine. It consists of a group of urinals attached on the side of a building. The only shelter is a strip of tin, hiding the person up to the chest. The town had a village square, as do most villages over here. A very small street carnival was constructed there. A few swings and ball games made it up. No engines or electricity were used in its workings.

We stopped by a French sign advertising a play to be given that night. It was difficult translating it all. Suddenly a little boy came up to us and asked if we understood its meaning. He said, "Understand?" We said we did, and then we began a conversation. He was twelve years old. In school he was studying English, and he did know a surprising amount. I could tell he was intelligent and must have come from a good family. Before long he invited us to his house for dinner. We were hungry. Cafes don't have enough food to serve us, and our K rations, which we had carried with us had been devoured even before our shopping tour. With a little coaxing, we consented to follow him home.

The house was only a few blocks away. We entered and were greeted with many bows and welcomes. The boy's mother and aunt were the only ones present. Between the four of us we managed to carry on a pretty good conversation. They were extraordinarily kind and hospitable. The family was going to eat in a short while, so they added four plates and we dined with them.

Time out

This time the interruption was due to an afternoon communion service. Every Sunday one of the chaplains conducts and administers communion. I attend most of the services if possible. They are always inspirational. After that I stopped off for a game of horseshoes. I'll have to practice. My shoe never opens correctly. I'd like to develop the plain 3/4 turn.

Ah yes, I'll continue with the French visit. Just as we began eating, the father came home. He was very, very nice to us, too. His business is being an auto mechanic. He joined us at the table. Here was our menu: soup (made up of potatoes, bread, a small amount of meat and some spices), egg omelet, bread and butter, and cider. It was good. The cider was a little hard. Cider takes the place of water, milk and coffee, I guess. The little boy drank it down eagerly. At the close of the meal, the father brought out some wine. I explained, as did one of my other friends, that I didn't care for it. He understood and acted as if he had met many other Americans who didn't care for liquor of any kind. The whole group was continually hopping about making sure we were satisfied. They really treated us as guests and yet as if we were members of the family. It was a wonderful experience.

They call their cider sweet cider. Comparing it with ours, it isn't sweet. I don't believe it has but very little alcoholic content, if any; but, still I think I shan't drink it again. It's not very good at all. They do drink milk at breakfast. I saw some in the neat, small kitchen. Perhaps they use coffee. We probably just didn't see it.

When we left we gave them a bar of soap and eight packages of cigarettes. They were so appreciative. They didn't expect anything at all, I'm sure. However, we had supplied ourselves with such items just in case such a situation should arrive. They insisted that we return again. We thanked them for everything and left.

Next we went to the three-act French play we had read about earlier in the evening. We paid forty francs and stayed five minutes. The rapidity with which they tossed words about was too much for us. We hiked back to camp. In fact, we hiked only half way. A truck gave us a ride. And that's the story of our pass. Educational, fun, and profitable!! We learned more about the French people, their customs and language, and we had fun and a dinner (chow-hounds) doing it.

Goodness, this has stretched out into a longer letter than I had expected it to be. There are still a couple of things I want to comment on, though. One is about Marcy's birthday gift, Mother. I'm sending a money order in the next letter. Please find something extra special nice for Marcy. Costume jewelry would be fine. Maybe a pair of small earrings with necklace or pin to match? I have too much money again. My new allotments don't begin till this month, so I got an extra large pay for February. Put whatever is left over in the drawer or bank.

So 50,000 miles have rolled up on the car. Ford is always going to be my brand.

This will probably reach you right after Easter. I hope the cablegrams I'm going to send reach you OK, just as I hope the one I sent you in Ann Arbor met you, Mother. I know Easter at home will be lovely. Hundreds of people will enjoy it immensely, both because of its symbolicness and the way you will present it, Daddy. It's a wonderful day.

Everything continues to be just swell here! I'll write again soon.

March 20, 1945
France V-Mail

The figures on the car were certainly interesting! I have passed them on to several of my friends, especially Ford enthusiasts. The total shows we've operated it for five years at a cost of a little more than three cents a mile. That's really a wonderfully low figure. Did you mean to add the initial cost? Last night along with your letter came two from Marcy. Her last semester's average was 4.00. To top it off, she has been initiated into Mortar Board!!! Isn't that really grand! When you realize all the extra curricular she has been carrying, it's even twice as marvelous. I sent her a cablegram of congratulations. Her sorority pledge class of about twenty-five produced twenty-three eligible for initiation. And, of those twenty-three, twenty had over a 3.00 average. Wow! I'm going to have trouble topping her record. In fact, I'm glad now that I decided quite awhile ago to concede the race in grades to her. Hmmm. She is truly marvelous! Your regular air-mail came in eleven days. That's the new record for speed. I do hope I'll soon learn that you have finally received mail from me. The weather continues to be lovely. It's much warmer than it was two weeks ago. Everything is still fine. Our ball league is half finished. We're leading with three wins and no losses. Food is still delicious. Yesterday I ate more chicken at one sitting than I have ever before in the army. All this food, all this sleep, plus the wonderful fresh air, is making a healthy group of us all. I'm probably getting fat. I'll write again soon.

March 23, 1945
France

I'm sure we're all caught up on our mail now. That is, your letters to me have finally all come. Mine are probably just beginning to struggle in. Letters of the 23rd, 1st, and 11th have arrived the last two days. All the letters are so interesting. The clippings were grand, too. Every man in the tent has gazed at both the pictures of Ellen. Also, I've let a couple of my buddies read your letter, Daddy, on the Menonite question. I was so sorry to hear about Eugene Canaday. We had been rather good friends. I used to kid him in band. The letters from Joanne and Ellen have arrived, also. It's soooo nice having a family of such wonderful corresponders. I have to smile at your remark about J.T.'s request for pancake flour. I'll bet you are laughing at my similar ask. The idea is we have neat little stoves just ideal for flipping pancakes during some quiet evening.

Reading first hand accounts of the river's recent escapades is fun. It must have given you a feeling of being isolated missing the usual things the rest of the world sends to Gallipolis for those couple of days. I was thinking of you. The "Stars and Stripes" kept us posted excellently. It even mentioned Point Pleasant in one write-up. News straight from Ohio was only a day late. Not bad at all!

Joanne's letter was interesting, especially about Doug's encounter with Tyrone Power and Commander Tunney. I do hope Joey has recovered from his cold. Goodness, he was really quite sick for awhile. I'm betting that he's a rascal now. This spring weather makes everyone feel just wonderful. Joanne's letters come a little more quickly than yours. However, yours of the 11th, mailed the 12th, arrived in only nine days. That's speed!

Yesterday afternoon we hiked to a nearby town and saw a movie. Then we hiked back, the round trip totaling some 11 or 12 miles. Now that's what I call adding incentive to the infantry hiking game. I hope we take more walks like that.

Last night a group of us argued for four whole hours over two questions. They were: the negro question, and the union question. I don't know how else to state them; they include so much. The time spent was well spent. I especially learned a lot about unions. Tell me, does Uncle Bob have "open" or "closed" shops? How does he operate on that question? And, speaking of Bob, how was everything at Ann Arbor, Mother? I'll bet you had a magnificent time. Was Ted there? Write me a good full-scale account. (Probably you have already done this.)

A nice letter came from Kenny last night. Also, the cutest Easter card came from Ellen. And, two more luscious letters from Marcy. She is going back to camp this summer, and the position she has is tops. She's going to be general program counselor. This means she'll be able to get the real low-down on making a camp interesting, and everything. It's really a grand job! I am happy to have her so interested in camps.

Did Joanne tell you Doug spent a day with Ernie Pyle? He is getting around. By the way, did I ever tell you that I have been to Le Havre? Maybe I'll get to see some more large foreign cities someday.

You mentioned that Joe E. Brown had said there was too much monotony in army life. You can dismiss that thought. For instance, just now I had an interruption of two hours while we of the first platoon put the clamps on the staff-sergeants in a hot game of baseball. Now we are the only undefeated team. Four straight wins make our record sparkle. Some outfits might be dull, but we never are. We always have something fascinating to do. Arguing, sports, reading, writing, many happy things more than fill our spare moments.

Just now it occurs to me that today marks one year of being a part of this division. It hardly seems possible. That means it's almost eleven months that I have been in swell M company. Army life couldn't have been more agreeable. I'll always remember M company as a wonderful bunch of

fellows who just can't be beaten. In all the time I've been here I don't recall a single fight. There have been a few scuffles, but never has there been real malice towards anyone by anybody. I can't imagine a more compatible and yet rugged bunch. We are a grand outfit. Always remember what a swell bunch I'm with. I wish you could meet them all. Maybe someday we can arrange a reunion of the squad at least.

I have read only the first 100 pages of "The Apostle." I do like it though and will continue to read it. I have a question. It, no doubt, displays ignorance; but, why are there 40 days in Lent?? We have church this evening. I'll be able to ask the chaplain. Funny how I've forgotten the reasoning there. None of us seem to know exactly.

Enough for now. I'll write again soon.

P.S. As soon as I get the money order I'll send it. Maybe I'll enclose it in here today. Send at least something to Marcy from the small box I'm sending. Even though the articles are rather cheap, I've told her to look for some French made souvenirs. She's expecting them.

CHAPTER ELEVEN

GERMANY

GERMANY
MARCH 27 - JUNE 1, 1945

March 27, 1945
Germany

The last batch of mail we received was surely flown to us in record time. In six short days word came all the way from Joanne and Marcy to me. Isn't that something though! That's almost as fast as it was in the states. Joanne's letter was numbered 4. That means I still have "3" to look forward to real soon. Also, Marcy mentioned sending a letter from Bob Rahn, which I haven't received yet. Joanne mentioned that you had written about receiving my first letters. That means, no doubt, there are lots of your letters in the mail for me. One of these days I'll probably get swamped properly. Naturally, I won't mind that in the least.

I've been reading more of The Apostle. I do like it immensely! My book is condensed to 550 pages, and I have 150 more to go. At first I was a little sorry that Paul had to experience his visions during his epileptic-type fits. However, I realize the significance of them isn't impaired by that malady. The visions were obviously not caused by the fits. Perhaps the fits were more the result of the terrific emotional strain of the wonderfulness of the sights. A Jewish friend of mine wants to read the book after I have finished.

The change of location means very little. I hope it doesn't frighten you. We're billeted ideally. It's difficult for me to believe I'm so far away from home. We're experiencing more of the comforts of home than I ever believed we would in army life. It's honestly amazing.

Joanne's letter was so, so wonderful. Perhaps if she remembers some of her topics she'll understand my enthusiasm. Joey is really going ahead by leaps and bounds. His vocabulary is much more complete than mine in French. I smiled at Mr. Feely's desire to retire someday and discuss topics with Grandpa. (Wuerfel) I do so much want to do the same. I'll bet we could fill a week of evenings right now. I've been thinking of him quite a bit recently. I am proud to be one of his grandsons. I'm extremely lucky having such wonderful families on all sides.

Easter is just around the corner. I hate to admit it, but I've been hoarding my candy ration looking forward to the end of Lent. Now I have a dozen or so candy bars. Sunday or Monday I'll feast on them. Hmmm. Is that defeating the purpose??

Marcy has some new stationery that really tickles me. In the corner is printed, "Especially for Scotty." I go overboard for stuff like that. (Egotistical, I guess.) Everybody seems to be going all out to make me just about burst with happiness over here. You are all so nice to me. Thanks for writing so often, and writing the things I like so much to hear about. I tell you, really you're spoiling me, even at this distance.

Tonight I was sergeant of the guard. It's a little late so I'll close early. Everything is really just fine here!! I hope everything is swell at home, too!

March 29, 1945
Germany V-Mail

Do you mind if I eat while we talk? In my left hand I have a delicious evening snack of sardines and hardtack. We found a large box of sardines. The hardtack was given to one of the Jewish boys to eat during this coming week, and we're all sharing some of the surplus tonight. Five of us make a gay scene all seated around a table eating and writing. Some Fun! A little while ago, Zig and I attempted to make up a string-duet. He had a mandolin and I was thumping on a zipher. Remember the instrument I had in the fourth grade called a psalter? This zipher is just like it only on a larger scale. We even located a harmonica tuner. Even if we couldn't play many tunes we were in tune. It took me a whole hour to tune mine, it has so many strings. These nights are beautiful! The moon is full and lovely. The weather is fine, too.! I'm betting on a perfect Easter Sunday. The coming of this special day brings about a closer than usual feeling. I have so many happy memories concerning Easter, music, etc. I'll will be with you in thought. Everything is swell here. I'll write again soon.

March 30, 1945
Germany

Another Good Friday! This year it seems more symbolic than ever. "A promise of salvation," fits in now especially. Surely light is beginning to filter in on these dark years, and we know the day is coming when life and constructing will take the place of death and destruction. We weren't able to have church services today. However, many of us remembered the day and thought and talked about it. Easter we will be able to worship together, I'm sure. Still, it isn't necessary to be in a group or in a church to worship and pray sufficiently. I will be with you in your songs and services Sunday as I am every Sunday.

Today has been such a swell one. Mail caught up with us once again. It was just like visiting with the entire family circle. A letter from you, Mother, written the 22nd, another from you, Daddy, penned the 22nd, an Easter card plus a note from Joanne, mailed the 21st, and a letter written the 17th from Ellen. Ellen enclosed a nice long letter from Chuck Whistler. Plus all the wonderful family news, I got four letters from Marcy. Such a big mail call gave me a solid hour of incomparable pleasure. Yep, nothing beats the words from you all and Marcy.

Mother, you are able to keep secrets! Such tight lipness is commendable. We all sort of smiled at your extra carefulness. It is wise, though. I see my cablegram didn't reach you while you were in Ann Arbor. Probably Grandmother and Grandfather will wonder what it's all about when it arrives. I hope my Easter cablegrams make better time. Just this minute I read the part of your letter which told Mrs. Russell's funny mistake. Gosh, but the boys did howl. Some of the ignorances civilians have about the army are screams!

Daddy, your letter was so interesting, as always. I'm glad Gallia Academy is attempting a music program in the school. I do wish the band could have been contiunued under good leadership. They're doing well considering everything, though. More and more I wonder about the negro-white problem. Sometimes the best solution seems to be separation with equal opportunity, as in the choir performance. One negro professor even advocated a 49th state made up of all colored folks. I thought that was a little rash, but maybe segregation will turn out to be one phase in solving the problem. Segregation might bring about equality of opportunity more quickly. Then after they have established themselves a little better, all the whites will accept them again more willingly. It's extremely interesting and involves generations.

I'm glad the church is continuing to be so successful. Nothing can compare with the strength and lastingness of the church. Everywhere I've been and ever expect to go I'll bet I'll see lots of signs of worshipping Christ. Lately I've seen lovely sketches of Christ and some beautiful churches or cathedrals. The buildings are rather torn and ragged, but they will be rebuilt, of course.

Now that we've changed countries, I've changed language studies(?). I'll probably end up knowing how to count to ten in French and ten in German. No doubt I'll retain very little. It is fun to try to learn certain words and phrases. I'll never be able to read it. Maybe I'll really learn it in college someday. German is an interesting language. French is prettier, though.

Marcy is so really wonderful. As I formulate more and more what I believe is most important in life, I see how perfectly she fits in. She stands for and is in favor of everything that's good and lasting. We are going to add to the armistice happiness our engagement. It is wiser to wait till then. I realize now it would be difficult to buy a ring at four thousand miles. Being with her for sure forever is essential, too, when I give her the ring.

Everything is coming along just swell here. We're living in buildings, and we do have all the conveniences of home. It would be impossible for the army to care for an infantry soldier any better than this. It is really OK!!! Check any of the other sources of info and they'll tell you the same.

Is my mail coming through OK? So far you seem to be getting them. If that box of perfume doesn't come, it isn't much lost. I didn't insure it, it was so little. I always think of "Micco," or Mark, and the funny mistake he made that day. Wasn't that funny? We men aren't up on stuff like that. Perfume and cosmetics are for zee opposite sex, yep. I'm glad to hear the news on Merrill, J.T., Kenny, Manning, and Tommy. I hope I see some of them sometime.

There isn't much writable news. I did a washing this afternoon and everything is now gleaming. It's nice to have everything clean. I also had a nice hot shower. We are being so well cared for.

For now, so long. I'll write again soon. I did like your closing sentence, Dad. "I feel confident that God will order all things to praise Him in the end and transform all sacrifices into a great blessing. Faith is victory."

P.S. "The Upper Room" arrived today, too. Right on time! Another box would be welcome! The first hasn't arrived, but I'm looking forward to it eagerly.

April 1, 1945
Germany

Another lovely Easter has arrived and almost gone. No one has remembered it's April Fool's Day, too. I don't recall a single joke played on anyone. Easter overshadows the lesser holiday. It has been a lovely day. We had a nice church service in a real church. The sun shone brightly most of the day, The Germans were all spruced up in their new or reconditioned Easter outfits. It was fun watching them go by. Some of them carried flowers. All were cleaned up for this glorious day. We had shaves and dusted our O.D.s before church. Naturally we didn't miss being without new clothing. The spirit of the day was enough.

After church I stopped and had a chat with the chaplain. He is extremely cordial and nice. My purpose was to ask him about the forty days in Lent. Before I left him, we had discussed many things, including The Apostle. This afternoon I finally finished the book. It was an easy and enjoyable way to learn about how and who did the writings of the New Testament. I liked the way it linked up all Paul's letters plus Mathew's, Mark's, and John's writings. Then, also, it made the split between the Jews and Christians more plain.

Another swell long letter came from Joanne today. It was written the 23rd. I was glad to hear that Joey's eye trouble has been diagnosed and is going to be fixed up. When she mentioned eye trouble in her last letter, I wondered what was up. I hope everything clears up easily for Joey. I do love to read about his latest tricks. He is advancing, singing "Super Suds" and everything.

We've been eating candy sort of heavily today. I had quite a collection from my rations which I haven't been eating. With Lent's finis and Easter's arrival, we dug in. Remember how we used to eat candy Sunday evenings after singing?

The fellows are calling me to join them in a big evening snack. They say chicken and vegetable, and meat and spaghetti, rations are just waiting to be eaten. I believe I'll join them. Tomorrow should bring another long letter from you, so I'll write a longer letter then.

P.S. I'm enclosing a mark and a half worth a dime and a nickel.

April 2, 1945
Germany

As I had hoped, a nice long letter came today from you. (And I do mean long!) It was written the 18th after Y. F. meeting. It was really fascinating! I haven't received the letter you wrote in Toledo, so I gulped up every bit of news about the happenings at Ann Arbor. You did have a wonderful time, Mother! I can't get over the feats of Hansie and Fritzie! That chess game Ted and Hansie played sounds unbelievable. Hansie beat me once at camp. I was ashamed! But now that he has defeated Grandfather, the real family champ, I feel better. Keeping track of every chess move mentally is an amazing ability.

News from this end is rather scarce. The news that we both know about already is truly wonderful, isn't it! The war is progressing sooo favorably!! I'm positive the year 1947 will find fighting a thing of the past. That no longer seems an optimistic statement or a dream. 1947 will surely find killing and conquest an awful thing of the past. However, you along with us must continue to realize that we still have far to go. And, you even more than us must fight the struggle for the right kind of peace. I know you know and are acting on these things already. "Civilian complacency" isn't a failure of many, I'm sure. It is wonderful to be able to see "finis" written so clearly on the wall, though.

Where was Grandfather born? I'd like to know more about his early life. Do any relatives of his still live near his birthplace?

Grm and Grmp are glorious. Continually I remember and am thankful for two wonderful family's traditions, reputations, and futures. It's a real privilege to have a part in continuing such a long line of worthwhile and good accomplishments. It would be impossible to let down an institution such as our family. I do hope I'll do my share. If I don't, maybe one of my big gang of children will. Hmm.

Another Wesleyan magazine came today. A wrong address on the envelope inspired me to at least say "hello" to the school itself for once. I'd still like to complete another year there at least. It is a fine school. Many swell kids go there and standards are high. As time goes by I'm realizing that standards and individual moral codes count a terrible lot in life. The small things (or seemingly small things) really add up.

In what are you going to invest your money, Mother? We have lost all appreciation for cash over here. I could actually get along on nothing. Stamps are the only thing we need and have to pay for. Even our PX rations are free now. If ever our mail clerk gets our money orders back I'll be sending more cash home for future reference. By the way, let me know when the new allotments start pouring in.

Sometime I may send home some souvenirs. The best ones are mental though. But, just to have some material proof around, maybe I'll wrap up a few items. Would you like something like a swastika, or like "that thar?" Just say so if you would.

Golly, I hope you are remembering Marcy's birthday of the 18th. Did you find a nice necklace-earring set, or something similar? I'll send a cablegram, as I will for Joanne, too. Hers is the 23rd, isn't it? Today brought two more letters from Marcy. She mentioned more mail from you, Mother. I hope she'll be able to see Joanne this summer when she goes east. Also, I hope you'll manage a get-together in Gallipolis sometime. You know, for a moment I forgot about her birthday. That was the reason for the exclamation at the beginning of the paragraph.

Everything continues to be just fine here. Please don't worry a bit. I promise you it's a worthless waste of energy. We're getting lots of food and rest. I'm positive I'm putting on weight. A haircut might cut me down a pound or two though. Enough for this eve. I'll write again first chance I get.

April 7, 1945
Germany

If you can stand green ink and notebook paper, I'll drop in for a visit tonight. The last couple of evenings have found me fooling around and neglecting pen thoughts. So,

I'll catch up a little this eve.

The countryside around here is perfectly beautiful. Rolling hills covered with pines help make up unbelievable scenery. It is lovely. The views even surpass those enjoyed in France. Spring is truly here, and we are enjoying it. It's fun enjoying the scenes and observing the German people. Being here is a most interesting and exciting adventure.

The other evening a pal popped in the door and threw two piccolos and a flute on my lap. My jaw fell clear down to the instruments. I attempted to toot them, and they are good pieces. The piccolos surpass the flute. All are of wood and have only sharps and flat keys. It's lots of fun trying to recall the fingering, etc. I may keep one of the piccolos.

Before the subject of Ted's wonderful offer grows old, I'd like to make a few additional comments about it. Here they are: There are two things I want in life. One is to be of service to others in a very valuable way. The other is to raise a fine family. Success to me will mean fulfillment of these two objectives. Many things are involved in the realization of both, so there are many things to be considered before a step is taken toward either.

Knowing about and appreciating the good things in life is a necessary requisite for happy, worthwhile living. If I can help people toward more worthwhile living, I'll feel as if I'm being of service. I want my vocation to be one of this type, one that offers opportunity for me to attempt guidance. And, I want to be positive my attempts are helping!

If the right set-up for objective #1 is found, objective #2 might be automatically taken care of. The job will have to supply enough cash for the family. However, the urge for family shouldn't guide the job hunting, nor the job hunting the family. There should be a sort of perfect equation. In other words, I want a position in which I can help others to the best of my ability and raise a family. It is a natural and common desire, I guess.

Our home life has, no doubt, formed my wishes. It has been ideal! I hope mine will be very similar. Probably I'm better suited for a different calling than the ministry, and I'd like a larger family. Those are the only differences I see.

Ted's offer is very appealing, exciting, and comforting. However, there is a big question in my mind. I can't recall but very few wealthy persons who seemed to have worthy goals in life. Money is too much the master. Drinking and personal splurging are too often their chief pleasures. Cash overshadows the real worths of life for them. Before I would accept a position serving the rich I would want to be positive I would be helping. I would have to know that I wouldn't be merely a tool instilling false culture which might later be guided completely by cash.

It's unfair to be harsh on people who have become wealthy because of their own initiative and brains. However, I would be working with their children who often gain fortunes merely through deaths or reaching the proper age. They are the offenders, I believe.

For Ted to put forth such a grand, wonderful offer so early is indeed an honor. I am honestly thankful and excited over it. Maybe the set-up he suggests would be ideal. The two-fold position is what I want someday. Also, maybe Marcy would have a chance to use her talent in such a set-up. But, we'll let time test it. Time is the test for everything. Later, if the direction seems wise, I'll happily take it. Of course, first I must prove myself worthy of it, and then I'll make sure it's what I really want. It's positively marvelous to know such an offer awaits. Wow!

Now it's a beautiful Sunday morning. Last night I stopped in the middle of the letter. This morning is georgeous!! Church is in about an hour, so I'll stop to wash up, etc., before going. We are located ideally. Never have a worry about us. Everything is just fine! Since there is a war, I'm happy that I got "overseas." It's a thrilling experience.

I'll be writing again soon.

April 10, 1945
Germany

The beauty of the day, plus three recent letters from you, puts me in the spirit to at least say "hello" tonight. The soft bed plus late hour makes me write hastily. So, stick around a minute while I just drop in for a short visit.

Three grand letters written the 20th, 26th (V-mail), and the 28th arrived last mail call. Everything seems swell at home. Mother, you certainly did exercise that day. Wow!! 129 sounds about perfect for you. I wouldn't worry about losing more. The contents of the box you are mailing sounded fine. Probably it will arrive very soon. You said it was mailed the 19th. We'll see how soon it makes it.

Want another request for a box? OK, I'll give it you top of the next page.

Tommy is still a fine basketball player. Twenty-four points isn't to be sneezed at. I hope he goes into athletic work of some kind. How is Kenny now? I wrote him a V-mail a short while ago.

Please send some stationery in a rather strong cardboard box. Brushless shaving cream can be used, too. Also, a tube of toothpaste. Candy and food is always welcome!

Thanks so very much for sending camellias. Marcy will love them! She mentions often the welcome letters you are writing her. Swell!

Daddy, can you spare another sermon? I'm getting anxious for another of the best I always like most. Send one sometime, please. Never do I hear anything compared to yours.

So, here it has been merely "hello." I'll say goodnight now. I'll be writing again much more lengthily soon.

April 16, 1945
Germany

I just wrote Marcy a lengthy letter. I had planned to do the same to you, but now I learn mail is going to be collected in a few minutes. So, I'll make this short and then continue another one to be mailed next chance.

Three swell V-mails came from you this morning. They were written the 24th, 28th, and 29th. Also, two came from Ellen written the 24th and 29th. Everything seems to be coming along so swell at home! All is tops here, too! We're gathering new worthwhile experiences. Each day finds us nearer the world's goal. The weather is delightful. Everything is "percolatin'" just grand! It was a surprise to hear about Roosevelt's death. That was a shock. However, I'm sure our representative type of government will ensure a continuation of smooth running, good living.

Germany is a beautiful country. This is an especially beautiful season, too. I can picture the plum tree at home! Rolling the lawn sounds like a good idea. It hasn't been very level, has it. Maybe you can put up a good croquet game again. How is the garden coming? Some sprouts should be coming up by now.

Marcy loved the gardenias. I'm sure she'll like her gift, too. She'll probably send on my today's letter to you, so I'll stop this one now to make sure it gets off. All is well, and we're happy and in fine spirits.

April 17, 1945
Germany

First of all, a report on the race between the air-mail and V-mail letters both written on the 28th. The air-mail arrived a week before the V-mail. As a rule, air-mails do seem to come much more quickly. A whole week must be rather unusual, though. Let's use the winner more. V-mails don't fill the bill as well as the longer regular letters. However, to remember the patriotic angle, I suppose we should alternate the two a little. Any word from home is wonderful regardless of the medium, of course!

It's nice to read about the lovely weather you are having. Ours is heavenly, too. I think spring is my favorite season. Blossoms, buds, sunrises, the roosters' crow, anything of nature's which signifies something better and more beautiful in the making is more significant to me now. The war in this advance stage is like the spring of the centuries. A better, brighter, more alive world is blossoming forth. We soldiers are like unto the roosters' crow. Each report of a weapon is broadcasting a new day. Such comparisons don't sound fair at first, but now that the end of the war is so plainly in sight, It's easier to look at the evil of war as a real good, or at least beginning of the good. If war is to be compared with the bud of goodness, the peace plan may well be called the rains or weather. The proper amount of the different combinations are positively necessary before the bud will bloom into the flower it should be. Let's hope and pray for that, too.

For the last five or six days I haven't been able to lift a pen. We have been very busy. The last couple of days I've been scrubbing up clothes, squad equipment, etc. We've had a real spring cleaning. It's lots of fun. Ever so often I'm going to insist that my wife let me do washings and some cooking. (Do I hear you laughing?) Really, I do enjoy jobs like that.

The thrills and experiences we've been having are wonderful. Without a doubt they are enlightening and revealing as to life's real worths. I can honestly say I wouldn't want to miss a phase I've experienced yet. You would agree with me, too. Someday I'll want to spend long hours relating lots of interesting stories. On the whole, people here are as people everywhere. Misguided, disappointed, and beaten, they still function spiritually as usual with an obvious faith in a brighter future. The last years have evidently changed former followers into slaves, shackled to a man who let them down. I blame Hitler and Nazism for this war, not the people. However, discipline, guidance, punishment, and a degree of tolerance will have to be combined to make them realize the seriousness of the cause they allowed to function. We must add kindness to the list of tools for rebuilding them. Maybe it should have been first. The whole question is one of importance and extreme interest. I like to turn it over in my mind ever so often. Helping to right such a topsy-turvy situation is something I wouldn't miss.

I got a nice long letter from Tommy yesterday. Everything is going well in San Diego. He knows he can get a scholarship for college because of his athletic ability now. The G. I. Bill of Rights should cover the cost angle pretty well, though. By the way, already I'm entitled to almost three years of college. The one year for 90 day service period and two school years of nine months each in recognition of eighteen months of service. Not bad at all!!! Working with people is absolutely going to be the object of the courses I want to take. The different chances I've had to view different peoples' reactions in varying cases will be even more beneficial when added to thought provoking, condensing school studies on the same subjects.

Wow, $10,000 is an awful lot of money to be made from honey. Hmmm, I do want something of that nature to make up for the sort of passive phases of studying. College is going to be wonderful to return to. The difficulties of readjusting to that life aren't going to be as many as most people believe, I think. Even though a year or two may have to pass by before book larnin' is taken up again, I don't believe it will be hard or distasteful. Not a bit!

Daddy, maybe your birthday will almost have arrived by the time this reaches you. I hope it's a most happy one!! If in my whole life I accomplish just half the good that you have already, I'll be most thankful. Your standards and ideals will always be mine. You are the most wonderful father a fellow could have! I wish I could be with you on May 1st to give you congrats; but, though I'm not, you'll know I'm thinking of you immensely. Happy, Happy Birthday. May you have as many more. 100 is a good age.

They're collecting mail, so I'll hand this in now. Till next time.

April 20, 1945
Germany

We're expecting a big mail call this evening. However, I'll write now to send one letter on its way today. Then tomorrow maybe I'll say "hello" again in answer to the many bound to arrive very soon. There's a good chance that your first box may arrive any day now, too. Several boxes have been coming to the fellows. Most of them are in fine shape, food unspoiled, etc. Naturally, I'm looking forward to yours.

The weather is so perfect it's almost unbelievable. Each day the sun shines forth full force. Now we're comfortably situated in a place where a sunbath is not uncommon. Many are running about minus shirts. You can actually see the results of the warm rays. Yep, we're gathering suntans. Our location is really very nice. I can register only one gripe. The fragrant aroma of cow manure is a little strong if the wind comes toward you. Hmmm.

I just completed this month's "Readers Digest." It was an interesting issue. "The Road to Serfdom" was especially revealing and thought provoking. I hadn't realized the many advantages competition offered in building the proper economy. It does seem wise to be careful of "planning" campaigns. Also, it looks as if we of the U. S. have already slipped off the path a bit.

Last night three of us stayed up rather late just talking. One of our topics was the "Have More" article in the Digest. "Tik," one of my ammo bearers, is going to be an orcharder. He loves the idea of having a big variety of things on a small farm. I'll bet you enjoyed that article, too, Mother. Does such an energetic set-up appeal to you and Daddy? By the way, "Tik," whose father has raised fruit for years, is most anxious to help you plan that fruit farm you've thought about. If you have a question or two, send it. He'd love answering you. And, he is an authority on the subject.

(I'm having ink troubles. This lighter blue is better, isn't it?)

How is everything and everyone at home? Is Elaine Lear still going to school at Cincy? Did I ever tell you that her clarinet was made by the same outfit that made my flute? I was surprised to know about it, as you will probably be too. Kohlert is an exclusive name.

I believe that we are now able to write that at one time we were in Cologne. Or maybe you guessed it already? You are rather psychic sometimes.

Sometimes during the week we have a church service. In just half an hour, another one is scheduled. You can count on at least two chances to worship every week. The chaplains are doing a fine job helping us to keep touch with the Almighty. Almost every evening I do have a chance to read from the "Upper Room." If ever I miss some days, I read those missed the first chance I get. It's nice knowing that we're worshipping with the same thoughts almost daily. Marcy is using the "Upper Room" now, too. Reading that booklet combines the reverence and singleness of personal devotions with the power and unity of group worshipping. It's a fine inspiring habit to have. I want to keep it always.

Ever so often I wonder a little about some of our censorship regulations. Any information I pass on to you is evaluated by me (and the censor, of course) as being safe to make known. It might be fun for you to try to picture my whereabouts ever so often. But, we aren't supposed to disclose that "info." Many times, however, by connecting rather irrelevant thoughts you may guess at approximate locations. If your guesses might seem right, probably it would be wise to withhold the speculations to the Westerman household. Do you follow my reasoning and hints?

-Time out for church. I'll be back in a few minutes.-

The service turned out to be a regular full-length worship period. Best of all, it was in a real church. The organ was rather battered and wheezy. Ever so often one of the keys would stick. It reminded me of that one Sunday when Mrs. Lanier almost went wild, with the rest of us, trying to unstick notes. Too bad someone around here hasn't your knowledge of an organ, Daddy. This church could surely use about a week's work on its music maker.

I'm enclosing a Cologne post card which advertises Fords. The German army's most used truck is a Ford V-8. At first it seemed outrageous; but, a little thought makes one realize there is nothing unpatriotic about it. Also, I'm sticking in a small cloth German symbol. Both of these items were found in Cologne.

To keep weight down I'll sign off here. Everything is fine here! I hope everything is very well at home, too.

P. S. Did I ever tell you I now have all seven of Joanne's letters? They arrived in the correct order, too, all except number three which followed number six.

May 1 & 2, 1945
Germany

A whole week has zoomed by since I last wrote. As yet we still aren't in a letter writing zone (area where letters are collected and mailed right after we write them), but I just have to - and now it's 24 hours later. No sooner did I pick up this pencil than we had to move again. So now it's May 2nd. But let me accomplish yesterday's mission, which was to say happy birthday, Daddy! I hope you had a gala, happy day. I thought of you all day. Through Ellen, you probably got a remembrance. I'm counting on being nearer to you for the next fifty or so birthdays.

Such a long period of not writing means the enemy is making us hurry to keep up with his retreat. The war is progressing magnificently! Even if the surrender doesn't come quickly, they are defeated, and their total occupation by us is only a matter of weeks. So, in a way it's good that I haven't been able to write sooner than this. Since the last letter, several censorship restrictions have been lifted. Now I can tell you some of our escapades. You were correct in connecting us up with the Fifteenth Army. However, we were with them for a very short period. At Cologne, where we first were introduced to combat, we transferred to the First Army. With that group, we worked in the Ruhr Pocket. There, at first, some of the resistance was rather fanatical, so we got a taste of the rougher phases of combat. After the finis of that area, we rested a few days at Altena, and then transferred to still another army. Our location now is restricted "info." I can say we've been moving quickly and successfully. After a week of being on the chase, I believe we'll have a chance to rest. I hope to write lots to make up for the long silence.

You may be sure that the long period of training we underwent in the states has paid dividends. Things have gone smoothly. The squad has performed nobly and is still intact. Naturally, the company has suffered casualties; but, we've been fortunate, and I am so very thankful. Perhaps my writing sounds as if we weren't expecting any more action here. I think we will have more skirmishes, but the end is so visible, one can't help but be optimistic. That's the reason for the sort of condensed report on happenings up-to-date.

In spite of all rumors and facts, I'm still optimistic concerning the future of the German people. A few crazy fanatics have been holding the positions of leadership. Anywhere, anytime, it's difficult for people to escape the influence and power of leaders. I've been trying to learn the score over here. Most of my conversations have been with country folks. With the language handicap, and the opportunity to converse with only the most stable group (country folks), my observations are apt to be quite wrong. Briefly, I've found these things to be true: Before the war, Hitler won the peoples' confidence completely by building and promising. After the war began, the nation slowly started to realize the mistake of trusting him. His attitude toward religion was a big factor in his downfall. Finally, now 75% know he is awful and bats, and they are totally happy to have the war end, even if it means their complete defeat. I don't think another of Hitler's type could begin here. The few supporters and S. S. troops are actually hated by the rest. The common folk urge us to destroy them all.

Perhaps I'm being soft and gullible; but, I do believe the German people will turn out all right in the next half century. We have to supply discipline and leadership. They do seem to thrive on and look for those two things. They realize their crime, and know years of repentance and labor are ahead of them. Also, this time they seem to know that they will be striving for something more permanent than that which they worked for before. The reason I have confidence in their future is because of their obvious strong religious beliefs. Millions have continued to worship secretly inspite of Hitler's threats. I hope and pray everything works out well. Basically, German people don't differ much from us. They believe in one God, everyone's God, too. My worry for future reference is Japan. I'm positive peace will win out in the end for everybody forever.

And, now let me turn to the four grand letters I have here from you. dated the 5th, 11th, 13th, and 16th. They cover a lot of swell days and news. The set for Marcy sounds tops!! And, already I have news from her telling me how much she likes it! Thanks a million, Mother. I'm so glad you were "extravagant." I can't think of a better investment. Hmmm. She was thrilled with it! You are A wonderful secretary, Mother. And, that reminds me, this will probably reach you almost on Mother's Day. I can hear you saying now, "Don't give me anything, please." It seems funny to even mention that you are the most wonderful mother anyplace. I'll be thinking of you, and will be with you all day the 14th, just as I think of you so very, very often.

Gosh, but the garden sounds wonderful. You are working on it! It would be nice if you discovered the thrill of fishing, Mother. -- Hot Dogs! I just heard someone yell mail call. I'll be back in a flash, maybe with more news from you.

A letter from Joanne and one from Kenny. Joanne's was number 11. Since I got 9 on Sunday, only 10 is missing. She sent two perfectly darling pictures of Joey. I'm sending them on to Marcy. You, no doubt, have them already. I didn't manage the birthday letter to Joanne the 23rd. I will get to write her soon, though. I'm so glad she is sending the dictionary. As yet I haven't received any packages. I will very soon, though, I'm sure.

I do want to talk to Grandfather sometime. I wonder if he would laugh too much at my faulty German. It is bad! We'll have many evenings of conversation. You and I have been doing many things too numerous and maybe too important to record in writing. It will be grand to talk about them. I'm still counting on the year 1947 as being the homecoming date for most of us.

Ol' man weather has been a rascal lately. Now the ground is covered with snow. Never has the weather been really discomforting - only a little rascally. Rain, hail, snow, and sunshine have been taking turns. It's about time for the sun now, too. Beautiful blossoms still rate first in catching our eyes. Spring is foremost, even if winter is trying to snow it under.

It's time for chow. Since I'm pretty sure I'll be saying "hello" again tomorrow, I'll close for today. The news and future is grand. All our prayers are bound to be answered soon.

(Note on bottom of letter written by Mother: "Joanne, please send these on to Ellen as soon as possible. The radio says the 86th will go to the Pacific, via U. S. in July.")

May 4, 1945
Germany

A full stomach, a warm room, and a rather quiet atmosphere send my thoughts spinning lazily homeward. Sunday afternoons after one of your super meals, Mother, I used to slump happily into this same mood. So expect this note to be one of rather mediocre content (as are most of my letters, I fear). I have things I want to talk with you about, but the mood might dull the "sharpness" of the conversation. If you'll put up with this sleepy attitude, I'd love to bother you for the next hour or so.

This morning I wrote Joanne a letter. Also, I slipped a V-mail in the mailbox to Kenny. Last evening's mail call brought two swell V-mails from Ellen and one from Westfield. Perhaps I can drop a line to Ellie yet today, too. Since she'll be home in a month or so, I sort of feel these letters to you are going directly to her also. I do appreciate the system of sending my notes to you around the family circle, but I like to say a direct "hello" ever so often if it's at all possible. By the way, speaking of services such as the letter rotation system, I do like the grand job my secretaries do for me. Mother, Ellen assists me, too, as you probably know. The two of you take care of my interests for special dates admirably. Thanks a million!

Recently I've been recalling your suggestions that it would be nice if I could be a member of the medical corp. They do perform a magnificent job. Over here they undergo all our hardships and actually take more chances. I've seen them go through their duties, and certainly their job is a most worthy one. If I had foreseen the important task they do I might have been more anxious to be one of such a helpful group, when I had the opportunity. Once or twice I've had a chance to help out in that capacity. One evening a surprise ambush caused us to seek cover quickly. Just as I was crawling into a ditch the man in front of me got hit. The bullet, a 20 mm tracer, knocked him into the ditch near me. The platoon medic was 30 yards away. The wound was simply a large hole easy to bandage. In a couple of minutes I was able to fix it up and give him his wound tablets. He wasn't in pain so the whole maneuver was simple. He had to wait only a short 15 or 20 minutes before we had neutralized the ambush making it possible for him to be evacuated. The handy first-aid packets we each carry makes the administration of first-aid a simple manner. Incidentally, yesterday we got a letter from the fellow, a buddy platoon member, and he's recovering excellently.

And here I wonder at the advisability of relating such a simple story. Does it cause you to worry more? You know I am in a combat area and you realize we are having experiences of this type. But I wonder if it is wise to write explicit events. You might imagine a thousand additional things that didn't take place at all. Hmmm. Let me know if you care to hear some of the more interesting exeriences. I don't believe in "combat story silence." It's natural to discuss events which are so powerful in ones mind. If ever you have any questions or fears please express them pronto.

Here I might tell you that I honestly believe combat to be less dangerous than I had thought. Veteran units attached to us have told us we were meeting "rugged resistance." I didn't think it was bad. So again I say, only this time with more of a background, please don't do any unnecessary worrying! We are safe here. You in civilian life have more things to worry about, I do believe.

You would laugh to see my moustache. It takes a full two weeks before it can even be put into that category. Another few days just to prove to myself that it can be done (why I want to do that I don't know) and I'll whisk it off.

One of my squad members, Tikvica, the orcharder, is on a seven day pass. He's spending it at the Riviera in France. An airplane transported him there. No matter where we are or what we're doing, if the order comes down for "one man for a pass," they find the man. In one of the rifle companies thc messenger received a slight wound crawling up to inform a lucky "Joe" that he was on schedule for a "vacation." Such unexpected pleasure has caused some humor loving G.I.'s to hope for a pass as "88's" are bursting about them. Ha-Ha.

Today we received some pay. For an entire month my expenditures have amounted to zero. Consequently I have over twenty dollars in my billfold in spite of the 78 dollars I'm saving monthly. Probably I'll be sending more home one of these days.

I have received two very interesting letters from Bob Rahn. I do want to re-continue our correspondence. Bob is a fine fellow. A glance at my watch (which is still running perfectly) shows it's only three o'clock. Maybe I can write two or three more letters today. Wow, six would be a record for me. Marcy is next, maybe then Ellen and Bob. Gee, I also owe Tommy a note, too. Did I tell you Mr. Shipps wrote a nice letter?

Perhaps the war in the E.T.O. will actually be finished in a few days. The news we get is wonderful. Still, it may be awhile yet. All our prayers and hopes are for a quick finis, naturally. May the next letter be written with even better news surrounding us. Till then.

May 8, 1945
Germany

It's six o'clock in the morning, and it is a beautiful morning! I just returned from guard duty. I don't feel the least bit sleepy, so I'm going to take advantage of this quiet atmosphere for a letter home. The rest of the boys won't be awake for another hour.

Last night we received word that the war is officially over. The last four or five days have been filled with rumors bearing the same glad tidings. Now with the arrival of the actual word, the men aren't showing much excitement. It's impossible to feel the immensity of the wonderfulness the change from fighting to peace brings. Everyone throughout the world is thanking God. Our prayers have been answered. The final goal toward which we are striving is coming nearer and nearer. I'm sure God will find it right to help us speedily find the complete finis we're concentrating our prayers on now.

Your letter of the 27th arrived last night. Needless to

say, I was shocked and so sorry to read of Merrill's death. He played a complete part in bringing about this surrender in Europe. In civilian life his influence did count. And in war I know his life was well spent. This peace for which he died is the beginning of a new and wonderful world. The price which he paid, along with the thousands of others who have sacrificed their lives, will certainly buy a better world. It's sometimes difficult to understand and justify such deaths. However, with a faith in the future and what we're aiming for, the many shortened earthly lives are accounted for. Hardships and sacrifices seem to always precede really worthwhile achievements. In today's upheaval the world is at stake. Thusly, human lives experience the hardships and are the sacrifices.

My thinking is muddled this morning. It's difficult for me to express adequately what I would like to say concerning Merrill's death. I am thankful such a vast area has once again had peace restored to it. And, I do know Merrill died knowing it was for the most worthwhile cause men have died for.

I'm so glad the box arrived in good condition. I hope the future finds me mailing more things home. I have a swastika I'd like to mail you. And I believe I could find several nick-nacks (sp?) to fill a box. Censorship regulations are pretty stiff on outgoing packages. However, it shouldn't be difficult to get some things by. Time has been the only real barrier up till now. We should be having more of that, so look for a package one of these days.

Saturday and Sunday found us moving about a little. That's why the no letter period. Yesterday was just a busy wash Monday. I love to travel in this country. It is beautiful over here. You know, I have seen the Alps! There is beauty! Yes, and I have been on the Danube River. I'm wondering if the Danube is what you were referring to in connection with the "Newsweek" and April 26th? I have traveled quite a bit here. The many places are terribly interesting. A few additional cities I have been in or near are Freising, Ingolstatt, and Hieberg. Maybe someday I'll be able to trace my whole route from Le Havre to Cologne to Altena to here. It is fun to look over.

With the finis of this part of the war, rumors are again flying as to what the future will find us doing. I'm very sure we'll have time on our hands for weeks to come. Some very fanatic S.S. men are still holding out in some sectors, but surely even they will cease their hostilities soon.

It's seven o'clock and I better wake the fellows up for breakfast. Be back in awhile.

Ah, a nice big, hot breakfast. Scrambled eggs, hot cereal, bacon, and grapefruit juice make me feel comfortably full. Many of the fellows are having tummy troubles. For over thirty days we had no more than ten prepared meals. The other 80 were K rations, C rations, and 10 in 1 rations. I think you are familiar with the K and C rations. The 10 in 1 ration is a large cardboard box full of food for a whole day for ten men. Our stomachs did become accustomed to smaller amounts of food. Going back on a more bulky diet has caused a little trouble. Two evenings ago my tummy acted up, but I have felt just swell since then.

Marcy continues to comment on her birthday present. She does like it! Thanks so much for finding such a nice gift, Mother. Have you found a suitable time for her to visit you yet?

Yesterday's mail brought another grand letter from Joanne. I had to smile at her mix up on the number for the letter. Twelve was correct, but she thought it might be ten. The home we're sharing with some people houses a baby boy named Hansie, age two. I keep comparing some of his tricks with what I imagine Joey to be doing. Gosh, Hansie is dumb! Joey knows ten times as much, really. But Hansie is cute, and I have lots of fun throwing him up into the air. He loves it, too. A nine year old girl named Anna lives here along with her eleven year old brother Siegfried. Both are nice and congenial. They are eager to learn English. I'm afraid some of the fellows have taught Siegfried some rather rough phrases. Hmmm. It was darling of Joey to call his mommy cooky. He is learning quickly. And, he can identify sentiments with his vocabulary, Mighty bright boy!!

The news on the annual meeting was interesting. I'm so glad everything is going so well. Your substituting sounds like great fun, Mother. Daddy, I'm surprised at your French. You translated the perfume label well. I have forgotten most of my French already. I'm still working on the German, though.

Perhaps a little later today I'll be back again. For now there are some duties to take care of. I will write again soon.

P.S. Please express my sympathies to the Nidays.

May 10, 1945
Germany

Since my last letter I've been doing some spring cleaning on my correspondence. A recent mail call brought letters from Wayne Gibson and Mother Crandall (Delta Tau Delta house mother at Ohio Wesleyan). So I answered theirs and also wrote Packy McFarland, Bob Rahn, and Jim Hader (all OWU friends). It's a nice feeling to have caught up a bit. The last few months I have been neglecting letters that I've wanted to write. We are having welcome time on our hands now. It's difficult to tell how long it will last, so I'm putting it to use while it's present. Yesterday's mail call brought two letters from you, an air mail of the 21st and a V-mail written the 20th. It is good to hear from you so regularly. The particualr thrill receiving letters from the family and Marcy brings will never die.

This afternoon we're making a ball diamond again. Isn't that great? It's symbolic of the change from war to peace over here. I am so very thankful for the ways things are progressing. You know, it will be exciting to get your letters telling about your celebrations and feelings upon receiving the actual word. I'll bet it was a gala day.

Before some recent experiences become faint in my mind, I'd like to record them. Diaries have been forbidden, but I don't think anyone would have any objections to a few stories. I'd rather spend a little time writing them rather than hurriedly relating them to you in letters.

I'm wondering exactly what my financial status is at home. March, April, May and this coming June should net the usual 30 dollars a month to you plus the $18.75 bond. Beginning in July, the 30 bucks will jump to $35. How much do I have, not including these overseas allotments? It's probably very little because of the gifts, furloughs, etc., that caused happy money to be drawn from that small collection of bonds. I'd like to know the amount, though. If ever you see some thrilling investment you would like to make, feel free to count me in. I'd love to put my cash with any you and Daddy are putting to work. In fact, I wish you would find something worthwhile to use my money on. Do use it at your own discretion.

I just returned from swinging a scythe for an hour and a half. It was fun! I stripped to the waist and let the sun beat on me full force. It was a wonderful feeling. We have the field cleared now for the diamond. As soon as we sink a few bases, we'll be ready to go. By then the athletic equipment should have arrived, too. With such wonderful weather, a swell ball league is bound to get off to a flying start. This time it's not apt to get interrupted by the duties that called us half way through our last baseball schedule. A lot of happy days are before us.

To be frank with you, I'm a little afraid of having too much free time. Inactivity is one of my worst enemies. I hate to just sit around. If such a seemingly preposterous fate does arrive, I have some plans to combat it. I want to read lots and lots. I'd like to write more, improving my style and vocabulary. (At times I'm positive I'm almost illiterate. I don't see how you stand such letters.) Also, I want to regain the habit of writing more interesting things, if censorship will allow it. Probably the army will take care of much more time than we wish it to. No doubt I'm outlining a problem impossible to arise.

How soon does Ellen actually arrive home? Her two V-mails of the 11th and 12th were interesting. The fellow who was overseas for three years and is now studying to raise fish must have been a dreamer and planner. Lots of guys will have good useful ideas after the war. Speaking of fish, the buddies tell me there's a stream a mile and a half from here just overflowing with trout. Maybe I'll have a chance to have a try at trout fishing.

The latest in C.R. (censorship regulations) allows us to tell about towns within a 25 mile radius. So, I will say that Salzburg isn't far off. And, today a group of fellows went sightseeing at Berchtesgarden. (sp.?) (I may get a chance to visit there.) Also, Branau, Hitler's birthplace, isn't far off. Guess where I am??? Hmmm.

I appreciate your regular air mail stamps which you enclose. Sometimes our mail clerk is unable to get them. Ever so often I almost run out. Please keep it up. I enjoyed John Donne's quotation. What a great preacher he must have been. I do wish you would mail me another complete sermon, Daddy. I really am hungry for words such as yours.

It's so queer seeing the many German soldiers walking the roads unescorted. Most of them are heading for predesignated points of discharge, processing, or something. Last night I got a thrill. For the first time since the U. S., we were allowed to show lights. The habitual black-out rules were out-moded. It was positively glorious to look out over the countryside seeing flickering lights shining forth from many a house. Vehicles drove around brazingly showing headlights which seemed much lighter than I ever remembered them to be. Each beam of light seemed to say, "Christ is the light of all darkness." Even the stars were shining brighter than usual. It was a moving, unforgettable evening.

Enough for today. A note to Marcy and then I will begin my notebook. Probably I'll mail the stories on to you as I write them. I hope everything is just super at home.

May 13, 1945
Germany

Today is Mothers' Day! And, we are remembering and thinking about it! I would so love to be with you actually, Mother. However, I feel sure that you know just how much I am thinking of you and loving you. It is easy to picture exactly what you'll be doing this morning. What an immense and wonderful job it is to be first lady of a church. All day today you'll be a mother to hundreds, just as you are really all week. And everybody connected with you will realize how wonderful you are. But, they can't know that as much as I do. It seems funny to even begin describing the love and devotion that a son has had for a mother for almost twenty years. In fact, it's almost impossible to reduce something so great and so everlasting to mere words. I don't believe I'll attempt it. I will tell you, Mother, that I know you are the most perfect of all mothers. I am thankful for you and the millions of things you have done and are constantly doing for me. I pray that I may be more worthy of being your son as time goes by.

The day is positively luscious. Each day this week has been perfect plus. Today seems to be the best yet, though. Mother nature is putting in her bid for recognition today. We are enjoying her, too.

Yesterday I wrote a rather dry account of the exciting sightseeing trip a group of us took the 11th. (See the Appendices for this.) I'm sending it in a separate envelope written crudely and in pencil. I'm mailing practically the same story to Marcy, so don't think of sending yours on. I wish I had had a camera and had taken hundreds of pictures. We saw some perfectly gorgeous scenery. I met Lewis Stevers at the lake I mention in retelling the trip. It was a nice surprise. We talked together for some five or ten minutes. He's looking fine. He was sightseeing with another medical officer and a chaplain. Do tell Mrs. Stevers that we got together for a short visit. Probably he'll be writing her about the beautiful scenery, too.

Yesterday's mail call brought two letters from you and one from Joanne. Yours were written the 18th and the 24th; Joanne's the 27th. How exciting that Mrs. Rawson is actually going to be Ted's cook. She sounds excellent for the job. I hope she still is there when I get a chance to return. This wonderful summer weather makes me eager for camp days. I've been talking with one of my buddies who lives near a Texas ranch which has been remade into a boys' camp. I wonder about the possibility of someday having a camp in the West. It would be wonderful for the boys to combine a long trip across the states plus a camp season. Truly ideal would be a camp over here for U. S. fellows.

Have you read about the point system? My total number will be in the thirties, depending on the number of battle stars we'll get. (It's rumored we may receive three.) The announcement of the huge sports program being introduced here is swell. Next I expect a similar program for education. The army is taking care of us in grand style, as usual.

In one of Marcy's three letters of yesterday, she told of a Wesleyan girl friend who is accompanying her to camp. I'm familiar with her and she is rather nice. They'll have a fine time together. Perhaps this might cause Marcy to miss out on a visit with Joanne. I hope not, though!

Jean Ratliffes' talk on college life sounded interesting. The future should find many more attending school. Yesterday afternoon a bunch of us talked over colleges we had attended. It was just a bull session with a lot of guys listening and adding their ideas. Yale, Texas U., Alabama, and O. W. U. were represented. Many other fellows have attended many other schools, but it just happened that those four had representatives yesterday. Several fellows still wonder about what they'll want to study. It is a tough problem. Lots of guys want to attend college who formerly didn't plan on it.

The conference at San Francisco is accomplishing things. All of us anxiously read every bit of news we can find. I'm especially interested in Mr. Molotov's words. He says so little, and is so careful. Do send on any interesting articles on the topic. We will have time to read, and certainly we're interested.

I'm hoping by now you will have read a line or two about the whereabouts of the Blackhawks. Several of the fellows have received news from home saying they have seen us mentioned in the papers.

It's almost time for church. I'll mail this and be on my way. I hope the service is dedicated to mothers, as I know church will be at home. The sermon won't be as good as Daddy's, but the sentiment will be present. I'll write again soon.

May 16, 1945

Germany.

I have missed writing you since Sunday. These past days have found us moving again and getting reorganized in our new setting. Now we are out of Austria and the countryside and in Germany near a city. The move was quite a long one. Our set-up took a definite change for the better, though. We are living in a large apartment house. Each squad has at least two rooms with a kitchen and bathroom to boot. We really couldn't ask for much better. We have no beds, but our arrangement for sleeping on the floor is fine. Beds became a luxury long ago anyhow. Right across the street is a soccer field which we are using for baseball. Yes, this set-up is OK!

We are back on a regular schedule. It reminds me a little bit of army days in the states. However, much more time is being given to athletics. Every afternoon from 2 o'clock till 4:30 we play baseball. A good battalion league has been formed. In fact, this afternoon we already played our first game. Sorry to report, a loss, too. We let "L" Company beat us 9 to 3. We had an "off" day, I guess.

Tonight one of our better educated officers (four years of college, mostly math) is conducting - and here you find me roaring with laughter. Just as I wrote "conducting," we stoogents were called to our class. The class was in calculus!! Did I understand much of it?? Oh, golly!! Trouble is, many of my comrades called it elementary. My head is swimming! We have eight elementary (???) problems for homework tonight. My whole trouble is very obvious. In calculus, algebra is used as a tool. Since this dope is a very "dull tool" when it comes to using that tool, it's plain to see that I am sunk!! Perhaps I'll try a couple more classes to see if I can swim out of this whirlpool. I do doubt it, though.

Your delightful letter written the 30th arrived this

evening. I'm glad you found some printed word about the 86th. It's fun to know that we were in the news. Most exciting of all the news you wrote was the possibility of a move from Gallipolis. I'll be just as anxious to get the word now as I ever was! I did chuckle at your little story about papa preachin' and mama packin'. By the way, anything you find of mine that looks like junk, throw it away. Feel free to clean up things in that room.

Speaking of moves, it may turn out that we will also be changing theaters of operations. It would mean a wonderful opportunity to view more of this fascinating world. However, my sightseeing urge isn't intense enough to make me really anxious to see that busy area. Whatever we do, or wherever we are, I do hope we play an important part in hastening that final day. I'm trusting things to turn out for the best, as they usually do. There's bound to be a period of question that will last a month or so anyhow. We'll see what comes.

Very recently I was actually in Munich. It's a fascinating city. Its architecture and design is unique. Although much of it is in ruins, It's easy to see that it was a place of beauty and interest. Also, I passed through Heidelberg. It was during the night, and I was unable to see much. I looked for college buildings, but couldn't spot any.

Do send the sermon "Peace on Earth." I really would love to read it. Probably you will when my other requests for one of your sermons start rolling in. Are my letters reaching you pretty regularly now? I hope so.

Tonight three more letters arrived from Marcy. In one she mentioned writing you. You've probably received it already. Goodness, but I do love Marcy!! She is as wonderful as possible. If by some chance (one in a million) I should get home before VJ day, I would like to give her a diamond. If I don't, though, I'm content to wait till I'm in "civies." She will be wearing it long enough, anyhow.

Although now the urge is to marry her as soon as possible, I know that will have to wait until after college. With that in view, school is apt to go by more swiftly and successfully, I know.

Today's mail brought a March Digest. I see I haven't read that issue, so there are some happy minutes ahead. I do enjoy reading good material. I'd love a magazine subscription for my birthday. Hmm.

Being on a regular schedule again makes for a better chance to write you more regularly. I hope I can keep a stream going your way in a more constant manner. This is enough for this evening. I want to write Marcy a note and then tackle those calculus problems. (Oh, me!) (I think more interesting courses are in the offing.) So till tomorrow, or soon, anyhow, I'll say "goodnight."

May 18, 1945
Germany.

Last night was truly an evening of pleasure. Right after a delicious supper (chow is extra-special now!), we had a small mail call. Two more fine letters came from you. The news that you had finally received three letters, after two and a half weeks of no mail from me, made me very happy. Just as I finished reading your letters the announcemnet came down that there was to be a movie shown at 7:30. The cinema was something we had forgotten about for the past two months, so that was good news, too. I planned to attend the movie, and decided to get real ritzy and clean up completely. Sooo, I heated lots of water and soaked in one of two bathtubs we have in the house for a whole half hour. What a luxurious feeling. It was the first bath or shower I had had since Cologne. 'Course I had washed in streams or from buckets, etc., since then; but a real bathtub or shower was another thing I hade almost forgotten about.   After scrubbing and soaking and scrubbing and soaking, I put on some new underwear I had found on the bottom of my pack. A shave and some hair oil even made me feel as if I were going on a date. It was fun to be so particular and leisurely in the usual routine procedure of cleaning up.

A whole gang of us went to the movies. Some good newsreels and football shorts were shown. The main feature was a "Phantom" show. It wasn't very good, so we left early. On returning to our apartments,   we found that the barracks bags which we had left in Cologne had caught up with us. It was fun unpacking them and finding that we had more things than we had recalled.

I never explained to you very fully the amount of equipment we carried with us. In preparing to move into reserve for combat duty, we stowed all extras in our barracks bags, and they were taken away to be stored for the duration. The essentials we placed in our packs along with our bed rolls. When we actually went on-line, our packs were stored in a rear area. All we carried was our raincoats over our belts. The sleeping bags were carried in our Jeep trailers which were always nearby.   With this system, it wasn't at all unusual to go a week or ten days without changing clothes. Most of the time we carried extra socks in our pockets or helmets. However, the rest of the clothes were worn continually till we were returned to a rest area where our packs would join us. I wore the same pair of O.D. trousers for six weeks without washing. (Do I hear a light gasp, Mother?) A regular dusting with louse powder, just in case, kept them in fine shape. The varying weather, such as washing rains and purifying sun, cleaned them pretty well on me, too. I happened to be short on trousers, with no substitutes to wear while scrubbing those. That's the reason for the long period of "no wash."

I smiled at your remarks about the censor. I think he

stopped reading my letters long ago, not because they were free from barred "info," but because the writing is too small and the letters are too long. In fact, he mentioned that fact to me quite awhile ago. I could probably tell you many things and get away with it. But, I don't think you would be very interested anyhow. Incidentally, don't fail to ask me questions of any sort. And, do tell me where my letters fall short. Not having any profs around to correct me, I count on your remarks to set me right on things in general.

I have a request for my birthday. The two pens I use alternately aren't very good. If you could find a better one, I would love to have one. Of course, that would do away with my only excuse for my poor writing. Hmm. But, I'm willing to trade.

It's now time for lunch. Since I have more to say, I'll drop out for a few minutes and then return.

Goodness, what a meal! A steak that actually covered the mess kit, and was tender, was the big thing on the menu. Diced carrots, mashed potatoes, lettuce, and crushed pineapple were the supporting dishes. A big cup of iced tea was the perfect drink for such a warm day. Really an excellent meal! Sounds good, too, doesn't it! Rumor has it that homemade ice cream is to be served tonight! There's a luxury I haven't even dreamed of since the states. Yum. Yum.

You can see that we are getting the very best of care now. Every possible thing that can be done for our pleasure is being acted upon. An announcement came out this noon that all those with brothers or sisters in the E. T. O. should hand in their names. Arrangements for a meeting would be made! Isn't that grand!!

Each day now two or three men from the platoon go on sightseeing tours to nearby places. The group that left today visited Heidelberg. Also, a few men are getting three day passes. They are zoomed into France for their frolicking. MIghty super, don't you agree! Since I went on the visit to Berchtesgaden, my turn for another jaunt similar to that won't come for awhile. 'Course I'll let you know when it does.

As I mentioned to you before, I believe we are no longer members of the army you mentioned. We switched to another fighting group just before the end of hostilities. You probably guessed that when I wrote of being in Austria.

Each day I'm adding to my vocabulary. The Readers Digest offers good words. If anything is apt to stand still in army life, it's ones vocabulary. Also, diction might slip a little. Bill Herndon, the brother Delt from Texas U., and I help each other on both of these. Maybe some interesting classes on similar subjects will develop after awhile.

Yesterday I figured up the amount of money I should have saved by the end of May. If all my war bonds were still intact, and all my allotments had reached you by June 1st, I should have $517.50. That includes the $90 in my soldiers' deposit. Have I sent enough money home via money orders to make up for the bonds I've used? Or, did I ever use any of those bonds? I'm not sure exactly what that status is. $517 is a pretty good sum, though.

I am glad you have made plans to have Marcy visit. Does she think she'll be able to make it then? I hope so!!

We play "I" Company in baseball in just a few minutes. We all have pretty good tans, or beginnings for good tans. The daily baseball period gives us lots of wonderful sun.

I'll write again Sunday or sooner. Do say "hello" to people for me. I think of many often to whom I'd like to send special greeting. So long for now.

May 21, 1945
Germany.

Saturday and Sunday were packed full of interesting and exciting events. I really don't know where to begin telling you about them all. Yesterday's announcement abrogating censorship leaves me with hundreds of things to say, too. Count on more lengthy letters for a couple of weeks.

Since I last wrote Friday, I'll begin recounting the many activities of the weekend starting with Saturday. In the afternoon we had our regular sports schedule. An hour of football plus a couple hours of baseball gave us all good rosy suntans. In the evening a group of us boarded trucks and drove to Mannheim (4 kilometers) for a movie. The theatre was much better than the Friday night building we attended. Soft seats, air conditioned, a seating capacity of 1500, it was a real honest-to-goodness theater. Luckily it hadn't been bombed. Most of the buildings in Mannheim are gutted. The air corp hit the city heavily. The movie was "To Have and Have Not." I had seen it before, but rather enjoyed it again. However, I have lost my enthusiasm for movies. Reading or conversing seem to be better ways to spend an evening.

Sunday morning I had a delightful detail. It was my duty to locate a good area for the battalion church service. Also, I placed guides to direct the church-going fellows to the site. We found a lovely shady spot. Not far away were enough boards and "horses" to make several bleachers. We managed to set up seats for almost one hundred. It was fun arranging things for church. It did remind me of home! The service was well attended. As many had to stand as there were seats. So, at least two hundred fellows were present.

In the afternoon, all who wished to visit Heidelberg were allowed to make the trip. Naturally, I eagerly accepted the offer. Heidelberg is only 11 miles from here, which is a short quick ride on the "Autobahn." In contrast to

Mannheim, Heidelberg had hardly a bomb dropped in its limits. It's a peaceful, picturesque city. Excellent facilities have been set up by the Red Cross to take care of visiting soldiers. A beautiful, large building is filled with waiting rooms, libraries, ping pong tables, pool tables, historic displays, sleeping rooms, information desks, coffee and donut bars, showers, and just everything. The building is built in the shape of a "U." In the center of the "U" is a garden complete with rows of beautiful flowers, fountains, brick walks, and a concert platform. Each Sunday afternoon the Heidelberg Symphony performs in this charming setting. And, you can bet that I took advantage of the opportunity to hear a group of German musicians. The orchestra had only thirty members. It was well balanced, though, and had a fine quality. I'm enclosing the program. Because we had more to see in the town, we listened only until the interval or intermission. It seemed rather queer to applaud heartily a conquered people. Surely it's appropriate to approve of good acts. And, we did clap loudly. By sanctioning the good, they will probably show more respect for our many disapprovals of their wrong actions. As Americans, we certainly should show no cruel affectations. We love good music and should show our appreciation for a good performance. We hate unworthy ideals which are against God, and we should show it. I think we're on the right track.

During the concert a German artist went through the audience sketching different soldiers. He was talented! He gave the fellows their sketches to keep. I wasn't one of the lucky guys. He no doubt thought my face was impossible.

Our next place for a visit was logically and absolutely the college. The name of Heidelberg has always stood out in my mind ever since Doug, Ruth, Frank, Joanne, Mr. and Mrs. Feely and I saw the "Student Prince." The whole operetta was built around the old city and school. Needless to say, it was a thrill to look at the buildings. The university isn't really very large. It covers only three blocks or so. Most of the buildings are now new or renewed. We walked through a couple of them. As far as I could tell, no classes are being conducted for civilians. Some army classes have been formed. An army group command occupies some of the buildings. The school didn't compare with many of ours. Wesleyan ia a hundred times better, of course!!

And, now for the really exciting event of the weekend. Last night for two colossal hours I listened to Jascha Heifitz, the world famous violinist. Four were allowed to attend from our company. Only five of us were familiar with the name. Naturally we all wanted to go, so we did. It wasn't difficult sneaking in the extra man. The entire program was perfect. I don't ever expect to hear a better violinist. The first hour he played numbers of his own choosing. The next hour he played classical requests. I copied down some of the titles to send on to you: Bach's "Prelude," "Spanish Symphony," a number by Tchaikovsky, "Jamaican Rhumba" by Benjamin, "Trip to the Sun" by Rimsky Korsakov, a Victor Herbert selection, and "Gipsy Airs." A few of the requests were "Air on the G String" by Bach, "Toccata," "Intermezzo," and "Ave Maria." He spoke of Bach's music as "musical spinach, whether we like it or not." When he was requested to play "Toccata," he growled and said, "Here's the horrible "Toccata." He kept his frown all through the piece. He is definitely a supcrb violinist. I am happy to say I have enjoyed hearing him. It was a wonderful experience.

Saturday two fine letters came from you. They arrived in record time being mailed the 6th and 8th and arriving here the 19th. It was a thrill to read your reactions concerning the peace news. Gallipolis acted sanely and wisely. I'm glad you spent the morning with Mrs. Niday. Has any news come concerning Baxter or Tommy? I do hope they are OK. One town we occupied, Acbs (sp.?), had many American air corps men there as former prisoners. It was exciting to see their happy expressions.

Do you still have that cheap print Dick Arentsen, Jack Sarvis and I had taken at Alexandria that summer? Dick, you will recall, is the fellow who loves forestry. His father is in charge of the second largest forest in the U.S., located in Wyoming. I hadn't seen Dick since the states. Of course, I see Jack quite often. Yesterday Jack passed on to me the alarming news of Dick's death. He was killed by a sniper after crossing the Danube. Since he was in a different regiment, we didn't learn of it till yesterday. I am happy that I had the chance to know Dick. He was a fine fellow and a real friend. His death makes another terrible loss.

Saturday we were given our Combat Infantryman badges. They look exactly like the Expert Infantryman badge except that a wreath encircles the rifle. You have seen them worn, no doubt. They signify "Satisfactory combat duty against the enemy." (Who else would it be against, anyhow?) Also, they mean a five dollar jump in pay. (Ten dollars for those who don't have the Expert badge.)

I'm glad Manning has recovered. His talk at Y. F. sounded interesting. I like to get all the news about the fellows that you can find. Do you know Johnny Lupton's division? BY the way, we're living in Rhineau which is a suburb of Mannheim. Can you find it on the map? Next letter I want to list the big cities in the order that we passed through them. Then if you wish you can follow our complete route from LeHavre to here.

Saturday's mail brought a V-mail from Joanne. I had another letter from her earlier, but seem to have mislaid it. I'm sure I read that Ruthie was going to the east coast to see Doug for ten days or so. Gosh, I didn't dream that, did I? I'm positive I read that startling good news somewhere. I am glad Marcy is planning on a visit during one of her 48 hour passes.

I liked Mrs. Brashares' comments on Ellen. As if we didn't know how wonderful she is. Say, aren't you home by now, Ellen?

Maybe this will be too heavy when I enclose the program too. We'll try it anyhow. It's going to be fun to lick my own envelope for a change. Only if we prepare for a move will censorship come back into effect. It's fun and much nicer knowing this is going direct from me to you with no third party involved.

Enough for today. I'm anxious to hear all the conference news.

May 24, 1945
Germany.

This morning a bunch of us began retracing our route of travel. Goodness, but we're finding it difficult. We can't even agree on the path taken to Cologne. Since we went from Doudeville to Cologne (a 48 hour ride) in box cars, we didn't see much scenery or many towns. Our medic says the medical officers kept a good record. He's going to investigate it for us. Maybe next letter I'll be able to take you on that promised tour.

Some dates and facts I do recall may interest you. We left San Luis Obispo Feb. 4th. We arrived at Camp Myles Standish near Boston on the 10th. February 18th we boarded the S. S. Lejune, and the next day we were sailing out of Boston Harbor. March 2nd we docked at LeHavre, France. However, we remained on the ship until March 5th. That day we drove to Camp Old Gold located five miles from Doudeville. March 25th we started for Cologne. The two day ride got us there the 27th. April 6th (?) we left that city. I'll have to check on the other dates more completely before I pass them on to you.

Yesterday we had a parade. Several citations were read. A dozen men from our battalion were awarded bronze stars. Four were given for work done on patrol duty across the Rhine at Cologne. The others were given for feats accomplished in the Ruhr pocket and with Patton's 3rd.

Would you like to know the exact number of points I have toward discharge? Hmm. Nineteen points for 19 months of service, four points for overseas service of four months, five points for one battle star, and possibly an additional five points for another battle star yet to come. So, my score is 28, with a possible 33. It's fun to figure it. 'Course I realize I'll not be back in civies till the finis. I thought you might be interested in the system, though. Men with children get 12 points per child up to three children. I like the set-up immensely. I believe it will discharge those most deserving it.

The weather has been cool for the last two days. It's rather a refreshing change. However, I'll welcome the return of the sun.

On one occasion during combat I had to go into a stream. I got completly wet, and several papers in my billfold were ruined. One of the items was Dr. Nicholson's address in England. Would you mind sending a repeat on that? A few passes are being given to the U. K.

My chances for one are one in a million, but I'd like to have the address just in case.

Recreational facilities are excellent. In fact, the recreational phase has almost overshadowed the educational set-up. Even our one instructor has been postponing classes to hear Heifitz, go to Heidelberg, etc. The idea of studying calculus does not appeal to me anyhow. A personal tutor with lots of patience might get me interested, but I doubt it. I think other classes will be formed in the future. Probably the hour won't be so conflicting with the recreation, too. The program as a whole is still just developing.

The non-fraternization policy isn't holding very well. In fact, it's almost humorous to see how completely it's disregarded. All of a sudden all the German girls have become "Ruscis," "Polskis," "French," or "Hollanders." So far the problem hasn't become serious. I think it might, though, and I'm not in favor of it. I believe a rather stern attitude should be taken, at least until movies, books, and other enlightening methods have been used to inform Germans of what's what. A too friendly attitude now might give the impression that really we don't abhor some of the atrocities the people have committed. And, that would be bad. So for the sake of the Germans and the world, I believe in keeping my distance. Their re-education must start with the realization of what terrible things they've been doing. Our smiles, and even overtures (in some cases), certainly don't help the cause, as yet. I'm for the $65 fine supposed to be given for any breach of the policy. I hope the law is made active. I may make the situation sound serious. As yet it isn't, but a continuation of present practice will make it serious. It's difficult to ignore such similar people (in many ways similar), but it's absolutely necessary. Don't you agree with me?

There's a piano upstairs. However, we have no music. Some other pals are sending for a few numbers. Would you like to mail a "Twice 55" or something similar? We would appreciate it. I still carry the piccolo. It has a lovely tone. One key is broken, but it's still in very playable condition. Ever so often I play it a little.

I'm betting on some letters from you in tonight's mail. I wonder if it's too early to expect the conference news? We'll see in a short while. I'll write again soon.

May 27, 1945
Germany.

First and foremost - - last night a letter came from Marcy bearing this good news: Marcy now is a Phi Beta Kappa! Pretty nice, eh wot? I am happy about it. She deserves it so completely! I wanted to send on the exciting news right away. Marcy probably won't mention it to you. One sentence told me about it. I wish I could send flowers or candy or anything. I wrote a letter of congrats. I know she'll appreciate the same from you. She sent me some recent pictures. She's getting even more lovely! I hope you do have a chance to visit together. Of course, sooner or later you'll know her as well as you do us children. For she is going to be a daughter of yours someday.

Today's mail brought my first box. Yippee! As queer as it may seem, it was from Joanne. Perhaps your early ones were sidetracked someplace. No doubt they will arrive, though, now that the stream has started to flow. In the box is a German-English dictionary of superb quality. Pop corn, maple sugar, sardines, anchovies, melba toast, and chewing gum made up a delightful box. It was wonderful to receive it. The dictionary will help me with my German. It's a little difficult learning the language with the non-fraternization policy in effect.

This evening two letters came from Marcy plus two delightful V-mails from Ellen. I do appreciate the good secretary service Ellen is providing. It's exciting to read about Ellen's bridal shopping tours. It's hard to believe that my other sweet sister is about to become a Mrs. She will make a perfect one. Has the place and exact date been set as yet? It will be at the end of the summer, won't it?

The Delts are planning a serenade for Marcy and

some other Delta queens. I'm wondering if there might be a way that you could find out the date so some flowers could be sent. I'm afraid I'll learn of it too late. Probably the brothers will furnish the girls with beautiful bouquets, anyhow.

Bed time has been rather late recently. Interesting talking sessions have been keeping us up late. So, I'll hurry to bed pronto. I'll be writing again soon.

May 28, 1945
Germany.

A scrumptious package has arrived from home. It contained pop corn, cookies, a luscious box of chocolates, and peanuts. Everything has disappeared except the pop corn. Perhaps even that will be demolished tonight. The cookies were great! They didn't have even the slightest taste of stalenesss. They were delicious! Did I mention the marshmallows? We ate them the lazy way, not bothering to roast them. Thanks a million for everything. And, all the squad thanks you too, of course.

Yesterday I had the nice church detail again. Rain threatened to break up any outdoor service we might hold, so we used a nearby theatre. Attendance wasn't very high. However, the service was nice and very impressive. The chaplain spoke on the differences between beliefs and convictions. He claimed that even though we die for certain beliefs, we don't live by them. Beliefs we live by are convictions. The sermon was better than usual, and I enjoyed it. The chaplain is young with flaming red hair. When he gets excited or enthusiastic, he presents a better sermon.

Yesterday I got a nice long letter from Joanne. I'm glad to know that Joey has had his eye operation and is getting along so well. I do love to read about some of his antics. His interest in cars makes me smile (and puff out my chest). Gosh, but he is sweet. It almost seems that each letter reports a year's jump in his achievements. He's growing up quickly.

I've been using the dictionary quite a bit. It's an excellent book, so very complete. Not wishing to fraternize too much with the Germans, I'm finding it a little difficult to advance beyond the counting, etc., stage. I have learned some of the language, anyhow. I'm looking forward to the grammar. That should help a lot!

When does Ellen's camp season begin and end? She plans on having the wedding right after camp, doesn't she? And, where will it be? Is that still such a question of controversy? Surely this letter will find you at home, Ellen. Your last swell V-mail, come to think of it, said you might be home before it reached me, and that was written the 15th. And, I'm wondering again, are we still living in Gallipolis??? Conference should be over by now. I'm anxious for the news. How's your cooking, Ellen? If you want an expert group of "tasters" to give you an unbiased opinion, ship some cookies this way. Hmmm.

Each day seems to point more and more toward the fact that we are returning to the U. S. before going on to the Pacific. Just when the big move will come I'm not sure. If ever there is a long lull in the mail supply from this end, perhaps it means that my next letters will be written in the same country where you are. No doubt that's rather far off as yet, anyhow.

I had completely resigned myself to the fact that we wouldn't be seeing each other till all the guns had ceased firing. However, if another delightful interlude should be tossed my way, I'll eagerly grab it, of course! But, I'm still concentrating my dreams on that final day. That's a surer bet! It's too possible that no furloughs will be given. After all, only five months ago today I was visiting you. The furlough schedule has been good to us already. It seems too much to expect another.

The mail clerk picks up our letters in a couple of minutes. I'll close now to add this to the bunch. I hope things are working out favorably at home during these conference days. Things are bound to come out for the best, as always

June 2, 1945
France. V-Mail.

We're pausing for a day or so on our miraculous journey homeward. Yes, my wildest dreams are becoming nearer an actuality each day! I am coming home! We will be together again for at least two or three glorious weeks. Still, it all seems like a dream It's difficult to grasp the wonderfulness of it all. In a letter from Marcy this evening, she told of reading the grand news in the paper. Surely you know the news, too, by now. My only desire for the vacation period is to spend as much time as possible with you and Marcy. If it's possible, I'd like to buy the diamond for Marcy before the furlough finishes. I'm hoping like everything that I'll be home for a period before Ellen goes to camp. In fact, I do believe I'll be talking to you actually before this reaches you. Gosh, I'm not even sure that we are still living in Gallipolis. That's a minor detail. A phone call will fix that up super! - Two of your letters of the 22nd and 17th reached me tonight. It was good to hear from you again. Since Tuesday we have been on the move from Mannheim. We came by Jeep - I'm hoping to have a minute to at least phone Joanne from New York (if we land there). In case this reaches you before I do, I'll guess that you'll be hearing from me verbally by the 20th at least. It will be so positively superb to see you all again. We'll have a trillion things to talk about. I'm counting the seconds till then. Hoping to see you real soon!! Excitedly!!

CHAPTER TWELVE

SALSBURG & BERCHTESGADEN

The Salzburg and Berchtesgaden Visit
May 11, 1945
As Described by Sgt. W. Scott Westerman, Jr.
on May 12, 1945

Since the famous Hitler's hideout, Berchtesgaden, is only a three hour ride from our present location, division recreation officers saw an opportunity to conduct a small sightseeing tour for a few of the men. The city of Salzburg ,on the Inn River, is situated enroute to Berchtesgaden. Being also a city of historical and modern interest, the trip is doubly interesting.

A perfectly glorious morning put us in an eager, excited mood for the coming jaunt. Nine a.m. was the hour for departure, but 8:30 found us ready to go. Armed with neckerchiefs, K rations and goggles, we were prepared for the dusty, long ride. Remembering recent dangers and the presence of the defeated enemy, we carried our small arms. Most of us borrowed pistols, getting out of the cumbersome job of carrying rifles or carbines.

Surprisingly, the trucks pulled up at exactly nine

o'clock. Everything seemed against the regular army principles: a free ride for pleasure beginning sharply on time. Three weapons carriers seated sixty of us from our battalion. With the proper amount of squirming and cooperation we were all comfortably situated and the trucks began to move.

The ride was dusty but beautiful. Weaving roads and steep grades kept us at a sightseeing pace. Stately forests bearing deer sharpened our interest. The nearing towering Alps kept us watching for breathtaking views. Small villages popping up every ten kilometers or so offered further variety to the already varied scenic ride. Needless to say, pretty frauleins brought the loudest exclamations of praise from our group of typical G.I's. All along, though, different eyes showed unspoken exclamations of wonder at the sight of some stretching, snow capped mountains.

War wasn't absent from our otherwise peaceful ride. Often our trucks were slowed or stopped by convoys of defeated Germans heading for stations of processing. And men in all styles of uniforms were constantly seen. French, English, Yugoslavs, and an unidentified group wearing tassels on their caps predominated in the mixture. Huge bomb craters gutted the earth in many spots. Many abandoned vehicles littered the roadsides. Although Austria was spared the intensity of warfare that other sections of Germany suffered, she still show hundreds of unbandaged wounds.

We arrived in Salzburg at 12:30 p.m. With knowledge of the exact roads, the trip could have been made much more quickly (as we learned on the return ride). The city is nestled in a valley with parts of it scattered on the surrounding hills. Not as large as the advertised name might lead one to believe, Salzburg, nevertheless impressed us favorably. Stores were open, shoppers walked the streets, things seemed to be returning to normal. Women wearing lipstick and upswept hairdos almost caused us to wreck several times. Salzburg was definitely one of the more modern towns we had viewed in Germany. Two women sunbathing in two piece bathing suits convinced us of this fact. Hmmmm.

Berchtesgaden is located twenty-five kilometers beyond Salzburg. That being our main objective, we drove on. A German airport with perhaps fifty Kraut planes sitting about intact caught our interest on the outskirts of Salzburg. American wing men now had control, of course. However, so many undamaged enemy crafts was a new sight. Driving out of the airport was a truck load of aviators. The boys had slick creases and were clean to the toenail. We filthy, dust covered doughboys were an obvious exact opposite. Smilingly, we felt the difference, as did they, no doubt. One of our talkative lads yelled, "I haven't seen you guys since the states." Of course this was untrue, but the air corps buddies waved and gave us smiles which matched their sparkling uniforms.

The roads from Salzburg to Berchtesgaden are equal to ours in the United States. Hard surfaced and wide, they offer an excellent path into unbelievable scenery. All around us now the Alps were hovering. The snow seemed so close we began talking of skiing, sledding and winter sports. The scenery is best described by a quite elementary comparison. Picture the most beautiful travelogue cover you have ever seen. Multiply the beauty of that by the intensifying loveliness actuality brings and you have the heavenly picture. Beyond that I can say no more. As is always the case, when something of God's creation is extraordinarily wonderful, words fail miserably.

The town of Berchtesgaden is small and picturesque. Built on a plateau and extending up the slanting mountain, it looks typical of what one would imagine a town in the

Alps to be. A war conscious village, it has memorials to the
last war and to this one all about. In the square one long
building has four murals depicting the fight and fall of
Germany during 1914-1918 "for the cause of freedom, etc."
Several groups of G.I.'s were looking around rather
obviously just sightseeing. Women, very blonde and
wearing checkered skirts with harness and white blouse,
and men in shorts , almost caused us to believe a costume of
clothes was being worn for us. It was easy to guess the
scenes of merriment and pleasure summer vacationers must
have had in the picturesque village years ago.

As further proof that Berchtesgaden must have been a
traveler's haven, we drove into a delightful colony of hotels
surrounding a mirror like lake. Constructed in chateau
style with intricate woodwork designs and with
fenestrations made for enjoying the lovely view outside, the
arrangement of buildings was something impossible to
forget. Bathhouses, boathouses, and docks likewise seem to
melt into the natural scene. Persons of wealth must have
spent hundreds for a week or two of being part of nature at
its loveliest. Now rear echelon troops of the 15th Corp were
enjoying the superb beauty. Eating in the ritzy dining room
(officers were being served by a tuxedoed German),
sleeping in carpeted rooms, spending leisure hours rowing
or riding in launches on the lake, these men are perhaps the
best billeted troops in Europe. They are thoroughly
fortunate.

Also sharing this peaceful scene was a girls' school.
Seventy-five or a hundred spick and span girls between the
ages of 11 and 14 sat stiffly around tables in one of the
smaller hotels. (Two large hotels and two small ones made
up the group). Crocheting and sewing, they looked very
prim and well disciplined. It was thought provoking to
wonder what ideals they had been taught.

The officer leading our tour wasn't familiar with the

direct route to Hitler's hideout. For this reason, we drove about searching for an hour or so. Such inefficiency paid off for we did view persons and places we might have missed otherwise.

At two o'clock we finally arrived at our destination. A long winding road climbing upward for a full two miles took us to the hideout gateway. Many interested visitors shared our curiosity. Colonels, WACS, nurses, a French woman correspondent, English oficers, brass of all types walked slowly around viewing what at one time must have been the most beautiful and complete hideaway for any persons. G. I. guards were scattered about watching over wire installations and unexplored areas. They also acted as guides identifying the different ruins as Hitler's home, S..S. barracks, etc. The amount of destruction left most of the original scene to one's imagination. However, many rooms were still intact. One large high ceilinged room had an immense window at the far end. Naturally, now only the frame remained. It wasn't difficult to picture persons standing in front of the glass looking down and out over the sheer beauty. Never have I such a large window area. It must have been extraordinary, as the whole place obviously had been.

We were allotted only a short thirty minutes to look over the ruins and the rubble. We sought out some souvenirs about which we might build fantastic stories, and left satisfied at seeing the one and only Berchtesgaden. While fighting our way to the peace that finally came three days ago, we had asked many a frightened frau, "Where's Hitler?" (Vo ist Hitler?) Most had answered, "Berchtesgaden." Now we had seen the hideout. And now we knew Hitler wasn't there, or if he was, he had probably met a death fittingly similar to the many he had caused.

Returning we paused once again at Salzburg to examine a huge castle which stood majestically on a hillside.

After hiking up the steep embankment, we learned the ancient building was being used to house returning slave workers. Off limits to G. I.'s, we stopped only to look out over the city. The height offered another thrilling view. The curving light green Inn River which flows through the center of Salzburg was fun to follow with the eye. For miles one could see it winding through the valley until at last it disappeared in a thick growth of trees. Perhaps Mozart had fished in the stream. (Salzburg is his home.) No doubt Hitler had crossed it many times. Surely more important historically, we are now occupying its banks looking forward to a peace similar to that which it naturally portrays.

A quick ride back finished the delightful excursion. This time we knew the route. Only the beaten Germans crowding the roads slowed the return. It had been an interesting, exciting day, another one spent in Germany, which I'll never forget.

CHAPTER THIRTEEN

COMMENTS CONCERNING COMBAT

EXPERIENCES

COMMENTS CONCERNING COMBAT EXPERIENCES

This section is designed to provide some descriptions of experiences which couldn't be reported in letters because of the the censorship rules. It should be emphasized that recollections fifty years later may not be accurate. Therefore, only those items have been selected which remain most vividly in memory.

Accommodations

Once we left Camp Old Gold, we regularly slept in houses or apartments owned by German citizens. Our officers would require the residents to leave and we would move in. Consequently, we were comfortably housed. Since we were rarely in a location for more than one night, the owners weren't too inconvenienced. For the most part, we didn't disturb the places too much. (On more than one occasion, we traveled all night, sleeping as best we could in the trucks and jeeps. Such travel was very slow, since no lights were allowed.))

There was one exception to the above. When we arrived in Cologne, we took over an apartment where we stayed for four or five days. My squad shared a unit with another squad. Members of the other squad threw many pieces of valuable furniture out of our third story rooms in order to provide more space for our weapons and equipment. I objected, but was quickly rebuked by the other squad members who asked if I was a Kraut (German) lover. They reminded me that the owners were our enemies.

We're Really in the War : Our first Casualty

We received our first combat assignment shortly after arriving in Cologne. Our battalion was asked to form a patrol which would cross the Rhine in an effort to capture some German prisoners. Volunteers were requested. Since a machine gun was not needed for this expedition, a priority was assigned to riflemen. Nevertheless, I remember well the tension I felt when the plan was announced.

Two pontoon boats carried the riflemen across the river during the night. One rifleman was left on shore when the boats returned, apparently the result of a misunderstanding. The officer in charge of the boat which had carried the GI had thought he was going to return with the other boat. The next morning his body was found floating in the Rhine. He had been shot. Word spread quickly. We knew we were really in the war.

Rape

Four or five days after we arrived in Cologne, I was the sergeant of the guard during the night. While I was checking to make certain that the guards were in their proper locations, I heard a woman screaming "Hilfe! Hilfe! Hilfe!" ("Help" in German). At that moment an MP (Military Police) appeared and entered the apartment from which the screams were coming.

The next morning we left Cologne to join the battle in a different location. In the jeep, in addition to me, was the squad driver, Al Woeltjen, the first gunner, "Zig" Aziglio, and the second gunner, Isaac Villar. Isaac reported with great pleasure how he and three others had had sex with a German women. When she began to scream, they all jumped out of a window to avoid being caught. I had perceived Isaac as being a loving husband and father and was really upset that he would do this. For much of the trip that day, Al, Zig, and I chastised Isaac angrily. He rationalized his actions describing the woman as the "enemy." As disturbed as I was, it never occurred to me to report his behavior. Our attention was riveted on the next encounter with the German army.

Being Shot At Personally

There were, of course, many occasions when we were shot at as a company or as a squad. The most common attack was with mortars or 88's. Ack ack (anti-aircraft) guns were also used against us sometimes. On these occasions we would seek protection in ditches, behind small hills or in buildings, until we could mount a counter-offensive to neutralize the source of the fire.

One day we were on the approach march when suddenly we were subjected to machine gun and rifle fire. We were in an exposed position. The origin of the shooting was no more than a thousand yards away at the crest of a hill overlooking the road we were traveling. Our platoon sergeant, the person who normally would direct the placement of the machine guns, was not nearby, so I ordered the gun placed on the berm of the road, planning to return the fire. Before we could get a shot off, we were drawing fire to our location. Consequently, I asked the squad to seek cover while I scouted for a better location. As I ran up a slight grade which was lightly wooded, I realized that I was being shot at. I quickly hugged the earth and tried to crawl to a safer, less exposed area. The bullets literally whistled over my head, clipping some small tree limbs in the process. This was the only occasion on which I knew that I was the sole object of someone's shooting.

Shortly after this surprise attack, some other unit was effective in stopping the effort. We never did set up the machine gun to help with the counter-attack.

Firing at the Enemy

It is difficult to remember how frequently we actually fired the machine gun at the enemy. I doubt it was more than 12 to 15 times. I do know that because we were moving so quickly, we never had time to dig a gun emplacement, a strategy we had learned during our training. Typically we would find a relatively protected area and fire the gun from there.

Because machine gun targets are generally a fair distance away (the gun was reasonably accurate up to 1500 yards), it was hard to determine whether or not the shooting actually inflicted harm or casualties. On one occasion, however, when we were firing on an enemy machine gun nest, a white flag came out waving surrender. We knew, therefore, we had hit our target.

As squad leader, I don't remember personally firing the machine gun in combat. The first and second gunners carried that responsibility, the first gunner pulling the trigger and the second gunner feeding the belt which contained the bullets. It was my role to determine where the gun should be placed, to make certain it was set up properly, to be sure ammunition and water (the gun was water-cooled) were supplied as needed (there were two squad members who were ammo and water carriers), and to help direct the

fire. I frequently carried the fifty pound tripod on which the gun was mounted. Also, I always double-checked to see that the gun was cleared (the bullet being removed from the chamber) before it was dismantled.

My personal combat weapon as squad leader was an M-1 rifle. I remember cleaning it regularly, suggesting I did fire it. However, I don't recall ever putting a specific enemy soldier in my gun sight.

Caught on the Jeep

The sudden sound of a German fighter plane strafing the roadway on which we were traveling caused us to abandon our jeep and jump into a ditch for protection. Three of the four of us exited successfully. Second gunner Isaac Villar did not. As he jumped over the side of the jeep, the handle of the shovel on his backpack interlocked with the handle on the side of the jeep. In his panic he didn't know how to extricate himself. Fortunately he was not hit.

I'll never forget the look of terror on his face as his arms and legs flailed and flopped as he tried to get free. We all kidded him about it after the episode was over.

The Role of Airplanes

We traveled many roads which showed evidence of the effectiveness of the strafing done by Allied planes. Destroyed weapons, vehicles and horses were scattered along the berms. There were also the bodies of dead German soldiers.

The event described above is the only occasion on which I recall being strafed by German planes.

By the time the 86th entered the war, I believe the air was controlled by Allied planes. I do remember witnessing, however, a dogfight between an American P-1 and a German fighter. Neither shot down the other, but it was fascinating to watch their aerial acrobatics.

While the air force was an important and essential ally for the ground forces, infantrymen generally disdained the "flyboys." Pilots were viewed as receiving undeserved recognition and pay since they were removed from the "real war," i.e., that which was fought on the ground.

Heroism after a Surprise Attack

One afternoon we were marching through a small German village where the residents greeted us warmly. I was impressed with their smiles and friendliness. A few hundred yards beyond the village, however, we were ambushed by an ack ack gun. (Ack ack guns which are normally used to shoot down aircraft were used by the Germans against ground forces toward the end of the war.) The man directly ahead of me was hit in his buttock tearing away a major portion of it. (I describe in one of my letters the way I was able to stanch the bleeding by wrapping the wound while we both were seeking protection in a small stream which ran along the side of the road.)

Suddenly I heard nearby machine gun fire. Fewer than 10 yards away on the other side of the road were Cy Troyan and Karl Spivak, first and second gunners in the companion machine gun squad in our platoon, standing upright fully visible and vulnerable, firing toward the location of the 20 mm gun. They rested their gun on a fence post and were blasting away fiercely and effectively. It was truly a miracle they were not killed. Apparently they hit their target so quickly it was impossible for the enemy to fire back. Their action was truly heroic.

Death and Dying

I was a few yards away from a German soldier courier who had been shot while riding a small motorcycle. We were alternatingly crawling and running across a field and roadway. While I was crawling near him, I realized he was still alive. He looked at me with fearful yet pleading eyes. I kept going wondering whether or not our medics would minister to him. I never found that out.

On another occasion, three or four of us were in a bomb crater seeking protection from enemy fire. In the crater was a recently killed German. One of the men took the German Lugar pistol from the dead man's holster "as a souvenier." I remember being uncomfortable with that action, just as I felt uneasy lying so close to a dead man.

While in a building to avoid mortar fire, I was in a room where a chaplain was administering last rites to a GI who was dying. I was aware of the peculiar sound emanating from his voice which I assumed to be the "death rattle."

I know I saw much less death than many of my age-mates who served with other combat units. While the 86th Division and "M" Company did suffer casualties, they were relatively few when compared with other infantry divisions and companies. After all, the Blackhawks were actually in combat for only 42 days or a total of six weeks. No member of my squad was wounded. While there were several in "M" Company who were awarded the Purple Heart, I there were only a few deaths. (I haven't been able to find specific data concerning these numbers.)

When we were in the Philippines after the war was

over, I was told that the entire rifle squad I had belonged to when I was in "L" Company before transferring to "M," had been killed while on patrol in the Ruhr Pocket. I never sought official confirmation for that rumor.

Fear

It's reasonable to expect that soldiers are likely to experience the emotions of panic, fear, tension, and concern. I know I never felt panic. Also, I don't remember ever being really afraid. I do recall feelings of tension and concern. On one occasion when we were in a house during a particularly intense mortar attack, our lieutenant claimed that we were surrounded and that our ammunition supply was low. I was concerned. We got out of that situation, suggesting to me that he was unnecessarily worried.

I attribute my absence of fear not to the presence of courage, but to the excellent training we had received. Almost everything we experienced in combat we had experienced before under simulated conditions. I think fear is most likely to occur in response to the unknown. It is likely, however, that I would have experienced fear, and maybe even panic, if I had been in combat situations in which I was observing first-hand many of my buddies being killed.

There was a man in our company with one of our mortar squads who was described by some as being absolutely fearless. What this meant was that he was foolhardy. He didn't take reasonable precautions. Some called him dumb. I admired him, nevertheless, believing that he was the type who might win a Medal of Honor if the right conditions presented themselves.

One of our tech-sergeants who had been particularly tough on us during the state-side training was relieved of his duties after about three weeks of combat. It was claimed that he had "trench foot," an ailment afflicting men whose feet were wet for extended periods. It was generally believed, however, that he was a coward who couldn't take it when his life was at risk. In his case, the training did not inoculate him against fear.

Tank Rides

I rode on the back of a tank a couple of times. I don't remember why I had that privilege, but I vividly recall doing it. I was amazed how the tank men looking out of the turret could hear airplanes above the roar of their own motors. I saw them looking up into the sky to confirm that planes were friendly. I couldn't hear the sound of the planes at all.

There were a few days when the tanks would blast houses before we entered the villages. This was prompted by the action of snipers who were firing at us from the houses.

Roosevelt's Death

I remember well the day we learned that President Roosevelt was dead. We were on the approach march (a column spread out on both sides of the road and led by our officers) when the word was passed from the front to the back. Sometimes messages became garbled while being transmitted verbally down the line. This time, however, the brief report was unaltered and emphatic. I worried about Truman's ability to lead - a worry which proved to be unfounded.

Moving from Place to Place

A word about how we moved from place to place: If

we were transferring from one army to another, or to a different section of the battle line, we were moved by trucks and jeeps. Sometimes this occurred under the cover of darkness. If we were in enemy territory but hadn't yet engaged them, we used the "approach march." This meant that most of us were walking, typically spread out so that enemy mortar fire, land mines, or strafing wouldn't hit "bunched" targets. I would walk in front of my squad with other squad members following according to rank and function. This meant that the gunners and I would take turns carrying the tripod which, as reported earlier, weighed fifty pounds. We would swing it from the ground to the shoulders by picking it up with the back leg in a manner which would allow the two front legs to be in front and grasped by both hands. Transferring it from person to person was even easier. Someone else would carry the gun itself, moving it from shoulder to shoulder. Ammunition carriers would lug a couple of boxes of ammo belts. Occasionally, machine gun and mortar squads would ride very slowly in their jeeps while riflemen walked, as happened when Villar got caught on the jeep during the strafing.

Food Provisions

As reported in the letters, because we moved so rapidly, mobile field kitchens couldn't catch up with us. We "feasted" mostly on "K" and "C" rations. However, we sometimes supplemented those foods with provisions found in the houses we commandeered. Moreover, there were actually a couple of occasions on which the German women whose houses we occupied would prepare some food for us. Fresh eggs for breakfast were cooked for us more than once. We actually went almost thirty days without receiving a meal prepared by a field kitchen

Prisoners

The 86th Division was credited with the capture of 53,354 German soldiers. Toward the end of the war, "M" Company entered a town only to be met by hundreds of unarmed Germans moving toward us with their hands over their heads. They had thrown all of their weapons in a stream in an act of surrender. As we passed over a bridge, we could see pistols, rifles, etc., lying on the stream bed. After we were billeted for the night, many of us went back to the stream to get "souvenirs." Pistols were the souvenirs of choice since they could be easily tucked into our packs. I still have the one I picked out.

CHAPTER FOURTEEN

POST V-E AND V-J EXPERIENCES

POST V-E AND V-J EXPERIENCES

What I report from this point forward is based largely on unaided recall since no letters were saved which would have described what actually happened.   However, the booklet, Black Hawks Over the Danube: The History of the 86th Infantry Division in World War II,   By Richard A. Briggs (The Western Recorder, Louisville, Kentucky, 1955, 127 pages), provides useful dates and information which help to fill in some of the gaps.

Returning to the United States

The division remained in the Austrian rural area not far from Salzburg until May 14.   On that day literally hundreds of trucks came to transport us some 200 miles to Mannheim.   All of the drivers were African Americans. Germans flocked to our encampment to openly stare at these black human beings. I suspect that most of them had never actually seen a black person. I was disturbed by their behavior, but the drivers didn't seem to mind.

It should be pointed out that the armed forces were

segregated throughout WW II. Regrettably, in those years such segregation was taken for granted. There were some opportunities for black personnel in the navy, but those positions were limited. All-black forces in the air corp, the army and the marines distinguished themselves in battle, although their heroic contributions were not highlighted until well after the war.   In 1948 President Truman integrated all the services by executive order.

The division remained in Mannheim from May 15 to May 30 at which time we all boarded 40 and 8 box cars (40 horses or 8 men) for the train ride to Yvetot, France. From Yvetot we took trucks again to Camp Old Gold which had become the processing center through which all Pacific-bound units were to pass.

A week later we were moved to Le Havre where the division boarded four troop ships. The USS General Parker carried the 343rd Infantry.

The USS General Parker

The Parker was a typical troopship. Sleeping bunks were stacked five high. If you were in the highest, you got there by stepping on the edges of the lower four. I was never on the highest or the lowest. The spaces between were very narrow. It was impossible to sit up. If you read in your bunk, you were either lying flat or leaning on an elbow.

We ate in a huge galley. Steel trays with imprinted sections to separate the different food items were used. Eating was done in a standing position, with the trays placed on continuous counters which were chest high. Sometimes when the boat was rocking those of us who were not sea-sick and were able to eat had to hold onto our trays to keep them from sliding down the counter.

Showers were taken in salt-water using special soap which was supposed to counter the negative effects of the salt. I remember the water as being cold.

The "head" or toilet was located in the bow of the ship. Twenty to thirty toilet seats were placed across two channels of moving water which ran along both sides of the bow. In effect, there was a constant flushing action as the water rushed under each person flowing from front to back. Not until the end of this stream did all of the feces and urine disappear. The head was populated not only by those who needed it, but also by men who wanted a smoke. Smoking was prohibited in the sleeping quarters. Frequently it was difficult to see because of the heavy haze of smoke.

It was in this setting that a humorous event took place. Someone created a large ball of toilet paper, lit it with a match and floated it on the water at the beginning of the stream. At least 10 to 15 men lept up from their seated positions as the fire passed under their butts. I witnessed this hilarious event. Fortunately, none was hurt by the prank.

Some activities were scheduled on shipboard. However, most of the time was spent reading, talking or walking on deck. While strolling one day I met Hugh Whitsell, a classmate from Dayton, Ohio. I had not known that he was in the 86th and it was an enjoyable reunion.

Eleven days after we left Le Havre we saw New York. The following five paragraphs taken from Black Hawks Over The Danube describe this joyous homecoming:

"Late in the evening of June 17, the four ships bringing the 86th Division home from war slipped past Long Island and anchored in the narrows off Staten Island shore, opposite Coney Island. As Winston Churchill once said, we were so near but yet so far. Residents of Staten Island came down to the waters edge and shouted greeting out to the men on board. It was good to be back in America again.

Hardly anyone on board ship slept that night.

Everyone was waiting for the next morning, when the boat would pull into dock at New York and the Black Hawks could put foot on American soil once again. But with all the excitement, no one, with the possible exception of the commanders, had the least idea of the welcome they would receive.

A thick fog covered lower New York Bay at 7 a.m. when the three transports, the Bliss, Parker and Brooke, pulled up anchors after waiting for dawn to break, and started moving up the harbor. As the transports and the accompanying vessels picked up speed they came abreast of the boat containing the WAC band. The roar from the tightly packed deck could be heard, it was said, for miles inland. The haze that covered the bay lifted as the vessels passed the Statue of Liberty.

The Old Lady never looked grander. As the New York skyline came into view, huge signs could be picked out reading "Welcome Home." As the ships slowly moved upstream in the Hudson River to Westside New York docks, the nations largest city gave the Black Hawks a typical welcome, such as they reserve for special occasions. Hundreds of boats kept a constant tooting of their horns, and factory whistles blasted while employees were dismissed to line the banks of the Hudson to welcome the first combat division to return from Europe.

The ships themselves were well decorated for the occasion. Atop the General Brooke was a huge banner, "ETO to Tokio." As the ships pulled into the dock, Secretary of the Army Patterson climbed aboard the Parker to extend a welcome to General Melasky, while the press service photographers flashed their cameras. After a brief ceremony in which the Division was hailed as the first combat division to return from the ETO, individual soldiers from the CG (Commanding General) to the lowest buck private came in for their share of attention, as thousands of newspaper men from all over the country interviewed the Black Hawks for their home town newspapers. Every newspaper in the country, and all of the magazines devoted pages during the next few issues to the 86th Division. The Black Hawks had indeed come into their own." (See the appendices for two newspaper articles.)

We welcomed and enjoyed all of the attention. In truth, however, it was disproportionate to our contribution to the war's end. We had been in the European Theater for less than four months and in actual combat for only six weeks (42 days). The veteran infantry divisions which returned later, particularly those involved continuously after D-Day (June 6, 1944), probably experienced a less joyous celebration when they returned home.

Furlough

After disembarking from the General Parker we were taken by train to Camp Kilmer in New Jersey where our thirty-day furloughs were authorized. We were instructed to report to Camp Gruber in Muskogee, Oklahoma no later than July 22, 1945.

It is difficult to reconstruct the activities which consumed the wonderful month-long vacation. Marcy and I spent much time together visiting in Lima, Gallipolis and Westfield, New Jersey. I don't think we went back to Ohio Wesleyan since school was not in session at that time.

The marker event was our engagement. That occurred on the afternoon of the10th of July, after we had celebrated my 20th birthday. Clearly that was the best birthday present I would ever receive. We knew that we would not get married until I had finished college. (We followed that schedule. I graduated from Northwestern in August of1948 and we were married on August 28th, some 37 months after our engagement. In those days living together or becoming "intimate" before marriage was considered wrong. Since that was the social norm it wasn't too stressful to abide by it.)

My departure for Camp Gruber was a lump-in-the-throat occasion. The separation from Marcy was very difficult. Moreover, I wasn't confident that I would ever see her again. I felt lucky to have returned from Europe without a scratch. It seemed unlikely that I would be so fortunate again.

Camp Gruber, Muskogee, Oklahoma (July 22 - August 8, 1945)

We arrived at Camp Gruber expecting eight weeks of training to prepare us to invade Japan.

The Muskogee population welcomed us with enthusiasm. Everyone on the streets and in stores treated us as if we were heroes. Each Sunday after church, we would be dinner guests in the homes of parishioners. I enjoyed such hospitality on at least two occasions.

A canopy-covered double-trailer pulled by a short-wheelbase truck transported us from camp to town. One Sunday my friend and squad jeep driver, Al Woeltjen, stepped off the trailer while it was still moving and fell to the pavement. (He jumped off in the opposite direction of the trailer's movement.) He suffered a serious fracture of his arm. That injury meant that he was removed from our squad and the division. He was a fine team member and we all missed him greatly.

On August 6, the first atom bomb was dropped on Hiroshima. The destruction was awesome - 92,000 citizens dead or missing. I remember struggling to find the right words when writing to my parents immediately after that historic event. At the time I naively thought that war had become an instrument of the past, that in the future only peaceful measures would be acceptable, the alternative being so terrible.

We were on our way to Camp Stoneman on August 8, the day before the second atom bomb fell on Nagasaki resulting in an additional 40,000 persons dead or missing.

In retrospect, this early departure leads me to believe that we were never actually scheduled for an eight week training period. Instead we were standing by awaiting the dropping of the bombs. It would have been impossible otherwise for the 27 troop trains to have been collected so quickly to transport us to Camp Stoneman in Pittsburg, California, the San Francisco Port of Embarkation.

Camp Stoneman, Pittsburg, California (August 10 - 19, 1945)

We were in Camp Stoneman for a little over a week, just long enough to be issued tropical clothing and to receive necessary inoculations. Then we were moved by truck and railroad to San Francisco Harbor where we boarded our troopships.

While at Camp Stoneman a number of the older GI's protested to Congressmen and to the press (especially Drew Pearson) the fact that the 86th was being sent overseas when the war was practically at an end. Those who anticipated an early discharge because of a high number of points were especially eager to be kept in the U.S. In spite of these pleadings, the division set sail for the Asiatic-Pacific Theater on August 19.

USS General Hugh Rodman (August 19 - September 11)

It was a thrill passing under the Golden Gate Bridge.

We didn't anticipate, however, that within 24 hours we would be passing under it two more times. We had not been gone very long before the Rodman turned around to return to San Francisco Bay. Some mechanical difficulty required repair before the ship could proceed with its long voyage. Initially some of the men thought a late decision had been made to keep the 86th in the U.S.

They were disappointed to learn the real purpose for the brief return to port.

I remember very little from this voyage. I do recall reflecting that the Pacific deserved its name; it was much smoother than the Atlantic had been. I remember, also, the special ceremony which took place when we crossed the International Dateline, losing a day in the process. All of us received engraved certificates signifying that we had been initiated into the "Domain of the Golden Dragon." (I have long since lost this piece of paper.)

Fifteen days out of San Francisco on September 2, 1945, the news was reported over the PA system that Japan had unconditionally surrendered to General MacArthur aboard the battleship Missouri in Tokyo Harbor. I don't recall any celebration; we had assumed that was inevitable after the two bombs were dropped. Nevertheless, that official announcement provided the final assurance that we would not be involved in an invasion of Japan, although we still did not know our destination or mission.

I think we probably spent most of our time reading, talking, watching the ocean, and, in general, taking it easy. Perhaps we had some lectures, although I don't remember them. There were some boxing matches on deck. In any case, I have no memory of being bored during the long 24 day journey.

I truly did enjoy all of the time we spent on water. As an infantry division, we eventually logged more than 75 days at sea counting our ship time while training amphibiously, the two trips across the Atlantic, and the two trips across the Pacific. I remember wondering if my pleasure was derived from some genetic predisposition since my father had spoken frequently of his love for the sea - a love which he had affirmed while traveling by boat to South America and to England. Also, I have a vague memory of hearing that one of my forebearers (on my father's side) captained a ship which sailed in the English Channel. I was also helped by being immune to sea-sickness.

According to Black Hawks Over the Danube, we dropped anchor in the harbor of Tacabolan, Leyte for two days before proceeding to the location which had just been announced as our ultimate destination, the Philippines. I do remember the scores of natives in their outrigger canoes who gathered around our ships.

Finally we moved on to the island of Luzon where we landed at a port on the southwest coast named Batangas, a city of some 30,000 inhabitants located about 60 miles south of Manila. We remained there for a little more than a month.

The Philippines (September 11, 1945 - May 1946)

Some of my memories of Batangas are as follows: setting up camp and living in tents, the tropical environment, the rain (the last two weeks we were there were the monsoon season), taking anti-malaria tablets which made our skin turn yellow, the comfort with which Filipinos assumed a squatting position sitting on their haunches for long periods of time, the houses built on stilts or columns with chickens and animals living underneath, the sounds of piano music coming from almost every home we walked by, the aggressive solicitation of soldiers by prostitutes, the public list of prostitutes who were "clean" according to some local health authority, the market with inexpensive bananas, the pungent smells in the market, the efforts to develop recreation programs for the division (this is when I began to box), and the cherished letters from home after the long hiatus while at sea (Marcy's came on the "Especially for Scotty" stationery).

We moved from Batangas to a camp near Marikina, a small town east of Manila on the Pasig River. Manila was only ten miles away. Although we were replacing the 38th Division which had previously occupied the camp and was returning to the United States, we had much work to do. We spent hours building tent platforms and digging drainage ditches.

The character of "M" Company began to change shortly after we arrived in Manila (Marikina). A few men who had accumulated more than enough points to be discharged went back with the 38th, confirming their judgments that they should have been kept in the U. S. In turn, some younger men were transferred to the 86th from the 38th. That transition, older men leaving, younger men coming, characterized the division and our company throughout our time in the Philippines.

A variety of recreational programs and opportunities were available to us. On weekends we would regularly go to the Roosevelt Club, the popular USO center. We also frequented Rizal Stadium where we could watch baseball games. "One peso only" clubs which featured second-rate comedians, magicians and "bump-and-grind" female dancers competed for our attendance. Shopping in the open-air markets for pina cloth (made out of pineapple) and other products unique to the Philippincs was a favorite activity. A divisional men's glee club was formed in which I participated for a brief period of time. Divisional study courses were offered. (I took one on creative writing.)

A major emphasis in the division was placed on boxing as a competitive sport. Each company was expected to train volunteers who would participate in boxing events on the weekends. I liked my boxing experiences in Batangas (I had also had some training in a phys ed class at Ohio Wesleyan) so I volunteered, as did seven or eight others. One of our officers served as our coach. A special training table was designated in the mess hall to make certain we got the food we needed. Also, a special time was established for sparring practice.

However, I never participated in one of the division-wide matches. During the third or fourth week of our training period my elbow on the left arm began to swell. (I had turned that elbow inside out when my arm was broken while playing basketball in high school.) On the recommendation of the coach, I went to sick call (for the second and last time of my army career) where the doctor advised against throwing punches with that arm. I continued with the program in the role of assistant coach and kept my favored position at the training table. I remember having mixed feelings about all this, acknowledging that it might not have been that much fun if I had been in the ring with someone from another company who was really good.

Jim Hader, a brother Delt from Ohio Wesleyan who was in another 86th regiment, contacted me. He was authorized to use a jeep, so we had an enjoyable reunion riding around the Manila area. We got together two or three different times.

I learned from my parents that there were Methodist missionaries living in Manila. They knew them and suggested I contact them. I did that, and was their guest one evening for dinner. I remember being surprised that their living quarters were so nice. For some reason I had thought that missionaries would be living in poverty.

On another occasion, my friend Bill Herndon and I visited a Filipino family who had known Rev. and Mrs. Brashares. We had a terrible time finding their residence. The houses had no numbers on them and street signs were available only occasionally. We finally did locate the house and spent a pleasant evening with them. I think that was the only opportunity I had to be in the home of Filipinos.

A major event for the division was an extended field exercise in northern Luzon. We arrived at the site for our maneuvers after a long day riding in trucks and jeeps. The farther north we traveled the more primitive the natives became. Bare-breasted women working in the fields became commonplace. We had a contest to see on which side of the jeep the most such women would appear. After we got to our destination and pitched our tents, a small group of us explored a nearby area where we found a family living on an open-air platform. The man wore only a G-string on which a bolo knife was attached. Two small children were totally naked.

One purpose of our exercise was to make our presence known to Huk Bala Haps (sp.?), an insurgent group of communists in the north who were a threat to the established Philippine government. While we didn't encounter any of them, and if we had I don't believe we would have engaged them in any combat, it's my understanding that we were there to convey the message that a major force was available to counter any initiative they might take.

An equally important purpose of the maneuvers was to provide training for the new members of the division and to keep our skills polished. I remember the time in the field as being a positive experience.

There was a small core of men in the company who

regularly made use of the Manila prostitutes. They would regale the rest of us with their experiences - offering to pay the costs of a first visit for any of us virgins, an offer we didn't take up. There were also a few who established relationships with Filipino women who were not prostitutes. These men became know as "pier husbands," meaning they acted like husbands until they went to the pier to go home to their real wives or girl friends. For the majority of us, we had no opportunity to be with women, except as we would talk with USO workers in the Roosevelt Club. I don't remember feeling deprived. My regular communication with Marcy via mail was sustaining and a constant source of joy.

As a result of the departure of the older men in the company, I was elevated to the position of company first-sergeant. If memory serves me correctly, I believe I was in that position for only the last three months. I was not given the full rank, although I was promoted to staff-sergeant. I was told that I would receive the rank if I would agree to stay in the Philippines for an extra six months, an offer I easily refused.

As reported in my Separation Qualification Record (See the appendices), my responsibilities as first-sergeant were as follows: "Was in charge of 156 men in a heavy weapons company, assigned duties to the men and checked their work. Supervised, making out the morning reports and payrolls, work done on service record books and changes or entries on classification cards. Handled incoming and outgoing military correspondence. Made out working schedules and saw that men were present for work details, parades and ceremonies."

My office was in the company headquarters tent. I had a company clerk who assisted me with clerical tasks. I reported directly to the company commander, a captain. As a twenty-year old, I benefited greatly from the experience.

Some of the experiences I had while in that position made a lasting impression on me.

The IG (Inspector General) Inspection

Every few months each company was visited by a team of officers led by a general who would inspect every aspect of the company's operation. The visit was pre-announced so that thorough preparation could be made. As company first-sergeant, it was my responsibility to see that we passed with flying colors. I remember staying up late at night for several days prior to the scheduled day working hard to see that everything was in proper order.

It was a tremendous relief when the official report proclaimed that we had met or exceeded all the standards. A negative remark appeared concerning the appearance of our morning reports. The night before the visit I discovered an error in the company clerks record which I attempted to correct through erasing . While it was factually correct, it was a sloppy work.

Counseling an AWOL soldier

Many of the men who had replaced our discharged veterans were inexperienced, young, and homesick. Their basic training had been minimal and they were typically 18 years old. Moreover, they wondered why they had been sent overseas since the war was over.

For the most part this group abided by the rules and, with the help of the training we provided, became good soldiers. On one occasion, however, a young man extended his weekend by going AWOL (absent without leave). The infraction was serious enough to warrant sending him to the stockade. I was talking with him in my office trying to determine what penalty to impose. I realized that he was a mixed up kid who needed help, but was mindful of the need to make an example of him. My decision was not to send him to the

Stockade, but to assign him to undesirable work details for an extended number of days. I thought I was alone in the tent; but as we were concluding our conversation, I saw the shoes of the company commander. The tent was divided by partitions, which were open at the top and the bottom; his office was adjacent to mine. I was relieved when he later told me that I had made the right decision.

A friend hallucinates

An age-mate soldier and friend who had been in "M" company since Louisiana, walked into headquarters' tent and asked me if he could talk to the captain. Normally GI's didn't talk with the company commander. If they needed to confer with an officer they would speak to their platoon lieutenant. However, I could tell something was seriously wrong with him. The captain agreed to see him. The conversation which I overheard was startling. He clearly had lost touch with reality. It was a mixture of incoherent religious references and comments about catastrophes which were about to happen to the division. I had known him as a deeply religious person. It was sad to witness first-hand this example of mental illness. I don't remember what happened to him after that, although I got a reassuring letter from him after we were both discharged in which he reported that he was doing well.

The battalion sergeant-major

Every weekday morning there would be a conference call which was the occasion for the battalion sergeant-major to give orders and information to the first-sergeants. These would typically last twenty to thirty minutes and were essentially a one-way, boring monologue. Much of what he said had also been provided in printed form by a battalion runner. I sometimes put the phone down on my desk without listening to him so that I could do work that needed to be done. That never got me into any trouble, but I was always fearful that he might address a remark specifically to me while I was doing this. I still feel a sense of guilt in recalling this behavior.

The influence of a fortune teller

One of the young men came to see me to talk about the "message" he had received from a fortune teller in Manila. He was told that his marriage wouldn't last and that he would marry a second time. He had been married just prior to entering the service. He said he was very much in love with his wife. Nevertheless, he believed the soothsayer's prediction had access to some authoritative knowledge about the future and believed her message to be true. He was greatly upset. It was the first occasion I had ever met anyone who respected a fortune teller. His "faith" in her prediction dumbfounded me and made an indelible impression. I don't remember how I counseled him. I do remember being startled by the gullibility of this seemingly rational human being.

Summing Up

My role as first-sergeant expanded my understanding of humanity and introduced me to administrative responsibilities. It was truly a growth experience.

I left the Philippines on March 19 arriving in the U. S. on April 16, 1946. I was discharged from the separation center at Camp Atterbury, Indiana on April 23.

I enrolled almost immediately in the spring quarter at Northwestern University. Ellen had enjoyed her time there and it had a national reputation for its excellence. My parents liked its Methodist origins, although that church relationship was not an active one. The primary reason for choosing it, however, was the fact that Marcy was serving as a Girl Scout executive in Rockford, Illinois, about fifty miles Evanston.

The friendships I developed during my thirty months in the service were meaningful and genuine. It is interesting, however, to reflect on how temporary they were. After I was discharged I had contact with only a half dozen of my buddies. Al Woeltjen, the man who broke his arm in Oklahoma, lived in the Chicago area. I visited him once while at Northwestern. He was enrolled in a pre-med program, I believe at the University of Chicago. Marcy and I also visited Bob (Slats, Jukebox) Gleason who lived on the south side of Chicago. He was the high school drop out who was my squad leader before I succeeded him. Most of our time was spent hearing him extoll the virtues of his younger brother who was making money on the streets in some kind of illegal racket. Karl Spivak, who had become a lawyer, stopped in Ann Arbor to see us while he was in the area on a business trip. I met one of our officers at a National Council for the Social Studies conference. He was in charge of one of the book displays there. The only person with whom I have had a continuing contact is Bill Herndon in Texas. Bill became a very successful lawyer. He visited us here in Ann Arbor many years ago. Marcy and I spent time with him later while I was attending a conference in Houston, Texas where he had his law firm.

I will always remember with great appreciation the relationships and experiences which were part of my time in the service. But life moves on. As I am about to celebrate my 70th birthday (July 10, 1995), I am very, very grateful for the exceptionally fortunate and happy life I have lived.

The letters and additional comments were typed during an eight-month period beginning in September, 1994 and ending in May, 1995. The pages were duplicated and bound during the first week of June, 1995.

In December of 2015, my son discovered the original manuscript on disk and transcribed it for publication.

==========

W. Scott Westerman, Jr. was born in Ann Arbor, Michigan on July 10, 1925. After his service in World War II he was educated at Ohio Wesleyan, Northwestern and the University of Michigan. He was a professor and educator, serving as Superintendent of the Ann Arbor Public Schools during a period of tumultuous change in the late 1960s. He concluded his career as Dean of the College of Education at Eastern Michigan University and has been active in community service and consulting ever since. The Dr. W. Scott Westerman Jr Preschool and Family Center was named in his honor by the Ann Arbor Public Schools in 2015.

W. Scott Westerman, III is Associate Vice President for Alumni Relations at Michigan State University.

Two Scott Westermans - Summer 2014

Made in the USA
Middletown, DE
04 January 2016